Civil War & Restoration in Monmouthshire

Civil War & Restoration in Monmouthshire

by
Jeremy Knight

Logaston Press

LOGASTON PRESS
Little Logaston Woonton Almeley
Herefordshire HR3 6QH

First published by Logaston Press 2005
Copyright © Jeremy Knight 2005

ISBN 1 904396 41 0

Set in Times by Logaston Press
and printed in Great Britain by
Biddles, King's Lynn

In Memory of Stan Knight
1906–1997
Man of Monmouthshire

Acknowledgements

This book could not have been written without the generous help of many people who answered queries, hunted down references, documents, pictures and objects and gave me access to material in their care. These include Edward Besly, Mark Redknap and John Kenyon (National Museums & Galleries of Wales); Tricia Buckingham (Bodleian Library); Chris Barber; Steve Clarke; Jane Cunningham (Courtauld Institute of Art); Con Manning; Alan Probert; Rachel Rogers (Abergavenny Museum); Kieran O'Conor (University College, Galway); Tom Lloyd; Pat Moseley; Frank Olding; Alf Webb (Dean Archaeology Group); Elizabeth Whittle; the staffs of Newport Reference Library (Haines and Monmouthshire Collections), Gwent County Record Office (particularly David Rimmer and Luned Mair Davies) and Cardiff Central Library. Liz Pitman took photographs specially for this book and Marilyn and Calvin Rees helped me with Welsh language sources. John Kenyon read the entire text and saved me from a number of errors and infelicities. Julian Mitchell read Chapters 6 and 7, which have benefited greatly from his comments, and sent me a typescript of his chapter on Monmouthshire politics 1660–1702 from the forthcoming Gwent County History Vol 3. At Logaston Press, Andy Johnson and Ron Shoesmith's relaxed but rigorous editing did much to improve my text. My greatest debt however is to Annie, who made the writing of this book possible in many different ways.

Contents

		page
	Acknowledgements	vi
	Introduction	1
Chapter 1	Religious Conflict in Stuart Monmouthshire	7
Chapter 2	The Anatomy of Stuart Monmouthshire	23
Chapter 3	The Great Pyramid: Grandees, Gentry & Others	49
Chapter 4	Community in Conflict: 1642–44	61
Chapter 5	The Royalist Ebb, 1644–45	83
Chapter 6	End Game; Raglan and Chepstow 1646–48	103
Chapter 7	A Reformation Too Far?	129
Chapter 8	Restoration and Reaction 1660–90. Plus ça Change	149
	Chronology of events	179
	References	183
	Bibliography	199
	Index	209

Hundred of Newport
1 Newport
2 Bassaleg
3 St Brides Wentloog
4 Peterstone Wentloog
5 Rumney
6 St Mellons
7 Marshfield
8 Coedkernew
9 Michaelston Y Fedw
10 Bedwas
11 Machen
12 Malpas
13 Bettws
14 Henllys
15 Risca
16 Mynyddislwyn
17 Bedwellty

Hundred of Usk
1 Usk
2 Gwehelog
3 Glascoed
4 Monkswood
5 Llanbadoc
6 Trostrey
7 Kemeys Commander
8 Llangibby
9 Panteg
10 Llanfihangel-Pont-y-Moel
11 Gwernesney
12 Llangeview
13 Llanllowel
14 Llantrisant
15 Llangwm
16 Kemeys Inferior
17 Caerleon
18 Llantarnam
19 Llanhennock
20 Tredunnock
21 Llandegveth
22 Llandewi Fach
23 Llanfrechva

Hunded of Caldicot
1 Chepstow
2 St Arvans
3 Penterry
4 Mounton
5 Mathern
6 St Pierre
7 Runston

8 Portskewett
9 Sudbrook
10 Caldicot
11 Ifton
12 Caerwent
13 Shirenewton
14 Newchurch
15 Itton
16 Howick
17 Dinham
18 Llanvair Dscoed
19 Llanvaches
20 Penhow
21 Langstone
22 Llanmartin
23 Llandevaud
24 Wilcrick
25 St Brides Netherwent
26 Llandevenny
27 Magor
28 Redwick
29 Llanwern
30 Bishton
31 Undy
32 Rogiet
33 Llanvihangel Rogiet
34 Goldcliff
35 Whitson
36 Nash
37 Christchurch
38 Crick

Hundred of Raglan
1 Raglan
2 Llandenny
3 Dingestow
4 Tregaer
5 Penrhos
6 Bryngwyn
7 Bettws Newydd
8 Clytha
9 Parc Grace Dieu
10 part of Llanfihangel
   Ystern Llewern

Hundred of Trellech
1 Trellech
2 Penallt
3 Mtchell Troy
4 Cwmcarfan
5 Pen-y-Clawdd
6 Llangoven

7 Llandogo
8 Llansoy
9 Llanfihangel-Tor-y-
   Mynydd
10 Wolvesnewton
11 Cilgwrrwg
12 Llanishen
13 Trellech Grange
14 Tintern Parva
15 Chapel Hill

Hunded of Skenfrith
1 Monmouth
2 Dixton
3 Rockfield
4 Wonastow
5 Llangattock vibion Avel
6 St Maughans
7 Skenfrith
8 Grosmont
9 Llangua
10 Llantilio Crossenny
11 Llanfihangel Ystern
   Llewern
12 Welsh Bicknor

Hundred of Abergavenny
1 Abergavenny
2 Llantilio Pertholey
3 Llanfihangel Crucorney
4 Oldcastle
5 Cwmyoy
6 Llangattock Lingoed
7 Llanvertherine
8 Llandewi Skyrrid
9 Llandewi Rydderch
10 Llanvapley
11 Llanarth
12 Llansantffraid
13 Llanvihangel nigh Usk
   (Gobion)
14 Llangattock nigh Usk
15 Llanwenarth
16 Llanfoist
17 Llanelen
18 Llanover
19 Llanvair Kilgedin
20 Goitre
21 Mamhilad
22 Trevethin
23 Llanhilleth
24 Aberystruth

The Hundreds and Parishes of Monmouthshire

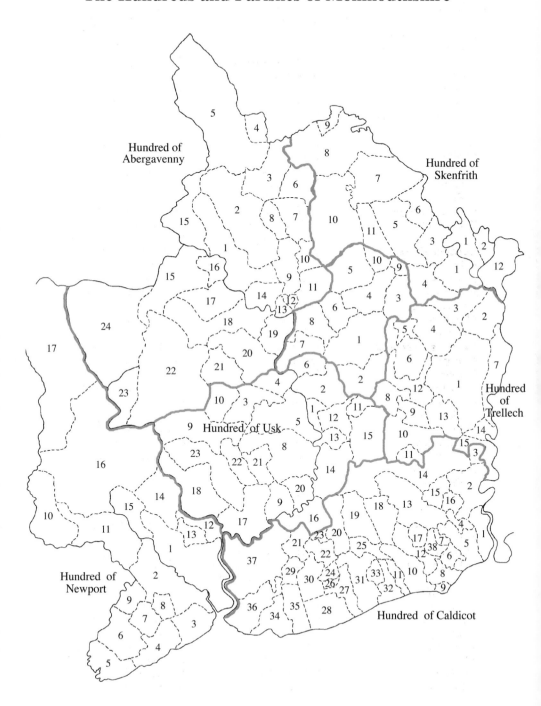

Introduction

On Wednesday 19 August 1646, Henry, the 76-year-old fifth Earl and first Marquis of Worcester, infirm and 'of great corpulency' waited with his family and household in the Hall of Raglan Castle to surrender the castle to Sir Thomas Fairfax, Commander-in-chief of Parliament's New Model Army. The heavy guns and mortars with which Captain Hooper had blasted its walls had fallen silent and as the household waited they saw 'through the window, the General, with all his officers, entering the Outward Court, as if a floodgate had been left open'. It was a flood that was to sweep away Raglan Castle and the semi-regal state which the Marquis kept there. By the end of the year, the Marquis was dead and Raglan a ruined shell.[1]

Monmouthshire has often been seen as a pre-eminently 'loyal' county, united in support of the King and the house of Worcester until destabilised by outside events. However, the bitter divisions within its community, between catholics and protestants, and between those loyal to the house of Worcester and those who felt excluded from its circle of power went back to at least the 1620s, and continued until almost the end of the century. Until Fairfax's arrival, the siege had been conducted by two Monmouthshire gentlemen, Sir Thomas Morgan of Llangattock Lingoed and Sir Trevor Williams of Llangibby, whilst in his courteous exchange of letters with Fairfax before the surrender, the Marquis claimed that his apprehension in surrendering the castle would be not of Fairfax himself, but of the enmity of 'the gentlemen on the County Committee'. Similarly, the leaders of the 1647 Glamorgan rising claimed that they had risen not against the central government, but against 'the unjust and arbitrary disposition of the Committee here'. Even Clarendon, no admirer of the Marquis's son, Edward Herbert, Earl of Glamorgan, spoke of 'notorious emulations and dissentions' among local families, based on 'prejudice against the house of Worcester and its religion' rather than on the 'civil and obliging nature' of Lord Herbert himself.[2]

Some academic historians might regard a 'county' history of the civil war as a dated concept,[3] but Peter Gaunt has commented on its intensely regional nature and it saw a complex interplay between regional, national or 'three kingdom' elements and its European dimension. There has been no book length study of Monmouthshire in this period since Arthur Clark's *Raglan Castle and the Civil War in Monmouthshire* of 1953 and recent studies of adjacent counties such as Gloucester and Somerset, analysing the ways in which they were affected and destabilized by the war, show the need for a similar study for Monmouthshire.[4] The present book cannot, however, offer similar close analysis. This is because of the absence of early sources such as Quarter Sessions records and Churchwardens accounts, the result of the weakness of parochial structures in the county and of the destruction of the library and archives at Raglan Castle after the siege. In 1650, the Parliamentary County Committee explained that it could not submit its accounts because 'by reason of the late troubles, the records of our county are so severed'.[5] These lacunae, and the lack of earlier work, other than Clark's, has made it necessary to concentrate on a detailed narrative account rather than a more structured analysis.

An exception to the dearth of private papers are those of Walter Powell of Llantilio Crossenny (1581–1656), particularly his diary, covering the years 1603–1654 . This is a private diary rather than an intended work of history, and some of his references to local affairs are frustratingly cryptic. It was 'a book of ould remembrances, collected by me, Walter Powell, of the ages of me and my ffrindes and children and of other matters happening in my occasions, collected out of my ould Almanacks, wch I have filed together from yeare to yeare, as in the blanks thereof they are written more at large', a 'shorte breviat to be caried about me to helpe my memorie concerning those things'.[6]

Interior view of kitchen court at Raglan Castle 1798 by Sir Richard Colt-Hoare from William Coxe's Historical Tour in Monmouthshire. *The library is believed to have been on the first floor of the central block, behind the row of large windows. Destroyed after the siege, it contained a major collection of early Welsh manuscripts and much of the archives of the county*

It begins not long after his move to Llantilio from Llanarth and his building of what is now Llantilio Court in 1611–12, with family notes taken from a lost parish register of Tregare covering the years 1560–1615. Powell, like many lesser gentry of the county, combined the role of landowner with that of steward and rent collector to a magnate family, in this case the Worcesters. His references to events of the war are useful chronological checks, but far more important is his day to day account of living through the war years in rural Monmouthshire, the ravages to his crops and livestock by the soldiers of both sides; his experiences as tax collector for the Royalist administration, ending with a spell in prison in Raglan Castle for his pains. He was eventually released through the siege lines, only to find that his house at Penrhos had been sacked by Parliamentary troops during his spell

Walter Powell of Llantilio Crossenny (1581–1656), from a portrait once in the possession of Lord Dunboyne

as a Royalist prisoner. Even after the end of the war, he was subject to the billeting of roundhead cavalry, heavy taxation and periodic searches for arms at the hands of local puritan officials. His experiences can be expanded by those of other minor Monmouthshire gentry whose estates were sequestrated after the war as 'malignants', or worse still papists, and who were forced to appeal to the London based Committee for Compounding against the decisions of the 'Usk Committee'. These tell not only of wartime hardships— looted cattle and horses, threats from soldiers, neighbours murdered—but also help us assess the activities of the hated committees, often accused of intimidation, of settling old scores, and of lining the pockets of its members from the confiscated estates of its social betters. The letterbook of the Caerleon customs official and lawyer John Byrd reminds us that Parliamentary sympathisers fared no better, either during the war or after, whilst the Chepstow parish registers and the diary of a soldier turned schoolmaster in Monmouth show us something of what it was like to live through the war years in a Monmouthshire town.

Unsurprisingly, much academic debate on the civil war has centred on the role of the gentry. Sources are plentiful in most counties, and have been worked over by generations of family and county historians—in Monmouthshire particularly by Sir Joseph Bradney. Many prominent county families had risen, as lawyers and property speculators, through the acquisition of monastic land. As Richard Symonds, the diarist and antiquarian who accompanied the King's army remarked of one North Wales family, the Kyffins, 'The ruine of the Abbeys was the raysing of them'. This applied equally to catholics like the Morgans of Llantarnam and to protestants like the Arnolds of Llanfihangel or the Williamses of Llangibby. The Herberts of Raglan, originally enriched by royal service in late medieval times, greatly increased their wealth with the former properties of Tintern Abbey. The second path to riches was service as steward to an existing magnate family. The Herberts had shown the way as stewards of royal lordships and manors in the fifteenth century. They were followed in the next century by other families within the county.

Below the two great Herbert magnates, the catholic Earl of Worcester and the protestant Earl of Pembroke, were around a dozen families, interlinked by marriage and kinship, who made up the core of the county gentry community. They and their kinsmen had sat as Knights of the Shire for the county in the Commons and served on the Commission of the Peace or as Sheriff. Most were protestants, but their relationship to their catholic cousins was not straightforward. 'Core' gentry families, like the Gunters of Abergavenny, had protestant and catholic branches. Philip Jones of Llanarth, at least nominally protestant, had an openly catholic wife, and a Kemeys of Cefn Mably, a Dominican priest from an otherwise protestant family, died in prison at the time of the Titus Oates plot. Henry Milborne of Wonastow, an old boy of Abergavenny Grammar School, with a protestant father and a catholic mother, had been raised a protestant. Another old boy of the school, the Jesuit William Gwyn, originally of Llanfair Kilgedin, whose parents were 'of the Middle or Yeoman class' had three brothers and three sisters and, he said, 'many relations some Catholics, some Schismatics'. He himself had been a protestant until the age of 20. Such families were normally Royalist during the war, particularly if they were linked by distant kinship or by clientage to the Herberts of Raglan.[7] Protestant families without such links, though conventionally Royalist at its outbreak became, under its pressure, neutralists like Thomas Morgan of Tredegar or opportunists like Sir Trevor Morgan of Llangibby. The modern scholar Philip Jenkins has called this group 'moderates', as opposed to the 'high Royalists' or 'ultras' of the Worcester interest on one hand, and the Parliamentarians with puritan links on the other.[8]

Monmouthshire was also rich in lesser 'parish' or 'township' gentry, more numerous than the 'county families', but less well documented. They filled a range of posts at Hundred and parish level, and sometimes served as stewards to greater families. When we find them complaining of the influence of the house of Worcester, it is more likely to be of the actions of Worcester's stewards than of the catholicism of Worcester himself, which was an accepted fact of life in the county.

The role of the steward as land agent helps to explain the almost schizophrenic divisions of opinion within the county regarding the Earl of Worcester. What Nathan Rogers, the puritan author of the anti-Worcester history *Memoirs of Monmouthshire*, would have made of the Earl's claim to the king that the supply of the court at Raglan was from his own resources, not those of the surrounding countryside, is hard to imagine, but at one level the Earl was correct. What he ignored however was the role of his stewards, Rogers's 'merciless Raglanders', in extorting those resources and dealing harshly with any who made difficulties about this. It was virtually the job description of the steward that he should fill this unpopular and unpleasant role precisely so that Worcester could distance himself from this, and appear as beneficent and gracious as he chose. The Welsh poet Twm o'r Nant wrote 'Between the law of the steward and the pride of the great ones, the tenant is caught between the devil and his tail.'[9] It was only when Worcester's grandson, by then Duke of Beaufort, in different post-war circumstances sought to re-coup his family's wartime losses and involved himself and his coercive power directly in the Wentwood disputes that the system broke down.

Any concept of a 'county community' requires heavy qualification. County boundaries were distinctly permeable barriers and the civil war made co-operation between the gentry of Monmouthshire and those of adjoining counties even closer. For Parliamentarians, links with puritan Gloucester and Bristol were central. Even today, as secretaries of county societies can sometimes be heard complaining, the focus of many local people is their town—Chepstow, Monmouth or Abergavenny—rather than the county as a whole. At a different level, any feuds or violence were no doubt against the young men of the next town or village rather than further afield.

The religious divisions between catholics and protestants within the county were repeatedly commented on by well informed outsiders in the pre-war years, but despite Parliamentary propaganda, the war was not a conflict between catholics and protestants. As in other counties, most catholics, other than courtiers or associates of Worcester, remained neutral, partly because of the penalties against 'Papists in Arms' but also because the Jesuit wing of the church refused to recognise formally the Stuart kings, making it illogical to fight for them on behalf of what was (despite puritan propaganda) a protestant church.

As what had started as a metropolitan political crisis, centred on Westminster and the City of London, began to open hidden fault lines in the country at large, how did people (or some people) at different levels of society choose whether to support King or Parliament, insofar as they had a choice in the matter? For the political classes, as for committed puritans, such a choice was relatively straightforward. Did those below the level of the gentry simply follow their leaders, or did some at least have their own views? Some groups, as defined by occupation, had decided views, based on economic grounds or their pre-war relationships with the Crown. Thus Cornish tin miners and Forest of Dean free miners took diametrically opposite stances due to royal involvement in their industries. One suggestion, going back to John Aubrey, is that the ecology and land use of particular areas may have influenced the mind sets of people, affecting their religious and political choices. This model can be tested against the varied landscape of 17th-century Monmouthshire.

As might be expected, the views of many changed considerably under the pressure of events. Rather than attempting to divide people into 'roundheads' and 'cavaliers', it might be more realistic to see them as the equivalent of voters in a modern Parliamentary election, 'voting' as the circumstances of the moment dictated, without being regarded as 'turncoats' or 'weathercocks'. Well below gentry level, we have the histories of two rank and file soldiers whose experiences were oddly parallel. Recruited into the Royalist army in rural Welsh speaking areas (Carmarthenshire and Blaenau Gwent), both were taken prisoner and later settled in Gloucester. One lived there for the rest of his days. The other, after undergoing religious conversion in Essex, served in the Parliamentarian army at the siege of Raglan and ended his days as a Welsh puritan elder. They remind us how so many below gentry level were uprooted from traditional rural communities by the war and brought into contact with new forms of society and new ideas. Sadly, such experiences are far harder to quantify than gentry allegiance.

One major problem in researching the Civil War period in Wales is that of the duplication of names due to 'family' Christian names and and the naming of children after close relatives. Even the Parliamentary County Committee sometimes confessed itself unsure which Anthony Morgan or Thomas Veale they had sequestrated. Contemporary practice (as in modern Wales) was to distinguish people of the same name by their place of residence or their farm, but these rarely appear in official documents. Such uncertainties, however, only serve to emphasise how much there is still to learn about the people of 17th-century Monmouthshire.

1 Religious Conflict in Stuart Monmouthshire

In February 1604, the year before the Gunpowder Plot, the Justices of Assize for Monmouthshire were informed of a scandalous and illegal episode in Caerleon churchyard:-

> One William Howell Thomas, a recusant deceased, was buried on a Sunday in the daytime, in the churchyard of Caerleon in Monmouthshire, being brought thither by many recusants, carrying wax candles, burning before the corpse [forbidden by statute] and no minister [Protestant clergyman] was present at the same burial. Thereupon one Morgan ap John, having some speech with Saunder William James, a recusant, touching that burial, the said Saunder said 'We shall have the Mass, and that very shortly, or else thou shalt see many bloody swords'.

William Howell Thomas and his wife Eleanora John had been fined as catholic recusants in the Armada year of 1588. They were no doubt respected Caerleon people, prominent members of its large catholic community. Yet that community could scarcely have picked a more conspicuous public place for the funeral than Caerleon churchyard on a Sunday afternoon. There was no shortage of secluded country churchyards in Gwent where they could have given William Thomas a catholic burial, and catholics had no reservations about burial in Anglican churchyards, which they regarded as having been legitimately consecrated before the Reformation. In the following year, a similar funeral in a Herefordshire country churchyard led to commotions which came to involve the king, the archbishop of Canterbury and the Earl of Worcester.[1]

Queen Elizabeth had died a year earlier, on 24 March 1603. Though she had been on the throne for virtually half a century, there was no certainty that her chosen successor, King James of Scotland, would enjoy an unchallenged succession, or that the Elizabethan religious settlement would survive the pressures from puritans within the established church on the one hand and catholic recusants on the other. When the churchwardens of Kemeys Inferior above Caerleon took down the medieval rood figure from the screen of their church at Elizabeth's accession, they hid it away beneath the rood loft stairs, perhaps out of reverence for the figure, but possibly because no one knew whether sometime they might be bidden to put it back, as their predecessors had been when Mary came to the throne. When news of Elizabeth's death reached Monmouthshire, there were rumours that Edward Morgan of Llantarnam, a hard-line catholic, had removed cartloads of arms and ammunition from the county armoury at Caerleon to his house at Penrhos. There were to be similar scares and rumours about armed papists for much of the century. As Lord Eure put it a few years later 'few causes arise in the shire which are not made a question between the Protestant and the Recusant.'[2]

The reign of Elizabeth I had seen a steady hardening of religious frontiers. The very first enactment of her reign in 1558 had been the Act of Supremacy (1 Elizabeth 1, cap.1), re-affirming the Queen's status as head of the Church and imposing fines for non-attendance at Sunday worship. In the early years of her reign, attachment to the old ways was still a conservative survivalism largely untouched by the ideas of the Counter Reformation. However, in 1563 the Council of Trent ruled it unlawful for British catholics to attend the services of heretics and three years later the Lancashire catholic Lawrence Vaux returned from Rome with a document setting this out in unambiguous terms. William Allen's foundation of the English seminary at Douai in 1568 was followed by the Pope Pius V's Bull *Regnans in Excelsis* (1570), declaring Elizabeth a heretic and urging her deposition. This 'papal declaration of war' was answered by the anti-Romanist Treason Act of the following year. The first Douai trained priests arrived in Britain in 1574, followed by the Jesuits Campion and Parsons in 1580, but antagonism between the 'mass priests' ordained under Mary, and the new hard line Romanist clergy, particularly the Jesuits, led to divisions among the catholics themselves. The arrival of the Jesuits was followed by fresh legislation—*An Act to retain the Queen's Majesties Subjects in due obedience* in 1581 and *An Act against Jesuits, Seminary Priests, and other disobedient persons* in 1585, (27 Eliz I, cap. 2) under which the majority of the catholic priests and laymen later executed for treason were condemned.[3]

Some catholic parish clergy of Queen Mary's time were still serving their flocks many years later. In January 1605, William Moore, Vicar Choral of Wells Cathedral, and Mary Sarney a recusant widow, landed at Chepstow from Bristol. They were on their way to Raglan to be married by Walter Powell, a catholic priest. Sadly for them, their letters to Powell had been intercepted and passed to the bishop of Llandaff, Francis Godwin. Powell was 'a priest ordered in Queene Marie's daies ... sometime beneficed in the diocese of Llandaff' — as vicar of Raglan perhaps—who had given over his living thirty years before. He was 'A common massmonger ... abiding in no certen place' but 'lurking about Raglan for marriages and christenings with masses'. Godwin had complained to the Lord President of the Council, the Archbishop of Canterbury and the Judges of Assize, but Powell was under the powerful protection of the Herberts of Raglan. Moore, subsequently summoned before the cathedral chapter at Wells, admitted that he had been married to a recusant by a catholic priest and was ordered to appear before the bishop. Another catholic, George Morris M.A. of Usk and Machen, had been 'a preacher in Queen Mary's days, who did forsake his living for his Romish religion'.[4] Younger men were travelling abroad to seminaries, for example the Blessed William Gunter, a Raglan boy born about 1560, who entered the seminary at Rheims in 1583. Arrested in London in the invasion scare of Armada year, he was executed near the Theatre at Shoreditch in August 1588.[5]

Catholics hoped for some relaxation of anti-catholic legislation on the accession of James I. His mother, Mary Queen of Scots, had been a catholic, and in the eyes of some a catholic martyr, whilst James's Queen, Anne of Denmark, born a catholic, refused to take Communion at the Coronation service. James was not unsympathetic towards those of his mother's faith, but the catholic clergy were divided on acquiesence in his rule. The secular clergy favoured this, but the Jesuits, following Papal directives, were opposed. The 'Bye Plot' of 1603, the year of James's accession, had an aftermath in Monmouthshire. William Watson, a secular priest, disappointed in his hopes of an end to penal legislation, joined with other catholics to hatch this crazy plot to kidnap the king and force him to grant toleration. A 'Mr Meredith of Abergavenny' told him that 10,000 catholics were ready to rise in the border counties. There were suspicious movements of armed catholics in Archenfield and talk of a march on London. When the Plot collapsed, Watson fled west, accompanied by a Pembrokeshire catholic, in the hope of reaching Ireland. In an Abergavenny inn he was questioned by a J.P., William Baker. Outside Abergavenny, Watson and his guide, 'a Catholick man of Wales called David Williams', stopped at a further alehouse for a drink. Williams was recognised by 'one Vaughan, a Justice of the Peace and his brother' and arrested. Williams was in prison for a long time and Watson hanged.[6]

The Caerleon episode, referred to at the start of this chapter, occurred the following year and with the Gunpowder Plot in 1605 reflected similar frustrations. After the latter, the king's proclamation was read in all market places in the county, and ports, roads and bridges watched for fugitives or suspicious travellers. 'Though the county abounds in recusants' the magistrates reported 'they seemed ignorant of the plot'. The gentlemen of the county wrote in similar vein to the earl of Worcester that 'this newes [of the plot] ys verie straunge … Neyther can we understand any maner of preparation [for] soe haynouse a treason in any place within this countie'.[7] Monmouthshire however, with its many recusants, was a possible place of refuge for catholic plotters. The Jesuit Robert Jones tried to save the lives of two minor Gunpowder

Plotters, Robert Winter and Humphrey Littleton, by having them guided to the Cwm at Welsh Newton by George Charnock, a Monmouth tailor. The escape attempt failed. Winter and Littleton were hanged, and Charnock ended up in Worcester Gaol.[8]

Monmouthshire had the highest proportion of catholic recusants in England or Wales, higher even than Lancashire which was known for its recusancy. Lists of 1603 and 1605 record the number in each Welsh diocese. Whilst such lists are notoriously inaccurate, they probably give a generally reliable picture and indicate that there were twice as many catholic recusants in Monmouthshire as in the rest of the dioceses of Llandaff and St Davids put together.[9]

The reasons for this strength are not immediately obvious. Lancashire was remote and with poor communications, its gentry 'introspective and self-sufficient', seldom marrying outside the county.[10] Monmouthshire was not particularly remote, and, whatever the shortcomings of its roads, enjoyed good communications, particularly by sea and river, with Bristol and Gloucester. Despite what Webb, speaking of neighbouring Herefordshire, called the 'universal cousinship among the gentry' a respectable number of outside families had bought or inherited land in the county. Tre-Owen, one of its great houses, had been built with money inherited from an uncle who was a London Merchant Venturer. James Gunter of Abergavenny and Roger Williams of Usk, founders of major county families, had lived and worked as lawyers in London. The Gainsfords of Upper Dyffryn, Grosmont were from Carshalton in Surrey; the recusant Milbornes of Wonastow, one of whom was a Middle Temple lawyer, were from Somerset. The priest hunter, John Arnold, was from an illegitimate branch of the Arnolds of Highnam outside Gloucester. When a small estate at Wilcrick was sequestrated under the Commonwealth, one claimant to it was a Dorset man. A Monmouthshire clergyman had a kinsman and namesake who was chaplain to the British trade factory in Aleppo and later bishop of Gloucester. John Byrd of Caerleon, customs official and tenant of the Earl of Pembroke, was a Bristolian, and many boys and some girls from Monmouthshire were apprenticed in Bristol. Sir Nicholas Kemeys lived in Llanvair Discoed on the fringes of Wentwood, but was listed by Symonds among the principal gentlemen of Glamorgan. William Wroth, the puritan rector of Llanvair Discoed, was presented to his living by another Glamorganshire gentleman, Sir Edward Lewis of the Van (they had been at Oxford together), whose family was resident at Edington in Wiltshire. Many gentry had been educated at Oxford, particularly at Jesus, 'The Welsh college'. Others, including catholics, attended the Inns of Court, where a gentleman could acquire the legal training useful in his role as landowner and magistrate and where religious tests and oaths of allegiance were not required.[11]

Nor was the catholicism purely a matter of conservative survivalism. At Abergavenny, the future saint David Lewis, his father Morgan Lewis and great uncle Augustine Baker, later a Benedictine monk, all initially conformed to the Elizabethan church settlement. In 1626, questions were asked in Parliament about the numbers of recusants among the pupils of Abergavenny Grammar School, where Morgan Lewis was headmaster. The House was assured that Lewis was a protestant and 'very conformable' to the established Church. Augustine Baker was reconciled to Rome in 1603, David Lewis in Paris 30 years later. The claims of alarmed protestants that the number of recusants was increasing were not wholly unfounded.[12]

Abergavenny Grammar School was housed in the disused church of St John from 1543 to 1898, when a new school was built. Morgan Lewis, father of St David Lewis, and Henry Vaughan, the displaced vicar of Panteg, were both headmasters here.
(Photograph by Jeremy Knight)

In 1586 Sir William Herbert of St Julians, a man of puritan sympathies, wrote to Sir Francis Walshingham explaining why so many in Monmouthshire were 'backward in religion'. He attributed it to 'want of instruction' (the shortage of Anglican parish clergy); 'want of correction' (the fines for recusancy were said to be ineffective); 'the over great countenance of men of great calling' (like the Earl of Worcester) and 'continual hopes of change'.[13] Queen Elizabeth was at an advanced age and unmarried, Mary Queen of Scots was still alive, and the succession to the throne undecided. Herbert was doing his best, but seminary priests were 'sowing the seeds of sedition and error' and undermining his efforts. Over 20 years later, Lord Eure, President of the Council in the Marches, was also concerned about the number of recusants. The Bishop of Llandaff, he wrote to Lord Salisbury, believed that 'the multitude of recusants ... groweth only by the scarcity of preaching ministers' made worse by the way in which lay impropriations of tithes and royal exactions left 'so small a proportion allowed for discharge of the cure as a minister will not accept thereof, as not being able to live by it'. Clergy were so scarce that the bishop was 'enforced to permitt lay people to execute that function'. Eure's scheme for raising £200 yearly from recusants' fines (which he implies often remained uncollected) to fund five or six 'proficient ministers' of the reformed Church in the main towns of Monmouthshire did not materialise, though something very similar was to be instituted by the puritans during the Interregnum.[14]

The lists of those fined as recusants for non-attendance at church were initially entered on the Pipe Rolls, but these became so cluttered that from 1592–3 special recusant rolls were opened. Pugh's maps show the distribution of catholics in the county, but the draconian anti-catholic legislation depended, in the absence of any effective police force, on the co-operation of local officials. Often administrative inertia, the influence of sympathetic local gentry and a desire for good neighbourliness could override religious differences. The main peaks of coercion are clear enough, particularly the Armada year of 1588 and the aftermath of the Gunpowder Treason in 1606–7. The many fines on families such as the Morgans of Llantarnam or the Morgans of the Garn show that resident catholic gentry could not always rely on parish officials to protect them. The Morgans of the Garn accounted for 44 of the 83 recusancy fines in Tredunnock, and their servants and dependants no doubt added to the total. The presence of zealous protestant gentry or clergy could also affect matters. In Llanhennock, the next parish to Tredunnock, there was a concerted campaign in 1596–1604, including the arraignment of a group of 11 women. It was not unknown for a husband, as head of the household, to attend church or take communion on behalf of the entire family, and this, rather than catholicism, could be reflected (strictly speaking, a recusant was someone who did not go to church, not necessarily a catholic), though it was often the women of the family who preserved the old faith. After 1604 there were only four convictions, all fresh names. Here, the motive force may have been Giles Morgan of Pencrug, a zealous Anglican (to use a convenient anachronism), to whom Llanhennock church was granted in 1599 on condition that he maintained it, and who left £5 in his will in 1638 towards a 'great bell' for it. In both parishes, the recusancy fines can thus be explained in terms of a resident gentry family. Some may have been fined for poor church attendance rather than for catholicism, as perhaps with a family of Grosmont coopers who were happy to use the services of the established Church for christenings and funerals.[15]

Urban Catholics Communities: Abergavenny and Caerleon

The towns of Monmouthshire show striking contrasts in religious affiliation. The ports of Chepstow and Newport, with their maritime links to Bristol and puritan south-west England had few or no recorded recusants. In contrast, Caerleon, only three miles from Newport, Monmouth, and Abergavenny had flourishing recusant communities. Monmouth is readily explained by the influence and patronage of the Worcesters, who controlled the town, and the many parish gentry in the area who claimed kinship with them. The contrast with Usk, a puritan-leaning town controlled by the rival Pembroke faction is marked.

Abergavenny was a flourishing inland market and wool town, a gateway to upland Wales, and a catholic stronghold. The absence of a resident lord and the shortcomings of the medieval alien Priory of St Mary had given the towns-people something of a tradition of self-help in religious matters. The number of recorded recusancy fines (75) is not particularly high, suggesting that in the pre-war period religious tensions were relatively low. In 1605 the Recorder of Abergavenny, David Baker, son of a major figure in its cloth industry, whose family had served as stewards to the lords of Abergavenny since the time of Henry VIII, left to become a Benedictine monk, Father Augustine Baker. Baker was a pioneer monastic historian of distinction. His six volumes of sources for the history of the Benedictine order in England survive in the Bodleian library and were used in a book published in 1626 of which he was joint author. We have a glimpse of him in the room outside Sir Robert Cotton's library in Westminster, sitting in fireside conversation with Cotton and William Camden.[16] His sister, Margaret, married Henry Pritchard, Gentleman, and was fined for recusancy in 1608. Of their children, John Pritchard became a Jesuit and Margaret wife of Morgan Lewis, headmaster of Abergavenny Grammar School.[17] Initially a protestant, Morgan Lewis became reconciled to Rome. On his last visit to Abergavenny in 1620, Augustine Baker stayed with his sister Margaret and would have met her three-year-old grandson, son of Margaret and Morgan Lewis, the future Jesuit martyr St David Lewis. Another of the family, the wealthy haberdasher and hat seller Nathaniel Pritchard, fined for recusancy in 1624, had his estate confiscated for recusancy under the Commonwealth.[18]

When David Lewis entered the English College in Rome about 1635 he described himself as follows (the danger of English agents entering under assumed identities obviously had to be guarded against):

> My name is David Lewis, alias Charles Baker. My father was Morgan Lewis and my mother Margaret Pritchard, both Catholics, who lately died of fever. I lived at Abergavenny, and was educated at the Royal Grammar School in that town, of which my father was Principal. He was of the middle class. Among my chief friends I number an uncle named John Pritchard, of the Society of Jesus. Up to my sixteenth year I was a heretic; about that time, leaving England, I crossed over to France with a noble youth, the son of Count Savage, with whom I lived for about three months in Paris, when by means of the Revd. Father Talbot, I embraced the Catholic faith, and on account of the war then raging [in France], I returned to England with the same nobleman, and lived nearly two years with my parents, on whose death, and assisted by the Revd. Father Brown, I bade adieu to my country on the 22nd of August and arrived in Rome on the 2nd November, and on the same day entered the college.[19]

The picture that emerges is one of a prosperous urban gentry, where those who accepted the Elizabethan church settlement and those loyal to the older faith were held together by ties of kinship. Augustine Baker's grandfather had been vicar of Abergavenny. The patron of the living, William Gunter of the Priory (with whom Charles I stayed in July 1645) represented the protestant branch of the family. He was the grandson of James Gunter, a London lawyer from a Breconshire family who, with his London father-in-law, speculated in abbey land. He bought the Priory and its demesne in 1546. Across the way from the Priory in High Street, Thomas Gunter (who had a common grandfather with William Gunter) had his house sequestrated for recusancy in 1648, though he was allowed to remain in it as tenant in view of his age and poverty.[20] His son, another Thomas Gunter, sheltered both David Lewis and his fellow martyr, Philip Evans, and had at the time of the Popish Plot a 'publick chappel ... adorned with the mark of the Jesuits [I H S] on the outside,where Mass was said'. His comment to the Anglican vicar at this time is deservedly well known: 'In Oliver's time of severity he kept a priest, and he would keep one now'.[21]

There were other catholic gentry in the countryside around Abergavenny. The Prodgers of Wernddu and of Gwernvale in Breconshire were professional courtiers who amassed a portfolio of court positions under James I, Charles I and Charles II. The progenitor of both branches was William ap John Prodger, M.P. for the county in 1588–9. His son, John William John Prodger, and daughter-in-law were fined as recusants in 1588 and the Wernddu Prodgers maintained a private catholic chapel until the 18th century. James Prodger served as a cornet in the Bishop's War of 1641. In the Civil War he raised James Prodger Herbert's Foot, with himself as Colonel and his younger brother, Charles Prodger, as Lt-Colonel, and fortified Abergavenny for the King. Charles Prodger may have been a 'church papist', for he was able to attend Oxford and to compound for his estate after the war.[22]

James Prodger or Prodger-Herbert claimed to represent the senior branch of the Herberts and was married to one of the Baker family. The recusant William Jones of the Hardwick was his cousin. The Joneses had been at Hardwick for two hundred years, and William's father, who had been at the Inns of Court, left him a small estate worth £300 a year. The medieval chapel at Hardwick still stood in 1621.[23]

In 1586, a wealthy Abergavenny tanner and landowner, John William Tanner, hoped in his will 'to be saved among the number of the elect'. This is our first glimpse of advanced Calvinist views in the town. Tanner was a kinsman of the Wroths, who despite the puritanism of William Wroth, himself a native of Abergavenny, included both protestants and catholics.[24] Signs of impending religious conflict in Abergavenny can be seen at the time of the Bye Plot in 1603, but the first clear view of this came in 1621. Eleazer Jackson was a protestant minister, possibly a curate in St Mary's. From his name he was not a local. He may have had links with the Wroths, and through them with the puritan community in Bristol.

In December 1621 Jackson complained to the House of Commons about the aggressive tactics of local recusants. He had upset the local *modus vivendi* and claimed that catholics had spread malicious rumours about him, denouncing his preaching and doctrines as blasphemous, and had intimidated his supporters with threats. One October evening two convicted recusants had burst into his room, engaged him in theological arguments about purgatory and the Virgin Mary, and rebuked him for 'handling matters of controversy in the pulpitt' and for obtaining a Warrant of the Peace against one Roger Howell. They assaulted him with a dagger and a candlestick and forced him to vow on his salvation that he would 'never preach more in that place' and leave the county forthwith.[25] Evidently, Abergavenny catholics were sufficiently integrated with the rest of the community to be concerned about what was said in the pulpit of the parish church, where previously doctrines such as purgatory and the worship of the Virgin Mary had evidently gone unchallenged. Two years later it was alleged that David Morgan, an Abergavenny recusant, was able to arrange the election of his fellow catholics as burgesses and bailiffs, and that they engaged in street fights with followers of William Morgan of Tredegar, the protestant Steward of Abergavenny and of his deputies, Henry and William Baker.[26] Over 30 years later, in the changed circumstances of the post-war period, another sermon in St Mary's was to spark off more controversy and a remarkable five hour public debate between Anglican clergy and puritan ministers on the subject of infant baptism.

Caerleon also had a large and influential recusant community. Indeed, Caerleon (119) and Llantarnam (157) had the highest number of convicted recusants in the county. The town had in the recent past been within the influence of the Morgans of Llantarnam. Thomas Churchyard in 1587 noted 'Maister Morgan of Lanternam in a fayre house dwelles two myle from Carleon' and 'A free schoole now erected by Maister Morgan of Lanternam', but they had been marginalised socially and financially by their recusancy, and their influence was on the wane. Even so, Edward Morgan's house at Penrhos outside Caerleon was a centre of rumours about armed papists and Jesuit priests and he and his wife were involved in the foundation of the Jesuit college at the Cwm.[27]

George Langley of Christchurch near Caerleon, a 'person of great power and abilitie' and member of a long established local family, was accused of keeping boats in Goldcliff Pill, 'an obscure place where no shipping used to resorte or people dwell', and of illegally exporting butter, leather, calf skins and hides 'for the benefitt and maintainance of other recusants beyond the seas'. However, as he was involved in quarrels over land enclosures in Christchurch, the allegations should be seen in relation to this. Goldcliff was one of the active small ports along the margins of the Gwent levels and the export of Welsh butter, though periodically declared illegal, was a major commerce in Monmouthshire. His trade was no doubt legitimate, but the implicit charge was that he was in touch with priests abroad, and that Goldcliff Pill, or Caerleon itself, were points at which catholic priests, and catholic books, could move in or out of the realm.[28]

Another Caerleon recusant had connections abroad even more alarming to anyone concerned about a possible catholic fifth column. Jane Pritchard was the sister of the Glamorgan catholic Royalist Sir Edward Stradling of St Donats, another alleged harbourer of priests. Her husband, William Pritchard, owned land in five Gwent Is Coed parishes. Jane evidently had a house at Caerwent, where she attracted five recusancy fines between 1592 and 1598, but her husband's will in 1598 describes him as 'of Caerleon'. Her brother, David, fled to Spain in 1573, her sister, Gwenllian, was in Louvain and another sister was companion to Jane Dormer, Duchess of Feria. Jane Dormer had been a friend and confidant of Mary Tudor and married the Duke of Feria, a grandee who had come to England with Philip II when he married Mary. The duke was Spanish ambassador in London at Queen Elizabeth's accession, and had suggested to Lord Cecil that the political situation might be resolved if Elizabeth married Philip. When Anglo-Spanish relations worsened, the duke and duchess moved to Flanders and then to the duke's estates at Zafra between Merida and Seville, which, after his death, became a centre for catholic exiles.[29]

Caerleon was a port with close contacts with Bristol, where many Caerleon boys were apprenticed, and had widespread maritime links. Under these circumstances, one might have expected few recusants, as in Chepstow or Newport. The wealthy gentry among the Caerleon catholics (what Barry Rea described as 'the devotional bookish Catholicism of the gentry household' and as 'a nonconformity of the gentry'), can only be explained by the proximity of the Morgans. This agrees with Richard Church's view, cited by Rea, that a recusant community below gentry level was 'almost always dependant on the proximity of a resident recusant gentleman'.[30]

The absence of church registers and similar sources makes it difficult to explore the relationships of the recusant community of Caerleon with their fellow townspeople. From the few sources available, it seems that families distinguished by master mariners, Bristol apprentices and (unsurprisingly) bequests to Caerleon church are absent from the recusant rolls. Against George Langley, we can set the career of an earlier member of his family. Philip Langley, the orphan son of a Caerleon husbandman, was apprenticed to a Bristol grocer in 1541. By the time of his death in 1592 he was an Alderman of the city of Bristol, armigerous, and with land in three counties. He was also a firm protestant, who began his will with a Biblical quotation and left his Bible and his law book ('Book of Statutes') to his son. He still regarded himself as a Caerleon man, as his bequests for the repair of roads and bridges around Caerleon show.

In Cromwellian times the business correspondence of John Byrd—a Bristolian, a Parliamentary sympathiser (who lost his post after the Restoration) and a customary tenant of the Earl of Pembroke—much of it dated from Caerleon, gives little indication of the catholic community there. His busy concern with merchant shipping (one son became a naval officer), customs dues and his official duties is the opposite side of the coin to the conservative catholic gentry of Caerleon and Llantarnam.[31]

The size of the recusant community in Caerleon can only be estimated from the Compton census of 1676, which lists 68 'conformists', 21 'papists' and 7 'nonconformists'. Though the intention was to list all adults aged over 16, often only the number of households was counted, and this seems to be case here. Using a multiplier of 4.25 (a widely used estimate for determining population size from the number of households) gives a figure of 96 households and 408 inhabitants. As Caerleon in 1545 had 400 'housling people' (communicants), this is surprisingly low for the population had doubtless grown in the intervening 130 years. Philip Jenkins has suggested that overall, Welsh figures from the Compton census are half what would be expected from Hearth Tax returns. In theory, all adults were legally bound to attend church and take communion, but in practice this was not the case. Other religious censuses invariably bring to light (with varying degrees of disapproval) a proportion of people outside the orbit of organized religion. For Caerleon, population figures often distinguish between the town itself and the parish as a whole, including the cross-river suburb of Ultra Pontem. A religious census in 1763 listed 126 families (x 4.2 = 635 people) for the town and 162 (= 689) for the parish. The Compton figures agree better with the former. It would seem that the population of Caerleon comprised around 90 recusants and 30 nonconformists, children included, about 290 Anglicans, and an unknown number, perhaps 150–200, outside the bounds of organized religion.[32]

By Law Established: The Anglican Clergy
William Herbert of St Julians (d.1593), who was so concerned about the weakness of the established Church in Monmouthshire, had three ambitions: to write a book, found a colony and establish a college. Whilst owner of much of the Fitzgerald lands of Munster, he translated parts of the Anglican service into Irish and briefly established a college there. When the lands for this were claimed by another planter, he moved this college to his house at Tintern, and endowed it with lands in Bassaleg, though the foundation ceased with his death. His Munster and Monmouthshire colleges were presumably intended to train clergy for areas where they were badly needed and in short supply.[33]

Monmouthshire livings were so poor that it was often difficult to find clergy who would accept them. The reformation had resulted in the large scale plunder of ecclesiastical lands. Not only had monastic lands transformed the economic and social status of those families able to acquire them, but at parish level the greater part of tithe payments had been diverted into the hands of lay impropriators, leaving only a small proportion for the support of parish clergy. Sir Edward Herbert of Chirbury made £140 a year from the rectories of Bedwellty and Mynyddislwyn, paying £10 a year to each curate. Nor were the impropriators necessarily supporters of the established Church. The militant catholic Edward Morgan of Llantarnam drew an annual profit of £173 6s. 8d. from the impropriations of eight Monmouthshire parishes, mostly a block in the Caerleon-Goldcliff area, after paying the salaries of the vicars and curates. Of 101 parishes listed by Godwin the profits of 79 were in the lands of local gentry, most of the rest in those of the Earls of Worcester and Pembroke.[34] The poorly paid curates who served the smaller parishes seldom appear in the records, and such churches often have no recorded clergy before the 18th century. Llanhennock, granted to Giles Morgan in 1599, has none before 1756.[35]

Monmouthshire was in the diocese of Llandaff, one of the poorest British sees and one which able men were reluctant to accept. George Carlton (bishop 1617–19) felt he could do little good because of his ignorance of the Welsh language and the opposition of powerful local catholics — 'some great ones that hate the truth'. Francis Godwin (bishop 1601–1617) was a notable scholar and church historian, a friend of William Camden and the first person to collect, and to record systematically, Roman inscriptions from Caerleon. His collection from Moynes Court still forms the core of the epigraphic collections in the Roman Legionary Museum at Caerleon. He could make little headway however against the catholic priests under Worcester's protection. Though he intercepted letters to suspected priests, his repeated complaints to the secular authorities about the activities of Walter Powell of Raglan were useless. Both Carleton and Godwin accepted, no doubt with relief, preferment to richer, but also more fruitful sees. Their successor, Theophilus Field, though from a puritan background, was one of the less satisfactory bishops of Llandaff. Appointed in 1619 under the patronage of Buckingham, his one success was to replace Laud as bishop of St Davids in 1627.[36]

William Laud, Archbishop of Canterbury from 1633, introduced what would now be described as 'High Church' reforms of the Anglican church, revising its liturgy, doctrines and church furnishings to create what he called 'the beauty of holiness'. His abrasive personality and brutal suppression of any opposition made him widely unpopular. Suspected by his puritan enemies of being a crypto-catholic (he had twice been offered a cardinal's hat by the pope) he was among the leading causes of the Civil War. The first Laudian bishop of

Llandaff, William Murray (bishop 1627–1639) was a Scot, previously an Irish bishop, who improved the fabric and liturgy of his cathedral, but puritans rather than catholics were now the main enemy. His successor, Morgan Owen, marked a return to the Elizabethan practice of appointing Welshmen to the see. Son of a Carmarthenshire clergyman and descendant of the famous doctors of Myddfai, his tenure was brief. Imprisoned in the Tower in 1641, he subsequently retired to his native Carmarthenshire, where he is said to have died of grief on hearing of the execution of Laud. The episcopates of Murray and Owen saw the appointment of new resident clergy of a Laudian stamp. George Crump, at Trellech from 1639, left his mark in a suite of Laudian style woodwork, including altar rails, much of which survives. The previous incumbent, the pluralist son of an earlier bishop of Llandaff, and Chancellor of Hereford cathedral, was presumably non-resident. Henry Vaughan, at Panteg from 1643, was an Oxford Fellow and a Laudian preacher of some repute.

Panteg church. Henry Vaughan, a former Fellow of Jesus College Oxford, was presented to Panteg church by the University of Oxford. At the outbreak of war, he joined the Royalists at Oxford, where he preached before Charles I. Expelled from his living by the puritans, he became headmaster of Abergavenny Grammar School. (Photograph by Jeremy Knight)

Despite their many problems, the educational standards of parish clergy had improved considerably under the early Stuarts; most beneficed parish clergy were now university graduates. This improved their social status and, despite the poverty of many curates, helped to reduce the pool of clerical unemployed who in later medieval times had depressed the economic status of chantry priests and other low paid clergy. Most Oxford colleges were represented among the Gwent clergy, though Jesus was, unsurprisingly (as 'the Welsh college'), best represented. When John Edwards, vicar of Tredunnock, a Jesus man, was deprived of his living by the puritans in 1648, he was replaced by Walter Prosser, another Jesus man.[37]

Something of the variety of men among the parish clergy is brought out by their relationships with the landowners who were patrons of their livings. John Dobbins of Llangattock vibion Avel was a Herefordshire man, appointed to the living by Thomas Evans, the principal parish landowner, whose wife was a Dobbins. Nathaniel Collington was given the lucrative living of Caldicot by Sir Nicholas Kemeys. Collington was a Kentish man, where he was vicar of his native Broughton, and Caldicot was served by a curate.[38] The majority were from Monmouthshire however, like the ambitious John Edwards, son of the curate of Caldicot, who, after Jesus College, acquired an impressive catalogue of Monmouthshire livings between 1608 and 1635, including Langstone,

Bryngwyn Church. The vicar, Robert Frampton, took refuge in Raglan Castle during the siege, along with his parish register. Restored to his living at the Restoration, he died in 1685 aged 83. (Photograph by Jeremy Knight)

Brass to Robert Frampton in Bryngwyn church, replacing an earlier marble slab with the same Latin inscription: 'Robert Frampton, Bachelor of Divinity, skilled in the Latin, Greek, Hebrew and Welsh tongues, long lived rector of this parish from 1632 to 1685. When living and in good health, he, out of gratitude to God and the Church, willed this monument. Dying on 6 January, his son William Frampton set it up.'
(Photograph by Jeremy Knight)

Llanmartin, Wilcrick, Tredunnock (where he purchased the living and appointed himself) and Magor. Deprived by the puritans for 'malignancy and persecution of the godly in his neighbourhood', he devoted his leisure to translating an anti-puritan religious book *The Marrow of Divinity* into Welsh, dedicated to the principal gentry families of the county.[39] Henry Vaughan, a Merioneth man and former fellow of Jesus, was presented to Panteg in 1643 by the University of Oxford, under legislation which forbad catholics (in this case the Morgans of Llantarnam) to appoint to Anglican livings. His parish register shows that he was resident until he joined the King in Oxford.[40] Robert Frampton of Bryngwyn was similarly resident and, though a Dorset man, added Welsh to his Latin, Greek and Hebrew. Though he had been present in Raglan Castle during the siege, the puritan committee for ejecting scandalous ministers found no fault with him, and initially allowed him to retain his living. His son became senior proctor of the University of Oxford and his kinsman and namesake was chaplain to the English Trade Factory at Aleppo and later a non-juring Bishop of Gloucester.[41] Though many curates and poor parish clergy lived on wholly inadequate stipends, many of those in the richer livings were comfortably well off, with good amounts of land and livestock, as wills confirm.[42]

Though curates were poorly paid, and are poorly represented in our sources, they were far from being nonentities. The great scholar-naturalist Gilbert White was only curate of Selborne, the living being in the hands of an Oxford college. Lewis James, the Royalist curate of Bedwellty, has left a record of his ministry in the parish records kept in the new register book which he bought in Bristol and in the way he continued the pastoral care of his flock after he had been deprived of his living by the puritans. On the other side of the divide, Henry Walter, a graduate of Jesus College, and perpetual curate of the family living of

Mounton, became an important puritan divine under the Commonwealth. Edmund Jones had heard handed down stories of 'Sir Philip', the pre-reformation curate of Aberystruth (and his pet goat), but he also recalled hearing of his father going with other young men of the parish to Bedwellty to hear a sermon from Hywel Williams, the curate there, in Cromwellian times. He also remembered Ambrose Moston, the puritan minister expelled from Aberystruth at the Restoration, preaching at the churchyard stile there, and being pelted with dead hedgehogs taken from yew trees in the churchyard.[43]

The Beginnings of Dissent

There had been religious radicals in the Gloucestershire weaving towns since the time of the Lollards, and the influence of Latimer among the Bristol merchants and of Bishop Hooper in Gloucester under Edward VI were to give Gloucestershire a strong protestant tradition. By Elizabethan times, wills show that puritan and Calvinist ideas were already appearing among some of the gentry of the coastal plains of southern Monmouthshire, mostly among wealthy men with metropolitan connections. John Robnett of St Bride's Netherwent, whose daughter married John Walter of Piercefield, hoped 'to be saved and counted among the elect' in 1562,[44] whilst Lewis Thomas of Newport, the overseer of whose will was a London saddler, hoped 'to be among the elected' in 1583–4. John Gyrlinge, Gent, of Caerleon who expressed similar sentiments in 1599 owned a house in London, and dealt in property and money lending.[45] Similar religious ideas were also reaching Abergavenny. John Williams, a wealthy Abergavenny tanner (alias John William Tanner), who owned a number of properties in the town, and land in eight other parishes, hoped in 1586 to be 'saved among the number of the elect'. Though such ideas reflect standard Elizabethan Calvinistic orthodoxy, and though doubts have been expressed as to whether phrases in wills reflect the beliefs of the testators, or of the clergy or others who drafted the wills, they at least show that such ideas were becoming current among some of the more outward looking of the well to do.[46]

2 The Anatomy of Stuart Monmouthshire

Apart from its high number of recusants, Monmouthshire was special in other ways. It was already regarded as neither wholly English nor wholly Welsh. A pamphlet of 1607 contained 'Lamentable newes out of Monmouthshire in Wales', but another of 1652 spoke more legalistically of 'the six counties of south Wales and the county of Monmouth'. Similarly, whilst according to the clergyman John Edwards, brought up in Caldicot, the Welsh language was already losing ground there, in Abergavenny, somewhat earlier, 'The main or principall language was the Welsh or British tongue'. Around 1580 the future Benedictine, Augustine Baker, had been sent by his father, a prominent Abergavenny cloth merchant, to school in London to learn English.

One major problem in studying Monmouthshire in the Civil War period in the absence of Quarter Sessions or parish records is the scarcity of sources for the population below gentry level. When war came, were most people prepared to follow the lead of their local magnates and gentry? Did they regard the whole thing as a tiresome and ruinous quarrel among their betters? Was there a class element—the 'middling sort' of townspeople, craftsmen and freeholders versus the nobility and gentry and elements of the labouring poor? Were there strong regional or localist elements, perhaps related to the ecology and land use of particular areas? The answer to all these questions is probably 'yes' and the views of well placed contemporary observers can be cited in support of all four. We are not dealing with a general election. People had no way of casting a vote, though we can make informed guesses about how particular areas might have voted. The best we can do is to look at what evidence there is from Monmouthshire with these far from mutually exclusive options in mind.[1]

The Market Towns
The settlement pattern of Gwent is determined by its rivers. On the east, it is divided from Gloucestershire by the Wye, flowing between the river cliffs and steep forested slopes which so impressed William Wordsworth and early Romantic travellers. The two crossing points at Monmouth and Chepstow

developed into medieval market towns on the sites of minor Roman settlements. During the Civil War, the Wye separated Royalist Monmouthshire from Parliamentarian Gloucester and, nearer at hand, from the Forest of Dean, whose inhabitants were noted for their dislike of the King, and of their Welsh neighbours. There were engagements along this front line at Beachley, Chepstow, Lancaut and Monmouth. Only when Chepstow and Monmouth, with Hereford further up the Wye, finally fell to Parliament late in 1645 were the gates to south Wales opened.

Further west, the pattern of Roman fortresses and forts determined much of the later urban geography, not least because the roads linking them were, with the rivers, the only effective means of communication within the county. Valentine Morris of Piercefield told the House of Commons that there were no roads in Monmouthshire; 'We travel in ditches' he added. Under Nero, a fortress for Legio XX was built at Usk in the geographical centre of the later county, where communication routes by land and water up the Usk Valley were joined by a road from a fort at Monmouth via the valleys of the Trothy and Olway. An auxiliary cavalry fort was added ten miles upstream, where the valley narrows sharply at its junction with the Gavenny, a stream which gives its name to the modern town of Abergavenny. In A.D. 74–78 Julius Frontinus replaced the Usk fortress with a new legionary base at Caerleon (*Isca*—named from the river) eight miles downstream. Here, ship-borne bulk supplies could be brought in at a good bridging point. These Roman settlements at Monmouth and Chepstow on the Wye, and forts in the Usk valley at Caerleon, Usk and Abergavenny provided the sites first for Anglo-Norman castles and then for the medieval market towns which grew up outside their gates.

To John Aubrey, Chepstow was 'the key of south Wales: a well walled town and a strong and stately castle; the foundation whereof on the east side is rooted in the River Wye, which washes it'.[2] It linked the river trade of the Wye with Bristol and the Atlantic seaways. Timber and oak bark from Wye and Dean forests, and iron and brass from the iron furnaces and forges around the Elizabethan wireworks at Tintern travelled through Chepstow to Bristol and beyond. Medieval Chepstow and Monmouth originated with castles built by the Norman conqueror William fitz Osbern (d.1071), Chepstow replacing the landlocked Roman town of *Venta Silurum* at Caerwent. As Leland explained:

> A great lykelyhod ys that when Cairguent began to decay then began Chepstow to florisch. For yt stondeth far better as upon Wy, there ebbyng and flowyng by the Rage cummyng owt of Severn. So that to Chepstow may cum great Shyppes.[3]

Chepstow's original Welsh name *Strigoil* or *Estriguel*, 'the bends of the river', already recorded in Domesday, was soon replaced by that of the town which

Map showing the natural features of Monmouthshire, and houses of the main participants

HEREFORDSHIRE

BRECONSHIRE

Monnow

Grosmont

•A

Skenfrith

•A

Hundred of Skenfrith

•B

Llantilio Crossenny

•C

Hundred of Abergavenny

Abergavenny •D

Monmouth

B C

•E
•F

G
L
O
U
C
E
S
T
E
R
S
H
I
R
E

Raglan Castle

Troddi

Usk

Hundred of Raglan

Trellech •B

•A

•A

Hundred of Trellech

C •Usk

B•

D•

Hundred of Usk

Wye

Wentwood

•A

H•

G• •B

Chepstow

E• •I •D •E •F

Caerleon

Ebbw

F•

Gwent Is Coed

A •C

Caldicot

•G

•A

•B

C• Newport

D•

Rhymney

Hundred of Newport

Hundred of Caldicot

E•

Gwent Levels

Wentloog Level

Land over 250 metres

GLAMORGAN

1   8 kms
1   5 miles

Hundred of Newport	**Hundred of Usk**	**Hundred of Skenfrith**
A Penllwyn Sarth (Morgan)	A Trostrey (Hughes)	A Upper Dyffryn (Gainsford)
B Machen (Morgan)	B Cilfeigan (Morgan)	B Treowen (Jones)
C Gwern Y Cleppa (Pretty)	C Cefn Ila (Williams)	C Wonastow (Milborne)
D Tredegar (Morgan)	D Llangibby (Williams)	
E Cefn Mably (Kemeys)	E Llantarnam (Morgan)	**Hundred of Abergavenny**
	F Penrhos (Morgan)	A Llanfihangel (Arnold)
Hundred of Caldicot	G Llansor (Morgan)	B Llantilio Pertholey (Parry)
A Pencoed (Morgan)	H Pencrug (Morgan)	C Wernddu (Prodger)
B Pen y Wyrlod (Morgan)	I Kemeys Inferior (Kemeys of	D Llandewi Rhydderch (Lewis)
C Merthyr Geryn (Nicholas)	Kemeys)	E Coldbrook (Herbert)
D Llanvair Discoed (Kemeys)		F Hardwick (Jones)
E Dinham (Blethin)	**Hundred of Trellech**	
F Moynes Court (Hughes)	A Llansoy (Jones)	
G St Pierre (Lewis)	B Pant Glas (Probert)	

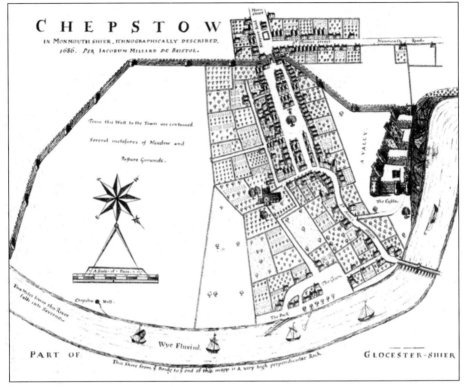

Millerd's map of Chepstow 1686

sprang up outside its gates: Cheap Stow—'The market town', as English as London's Cheapside. In Edwardian times, Chepstow acquired impressive town walls, though how effective these were in any military sense is uncertain. The town gate, with its wide arch, lacked any serious defences and in the absence of a ditch, a simple ladder would have served to scale the walls at any point along their lengthy circuit.

Partly for tenurial reasons, Monmouth never developed into a major medieval castle on the scale of Chepstow, though as a town with strong royal connections it emerged as the shire town and administrative and assize centre in the 16th century. Sited in a river loop at the junction of the Wye and Monnow, its defences were not particularly strong. The medieval fortified Monnow Bridge is an impressive piece of military architecture, but today in summer it is possible to wade across the river upstream of the bridge dryshod in Wellingtons. The higher ground in the neck of the river loop contained the castle and Edwardian town walls. Both were operational during the Civil War, though the frequency with which Monmouth changed hands shows their military limitations. Perhaps because of the weakness of the river defences, the cross-river suburb of Overmonnow, outside the Monnow Bridge, was

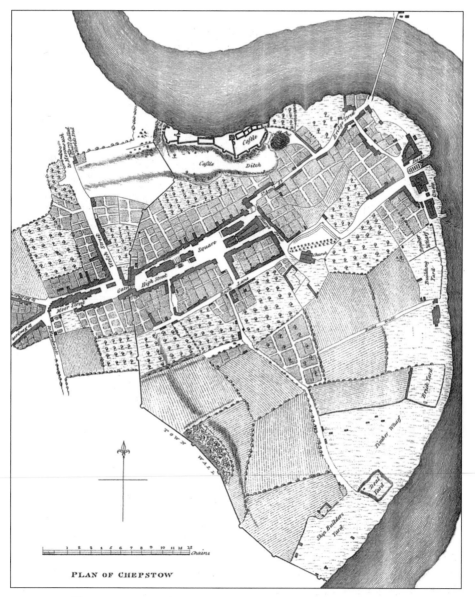

Chepstow town plan of 1798, surveyed by Thomas Morrice
(from Coxe's Historical Tour in Monmouthshire*)*

protected by a semi-circle of wet ditch known as the Clawdd Ddu ('Black ditch').

From Monmouth and Chepstow, Roman roads ran westward towards the next river crossing, that of the Usk. The road from Chepstow ran through the fertile lowland plain of Gwent Is-Coed (Gwent under (Went)wood) to the former Roman civitas capital of Caerwent (*Venta Silurum*) and thence to

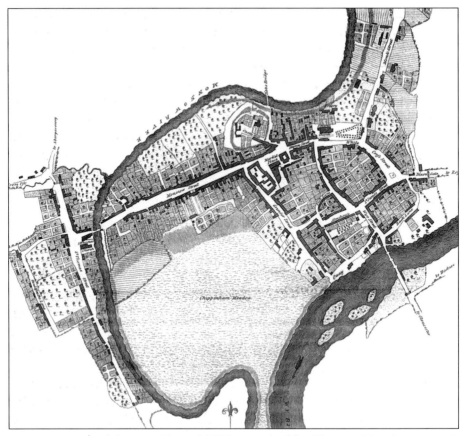

Monmouth town Plan of 1798, surveyed by Thomas Morrice
(from Coxe's Historical Tour in Monmouthshire*)*

Caerleon. Caerleon castle was there by Domesday, but it lay on the margins of the lordship of Chepstow and changed hands between Welsh and English several times before it was finally wrested from its last Welsh lord, Hywel ap Iorwerth, by William Marshall the Elder in 1217. Though an active medieval port, Caerleon never became the centre of a marcher lordship. Its marginal position is brought out by Leland:

> some say that Caerleon is in Base Ventland [Gwent Is Coed] and some say nay. [t stood] magnificently on the farther side of Wische [Usk] … So that very great Shyppes might wel cum now to the Town, as they did in the Romaynes Tyme, but that Newport Bridge is a Lette. Nevertheless, bygge Botes cummeth to the Towne. The Ruines of the [Roman] Walles of the Town yet remayne, and also of the Castel.[4]

When the lordship of Chepstow was divided in 1246, Usk became caput of a new lordship, which included Caerleon. Usk Castle, on higher ground above the legionary fortress, was largely built by William Marshall the Elder in the early 13th century. The massive 15th-century gatehouse is still inhabited. By the 16th century, Caerleon and Usk castles were largely ruinous, eclipsed by the fortress-palace of the Herberts at Raglan five miles from Usk. Neither played any significant role in the Civil War. The gatehouse at Usk was the residence of Thomas Herbert, steward of the lordship, and half-brother of the Parliamentary Colonel Henry Herbert of Coldbrook. The town retained some importance (as it still does) as a convenient central place at which county organizations could hold meetings. The activities of the Parliamentary 'Committee in Usk' were a constant cause of complaint from former Royalists after the first Civil War and a major irritant leading to the second Civil War in 1647–8.

Newport, downstream on the Usk from Caerleon, had a different history. Gwynlliog, the most easterly of the 'seven cantrefs of Glamorgan', formed part of the Honour and Lordship of Glamorgan until the death of Gilbert de Clare at Bannockburn in 1314. Thereafter, Newport developed as a separate lordship, in Royal hands from 1521, and under Henry VIII was allotted to the new county of Monmouthshire. Its castle boasted an impressive riverward façade (where defence was hardly needed), but elsewhere had only weak defences, probably unfinished. By Stuart times it was largely disused, though it had a small garrison, guarding the river crossing, during the war.[5]

Abergavenny, commanding the Usk valley where it narrows sharply as it enters the Welsh uplands, was a separate Marcher lordship, conquered by Hamelin de Ballon early in the reign of William Rufus. A wool town, Tudor and Stuart wills record bequests of at least six fulling mills in Abergavenny itself, several tucking mills, tucker's shears and cards and large flocks of sheep in the surrounding countryside. Abergavenny flannel was a major item of commerce.[6] It was also an important market town, at the gateway to upland Wales. In 1801 it was described as 'once the chief mart for supplying the midland parts of Wales with shop goods'. Convicted catholic recusants included a glover, a draper, a tailor, a haberdasher and a hatter. It had no resident lord, the Nevilles, who held the title of Lord Bergevenny, living in Kent. St Mary's was an alien priory, a daughter of St Vincent at Le Mans, with a mixed reputation (one 14th-century prior had fled with the house's valuables when faced with an official visitation and enquiry). The absence of a resident lord, and the lax state of the priory, meant that Abergavenny had a tradition of independence, particularly in religious matters. Although in the 15th century the priory underwent something of a renaissance, thanks to the patronage of the Herbert family, when the townspeople collected money for new church bells, even performing fundraising plays in surrounding villages, the monks contributed not a penny. 'And this' as Professor Sir Glanmor Williams remarked 'in their own Priory church'.[7]

*Abergavenny Town Plan of 1798, surveyed by Thomas Morrice
(from Coxe's* Historical Tour in Monmouthshire*)*

By Stuart times Abergavenny was the most populous town in the county. Clarendon called it 'the chief town in Monmouthshire'. Tax returns and the like consistently rank it first, with Newport and Monmouth vying for second place and the remaining towns lagging far behind.[8] Recorded wills proved in the prerogative court of Canterbury between 1560 and 1601 give a similar ranking, with Abergavenny (19), followed by Monmouth (13) and Newport (7). Usk had six testators, Chepstow five. A survey of 1545 gives a similar picture for the smaller towns. Newport had 660 'housling people' (communicants), Chepstow

440, Caerleon 400 and Usk 350. A different ranking order, reflecting commerce rather than land and property, is provided by the number of tradesmen issuing copper alloy tokens between 1656 and 1672. Chepstow had seven, Monmouth five, Abergavenny four and Caerleon one. There were none from Newport. Chepstow was outranked only by the ports of Carmarthen and Haverfordwest in south Wales and by Wrexham in the north. In addition, several Monmouth tokens have been found in Abergavenny, presumably reflecting Abergavenny people visiting the county town on business, and doing some shopping there.[9]

Lordships and Hundreds

The medieval Marcher lordships survived until the shiring of Monmouthshire in 1536, when they were replaced by Hundreds on the English model. Each had two Chief Constables — 'substantial gentlemen or yeomen' — appointed annually by the Justices of the Peace, sitting in Quarter Sessions, and an array of petty or parish constables. These formed the essential framework of Tudor and Stuart local government, responsible for local administration of justice and policing; military musters; 'contributions' and taxation; public order and the repair of highways. In 1631, when two bad harvests and soaring corn prices led to hoarding and bread riots, sheriffs were required to hold regular meetings with the Chief Constables and report to the government the numbers of vagrants punished, unlicensed alehouses shut down, young men and women apprenticed and measures taken for the relief of the poor and the control of corn prices in each Hundred, However the initiative was short lived.[10]

The lordship of Monmouth, a Crown possession since 1399, became the Hundred of Skenfrith. The much larger lordship of Chepstow (Strigoil) had been divided in medieval times into the lordships of Chepstow, Caldicot, Usk and Trellech. These became the four Hundreds of Caldicot (including Chepstow), Usk, Raglan and Trellech. In the Upper Usk valley, Hamelin de Ballon's lordship survived as the Hundred of Abergavenny. Gwynllwg (anglicised as Wentloog), the western fringes of the county between the river Rhymney and Newport, was now the Hundred of Newport. Edward VI granted it to William Herbert, fourth Earl of Pembroke by the second creation, along with Usk, Trellech and Caerleon. None of the castles involved were habitable, or in good repair. The main local seat of the Earls of Pembroke was at Cardiff Castle, though their kinsman Lord Herbert of Chirbury had a house at St Julians outside Newport. In contrast, their rivals the Herberts of Raglan controlled not only the central palace-fortress of Raglan, but the castles which formed the keys to the county at Chepstow and Monmouth and, indirectly, that at Abergavenny, where impressive church monuments and heraldic stained glass proclaimed the ancient glories of the house of Herbert.

The Hundred centres were not administrative antiquarianism, but convenient central meeting places within distinct geographic areas of the county. This explains the choice of Skenfrith for the Monnow Valley area, for Monmouth is on its very fringe, separated by ten miles of difficult and hilly country from White Castle or Grosmont, both of which are only half that distance from Skenfrith. Something similar may account for the choice of Caldicot rather than Chepstow as the hundredal centre for Gwent-Is-Coed, although Chepstow has always been the natural centre for this area, and was, with Usk, the meeting place of the County Committee during the Civil War. In both cases there may also have been a wish to separate the Hundred Court from the magnate influences that could have been brought to bear at Chepstow or Monmouth. Usk, at the geographical centre of the county; Raglan with its great Herbert castle; and Abergavenny are the natural centres for their sectors of the Usk Valley, even today. Trellech served the remote and wooded Trellech uplands west of the Wye between Monmouth and Chepstow and the Hundred of Newport comprised the old Lordship of Gwynllwg between the Rhymney and the Afon Llwyd.

Ecology, Economy and Religious Allegiance

The east/west pattern of road routes and river crossings is matched by a north/south pattern of geology and elevation. The forested Wentwood ridge separates two of the three main divisions of the county. On the south is Gwent Is Coed — 'Gwent under [Went] wood'. North of the ridge is Gwent Uwch Coed — 'Gwent above [Went]wood'. The western parts, adjoining Glamorgan, make up the third natural division, Gwynllwg, named after an alleged early ruler, Gwynllyw.

Gwent Is Coed

On the south, along the border of the Severn, are the Gwent levels, a geologically recent landscape of alluvial flats, whose settlement history has been the subject of much recent study.[11] Extensively settled and cultivated in Roman times, the area was later inundated by marine transgression. It was gradually re-settled in the medieval climatic optimum with nucleated villages with English names like Redwick (*Hreod-Wic*, 'the dairy farm where the reeds grow'), Whitson, Nash, Goldcliff or Peterston, protected by elaborate systems of drainage channels (reens) and a sea wall. Surprisingly large churches standing in an empty landscape suggest medieval prosperity and later decline. The sea defences had not saved the area in January 1607 (1606 Old Style) when climatic conditions and an exceptionally high tide led to a bursting of the sea walls, the flooding of over 20 parishes and heavy loss of life. This event is commemorated by inscriptions in many of the churches on the levels, whilst a pamphlet *Lamentable newes out of Monmouthshire in Wales* by W.W. (probably William Wroth, then a young clergyman fresh from University) recounted the disaster at length, with much puritan moralizing and a graphic woodcut of the flood. Henry Herbert, the future fifth Earl of Worcester and defender of Raglan Castle, and Sir Walter Montague led the rescue effort with boats 'fetched ten miles compasse upon waines'.

Something of the potential for conflict between improving landlords and their tenants seen in the forest edge areas to the north also existed on these

1 6 0 7

Lamentable newes out of Monmouth-
shire in Wales.

CONTAYNING,

The wonderfull and moſt fearefull accidents of
the great ouerflowing of waters in the ſaide Countye,
drowning infinite numbers of Cattell of all kinds, as Sheepe,
Oxen, Kine and horſes, with others: together
with the loſſe of many men, women and
Children, and the ſubuerſion of xxvi
Pariſhes in Ianuary laſt
1 6 0 7.

LONDON
Printed for W.W. and are to be ſolde in Paules Church
yarde at the ſigne of the Grey hound.

'Lamentable newes out of Monmouth-shire in Wales'. *Woodcut from the pamphlet describing the flood of January 1607. The calamity affecting the people and countryside could almost be symbolic of the effects of the Civil War. The author 'W.W.' is almost certainly the puritan William Wroth. (Newport Public Library)* coastal wetlands, but the situation was in reality rather different. In 1612, James I granted the manor of Caldicot to the Earl of Worcester. In 1640, a Royal auditor reported that 'large moors and commons belong to that manor, but he has no records of their acreage or fertility. No improvements can be made during the lives now in being, nor hardly afterwards, as divers other parishes common on the said moor'.[12] Most tenants and leaseholders had legal title rather than mere rights of common, many rights of common appertained to manors in different ownerships, and there was no valuable standing timber to tempt speculators who hoped to make money by felling the trees. Recent work on the Caroline enclosures in Dean has shown how, even there, the rights of existing tenants were respected, and that the conflict and unrest came rather from the large numbers of poor forest-edge squatters and commoners, the results of the 16th-century population explosion, whose rights were customary rather than of law.

North of these coastal levels is the lowland of Gwent Is Coed, fertile arable land, much of it on limestone, forming a corridor between the Vale of Gloucester and the very similar landscape of the Vale of Glamorgan to the west. This is a land of nucleated villages and hamlets, with a few stone-built medieval hall houses, those of higher status, like Penhow or Pencoed, fortified, more for show than defence. Links with Bristol, Somerset and Gloucestershire are strong, as the church towers show. This was the most highly anglicised part of Gwent, and Revd John Edwards of Tredunnock, writing in Cromwellian times, explained (though writing in Welsh) that his Welsh was not as fluent as it might be since around his native Caldicot its use was not widespread and English was more common. Similarly, Edward Lhwyd's correspondent at Caerwent claimed near the end of the century that 'none born in this parish speak Welsh'.[13]

Whilst the Gwent levels were dairy country, northern Gwent Is Coed was an area of mixed farming. Defoe commented on the large scale of corn exports from eastern Monmouthshire and when Nathan Rogers of Llanvair Discoed was arrested in 1678 during post-war disputes over the enclosure of Wentwood, one of his bitterest complaints was that this had taken place on the first day of harvest, at a time when he had 50 reapers at work. According to Edward Lhwyd's correspondent, the country around Caerwent grew 'Wheat, barley, pease [and] all sorts of grain' and 'As good Hay as any in ye county.[14] The milch cows, butter and cheese in wills from parishes like Magor, Piercefield, Newport, Caldicot and Christchurch show that this was also dairy country. In 1590, John Walter of Piercefield, of what was to become a noted puritan family, bequeathed to his wife a kilderkin (barrel) of butter and '20 cheeses made at my dairy on the Moor, and 4 of the best cheeses there'.[15] There was no exclusive connection between dairying and puritans however. The militant catholic George Langley of Christchurch was accused in 1609 of exporting large quantities of butter, leather, calf skins and raw hides through Goldcliff Pill, one cargo being worth £500.[16] The merchants of Bristol had a strong vested interest in Welsh butter.[17] and the value of butter exports from Monmouthshire and Glamorgan to south-west England were estimated to be £12,000 a year.[18] This again brought south Gwent into contact with Bristol, and with the ports of northern Somerset and north Devon, which had strong puritan traditions. David Underwood's concept of arable 'chalk' country, with more nucleation of settlement, seigneurial control and political and social conservatism, and contrasting 'cheese' country with pasture, scattered settlement, weaker seigneurial control and more independent and radical social structures is difficult to apply in this mixed environment.

The influence of Bristol was all important. Many Monmouthshire boys, and some girls, were bound apprentice there and by the end of the century a weekly market boat plied between Caerleon and the Welsh Back, the Bristol quay from which such boats sailed to Wales. The puritan church at Whitemeads was an elder sister to the separatist puritan congregation at Llanvaches, whose founder, William Wroth, was a familiar figure in the puritan pulpits of Bristol. One of the witnesses to his will in 1638 was the Chepstow born Bristol 'minister of God' Richard Blindman, vicar of Chepstow during the Interregnum. In August 1645, near the end of the war, the Royalist commander Jacob Astley complained to the courtier Lord Digby that Monmouthshire people, 'seeing Bristol blocked up and the river [Severn] for trade taken from them do incline to Parliament for their advantage'. When Bristol changed hands, it was the signal for leading gentry to change sides, as Kyrle and William Pretty did in 1643 when the Royalists took Bristol, and Trevor Williams and the Glamorgan Peaceable Army did in 1645 after Rupert surrendered it.

As we have seen, puritan Calvinist ideas were already reaching lowland Monmouthhire in Elizabethan times, among gentry and merchants with metropolitan connections. By the following century, many gentry in Caldicot Hundred were puritan in sympathy, perhaps because of the proximity of Bristol and Gloucester. In the Wye Valley above Chepstow, Henry Walter of Piercefield became the Cromwellian vicar of Newport, whilst three of the Morris family of Piercefield and Tintern served in the Parliamentary army, later emigrating to America.[19] The lawyer Sir Thomas Hughes of Moynes Court was a Parliamentary Colonel, Governor of Chepstow and M.P. for the county during the Interregnum though his brother Charles Hughes of Trostrey was a Royalist Major. The tone for the area was set by the carved oak pulpit which Sir Charles Williams of Llangybi, father of Sir Trevor Williams, gave to Caerwent church in 1632, with the uncompromising text 'Woe Be to Me if I Preach not the Gospel', and identifying the text in true Puritan style as I Corinthians 9.16, though a small carved shield with a view of Llandaff cathedral made it clear that he belonged to the Church by law established. The first separated Puritan cause (so-named as meeting outside the ambit of the established Church) in Wales was at Llanvaches in 1639. In contrast, there were very few convicted catholic recusants in Gwent Is Coed—none in Chepstow or the Gwent levels and only a handful in Magor and Caldicot.

Llanvaches lies on the margins of the Forest of Wentwood. Later reli-gious radicalism was associated with forest edge communities in this area, down to the time of the 19th-century Bible Christians. Here, a deter-mining factor was opposi-tion by such communities to de-afforestation and interference with rights of common by the catholic courtiers the Marquises of Worcester (later Dukes of Beaufort) in Wentwood,

Caerwent church pulpit of 1632, with details of the inscription opposite.
(Photographs by Elizabeth Pitman)

and their kinsman Sir John Wintour across the Gloucestershire border in Dean. Everyone, from the King down, admitted that the foresters of Dean were hostile to the Royalist cause. The Royalist *Mercurius Aulicus* called them 'most noto-rious rebels' and 'the rebel foresters'. Nor were they fond of their Welsh neigh-bours. The sharp population growth of the later 16th century created a large population of squatters and cottagers on the wastes of Dean, and these, together with the free miners and foresters, were threatened by Wintour's activities, leading to widespread riots in the pre-war era. Despite these, Lord Edward Herbert optimistically offered Prince Rupert Forest of Dean miners for his assault on Bristol in 1643, assuming that deference would overcome hostility.[20]

The forested Wentwood ridge merges to the east, across the Wye and the English border, with the Forest of Dean, and runs westwards to end in a wooded escarpment above the Usk between Caerleon and Usk. The feuds of this forest edge area were in full swing well before the war. In 1624, there were claims that Wintour—catholic nephew of the third Earl of Worcester, kinsman of a leader of the Gunpowder Plot, secretary to Queen Henrietta Maria, 'one of the Queen's White Boys '(Irish rebels), and partner in royal monopolies and dis-afforestations which interfered with the common rights of the Foresters—'and other Papists' had large stores of powder and ammunition in Raglan Castle and were plotting rebellion.[21] Three years later John Harry of Dinham in Wentwood was alleged to have said before witnesses that 'he cared not if these and the King were hanged'. George Jones, the parish constable, reported his words to Nicholas Kemeys of Llanvair Discoed, who warned him to say no more about it, since Harry was a friend of his. This might have been no more than a piece of good neighbourliness, but the way that the quarrel then escalated suggests that other factors were involved. Two other J.P.s committed Harry to prison, whereupon Kemeys summoned Jones and the

other witnesses, and threatened them. At Monmouth assizes they nevertheless gave evidence, only to see Harry acquitted by 'a compact Jury'. They were then threatened with arrest for perjury, forcing them, they claimed, to flee the county.[22]

In about 1630 the Earl of Worcester advanced £40,000 to the King in return for a grant of a third of Wentwood, comprising 3,000 acres in Chepstow Park Wood, Coed Lluvas, Cefn Garrow and the Veddw. The area contained many squatters and commoners, who survived around Shirenewton and the Veddw into recent times. The grant was opposed by landowners with rights in Wentwood, including Sir Nicholas Kemeys, William Wroth, Wroth Rogers and William Blethin of Dinham. All save the first were to be active Parliamentarians, though Wroth died at the beginning of the war. Rogers was to be a Parliamentary Colonel, Cromwellian governor of Hereford, and Deputy Major General. They failed to obtain redress at Common Law or an Injunction at Chancery, and were harassed by the 'Merciless Raglanders'. Rogers' estate was seized in an action for contempt and his wife and two small children forced to seek refuge at her mother's home in Glamorgan, where she died shortly after.[23]

The popular culture of the upland and forest-edge communities of western Britain had been under attack from puritans in the pre-war period. William Wroth (1576–1641) graduated from Jesus College Oxford in 1605 and some-time between 1611 and 1617 was appointed rector of Llanvaches by Sir Edward Lewis of the Van, Caerphilly. Wroth had been at Oxford with Lewis and was later chaplain to his widowed daughter-in-law and tutor to her children. Charles I's re-issue of his father's 1618 *Declaration of Sports* (*Book of Sports*) in 1633, permitting sports and relaxations on the sabbath, was in response to a puritan enactment in Somerset, with little legal backing, banning these, and the resulting opposition to the ban by the Laudian bishop of Bath and Wells. Sunday ball games in the churchyard were not unknown in the area, and William Wroth's riposte, originally the churchyard stile, can still be seen in the porch of Llanvair Discoed Church:

> Who Ever hear on Sonday
> Will Practis Playing At Ball,
> It May be before Monday
> The Devil Will Have you All

In 1635 Wroth was summoned to appear before the Court of High Commission for refusing to read *The Book of Sports* during divine service, as Laud had commanded. He submitted in 1638, and probably surrendered his living. In the following year, the puritan Henry Jessey visited Llanvaches and helped set up the first separated Church in Wales 'in the New England (*i.e.*

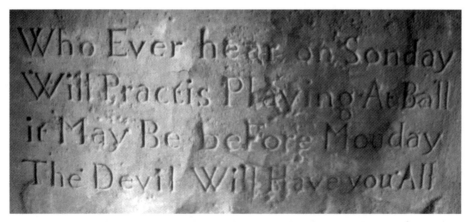

Inscription at Llanvair Discoed church, originally the churchyard stile: 'Who Ever Hear on Sonday' was William Wroth's counterblast to Laud's re-issue of James I's Book of Sports. (Photograph by Elizabeth Pitman)

Congregational) way', as 'the mother church of Antioch in the Gentile country of Wales'.[24]

If a puritan minister had to contend so hard with his own parishioners on the issue of Sunday sports, such sports must have been widespread elsewhere, not least for example in the parishes of the anti-puritan pluralist John Edwards. In another part of the county, after the war, some young men from Aberystruth in upland Gwent went to hear Hywel Williams, curate of Bedwellty, preaching there. They arrived early, and 'according to their manner at home' began to play ball (probably stoolball, a form of rounders or baseball) in the churchyard, for which they were soundly reproved by the curate. In the 18th century, the Mabsaint or parish festival was still kept up at Aberystruth, although by 1779

The William Wroth Chapel at Llanvaches, a modern chapel not on the original site. (Photograph by Jeremy Knight)

its date had been changed from the date of dedication in February to St Peter's Day (29 June). There were 'no acts of devotion, but much sinning' and its abolition was much desired by the minister and 'the sober part of the parishioners'. Though evidence is too scarce for analysis, conflict between puritan sabbatarianism and popular culture was not absent in the wooded and upland areas of the county.[25]

Gwent Uwch Coed

North of the Wentwood ridge, between the Wye and the Usk, is Gwent Uwch Coed—Gwent above the Wood, in many ways the Monmouthshire heartland. The fertile red sandstone soil, very like that of neighbouring Herefordshire, supports a mixed agriculture, with pasture predominating, and the Devonian sandstone, with timber from the many oakwoods, provided building materials for the solidly built vernacular farmhouses of the 16th and early 17th century that form the older units of settlement in most parishes. Edward Lhwyd's correspondent from Llantilio Pertholey near Abergavenny described the natural resources of his parish, with meadows, pasture (the number of cattle had been greatly increased by sowing clover), arable fields of wheat and barley, oak and ash woodland together with black and red grouse, bilberries and building stone from the Skyrydd and Sugarloaf.[26] Most parishes were small, suggesting modest medieval manorial settlements, with around four to half a dozen vernacular farmhouses per parish. They show the rise of a prosperous Tudor and early Stuart yeoman class, evidently geared to the market production of corn, livestock and wool. Defoe, later in the century, described large scale corn exports from eastern Monmouthshire through Bristol, and Fox related the chronology of the vernacular farmhouses to the rising price of corn between 1530 and 1640. Hoskins' comments on their Devon counterparts applied equally in Monmouthshire:

> The typical farmer of Stuart times lived in an isolated farmstead some distance from his neighbour … His farmhouse, barns and stables had probably all been rebuilt since 1580, and the buildings of his medieval predecessors swept away. He lived in the midst of his enclosed fields, arable and pasture, though his pasture was tending to become more important. In the higher parishes … tracts of rough heath and moor separated him from his neighbours, and made social intercourse next to impossible for several months of the year. There were however, more favoured parts … where villages were more common, and where there was little isolating waste. Here life was a more sociable business.

At times, these single farms may have replaced small late medieval hamlets.[27]

The eastern part of Gwent Uwch Coed comprised the Hundred of Trellech, an area of wooded upland, cold and wet in winter. Around Trellech itself were extensive commons of heather moor, with Blackcock, herds of goats, and scattered millstone quarries utilising the local 'puddingstone' conglomerate for large millstones which were exported as far as Ireland. The lordship belonged to the Parliamentarian Earl of Pembroke. Trellech had been an important borough in the earlier Middle Ages, perhaps an artificial planted creation, but suffered a population collapse after the climatic downturn of the early 14th century, partly due to pestilence and destruction by fire in the Anglo-Welsh wars. Whereas places like Usk suffered the same vicissitudes, they largely recovered. Marginal upland land was now less viable, and tenants were glad to move to vacant burgages in Usk or Monmouth.[28]

Despite this, there were a respectable number of resident gentry around Trellech, often with Parliamentary sympathies. The lawyer Christopher Catchmay of Trellech served on the County Committee for Monmouthshire and Thomas Evans of Trellech (d.1656) was a Commissioner for Sequestrated Estates. Another Catchmay served as an officer in Sir Trevor Williams's nominally Royalist regiment of foot. Firmly on the Royalist side were the Proberts of Pant-Glas and Henry Herbert of Trellech Grange. Henry Probert and his son Sir George Probert both served as Royalist Commissioners of Array. Sir George Probert fought for the King and was M.P. for Monmouth in the Restoration Parliament. His wife Magdalene, sister of Sir Trevor Williams, set up the remarkable sundial of 1689 now in Trellech church.[29]

Few clergy in this area proved unsatisfactory to the puritans. Of those who did, George Crump at Trellech, appointed in 1639, had been impressively successful. His surviving carved oak pulpit of 1640 and Laudian communion rails were part of a more elaborate ensemble, elements of which, dated 1639, also remain. In 1642 the church acquired a new bell, a matter requiring fund raising and parish organization. His very effectiveness as a Laudian vicar probably led to his removal by the puritans. Otherwise only Walter Harris of Wolvesnewton was evicted after the civil war, for 'drunkennes and assisting the King'.[30]

Trellech and the Wye Valley had an iron industry of medieval origin. An Elizabethan wireworks had been established on former land of Tintern Abbey belonging to the Earl of Worcester. In 1593 George Catchmay of Bigsweir was expressing an interest in taking over the lease.[31] By 1634 he was also involved in Coed Ithel blast furnace, opposite Catchmay's Court at Llandogo, which can be identified in a lease of 1651.[32] In 1646 Tintern and Whitebrook, in a depressed state due to the war, were taken over by the west midlands Parliamentarian ironmaster Thomas Foley, along with the derelict royal furnaces and forges in the Forest of Dean which had once belonged to Sir John Wintour.[33] In the same period Monmouth and Redbrook forges were in the hands of Robert Kyrle of Ross, who, after several changes of allegiance, ended the war as Parliamentary governor of Monmouth. Charcoal iron making was a normal part of a landed estate where timber and water power were available. In

1649 William Herbert of Coldbrook was accused of profiting from the Earl of Worcester's estate 'out of his woods, converted to charcoal, his iron mills etc.' and Thomas Hughes, Governor of Chepstow, of possessing materials belonging to Worcester and his son for making iron 'which he did'. This might refer to attempts by the scientifically minded Edward Herbert to make armaments at Chepstow.[34] The blast furnaces consumed vast quantities of standing timber for their charcoal fuel and felling of this highly profitable resource often brought landowners into conflict with the multitude of tenants and cottagers claiming rights of common. Under Elizabeth, Henry, Earl of Pembroke, found himself in conflict with commoners in the woods of Glascoed and Gwehelog above Usk, who disputed his cutting of timber 'to make coals' (charcoal).[35]

In contrast to Trellech, Skenfrith Hundred, along the Monnow Valley and the Herefordshire border, was recusant heartland. Elizabethan and Jacobean recusant rolls and the Compton census of 1676 alike show a cluster of strongly catholic parishes between Monmouth and Skenfrith. These include Skenfrith itself; Llangattock vibion Avel; Wonastow; St Maughans and Rockfield. Adjacent parishes like Grosmont and Llangua show much lower numbers of recusants. Llangattock vibion Avel had the highest number of convicted recusants in the county, save for Caerleon and Llanhennock and in 1676 'papistae' in the 'catholic' parishes were usually between 20% and 30% of the combined catholic and anglican total. In neighbouring Grosmont it was 5%.[36]

This was a land of mixed farming, with much arable. Defoe mentions large scale corn production in eastern Monmouthshire, and its export through Bristol merchants. Llangattock vibion Avel was 'red clay, good land ... for corn', with wheat, oats and peas, much like adjacent parts of Herefordshire.[37] 'Chalk' rather than 'cheese', the area supported a prosperous gentry, many of them catholics. Under Mary, Blackbrook in Skenfrith was owned by Sir Richard Morgan, M.P. for Gloucester and a leading supporter of the queen. Later catholic owners included Thomas Bodenham of Rotherwas outside Hereford, and William Baskerville, who bought the house from Bodenham's widow. Before the Titus Oates plot William Pugh was priest here, and the chapel of St Noye survived into the 18th century.[38] Blackbrook was rebuilt about 1800, but Llantellen, the other main house in the parish, survives in its 17th-century form. George Vaughan of Llantellen was sequestrated as a papist after the Civil War. Walter James of Trivor (Tre-Ifor) in St Maughans had a chapel in the roof of his house served by St John Lloyd, martyred at Cardiff in 1679. Across the border, neighbouring Archenfield held a third of the recusants from Herefordshire's eight deaneries, and this cannot simply be explained in terms of resident gentry.[39]

Monmouth, controlled by the Worcesters, had many catholics. Its situation on the boundaries of the sees of Hereford and Llandaff (Monmouth was in the see of Hereford until 1843) helped in the evasion of ecclesiastical authority when necessary. In the 19th century, the Monmouth based Royal Monmouthshire Engineers were known locally as 'The Royal Monmouthshire Militia (The Pope's Own)'. A number of manors around Monmouth had belonged to the medieval priory and after the Dissolution came into the hands of minor branches of the Herberts. Other families, often catholic like the Powells of Porth-Hir in Rockfield, or the Joneses of Trivor, intermarried with Herberts and bore the Herbert arms. Whereas 'loyalist' families emphasised their links with the Herberts by bearing their arms, several 'opposition' families, like Williams of Llangibby or Nicholas of Llanfihangel-Tor-Y-Mynydd asserted their status differently, by claiming descent from ancient Welsh princes like Ynyr Gwent or Brychan Brycheiniog.[40]

John Jones of Dingestow, in Raglan during the siege, had his estate confiscated as a 'Papist in arms', but recovered it at the Restoration; the last of the family died as a nun in Ghent in the mid-18th century.[41] His neighbour Henry Milborne of Wonastow, Worcester's steward and a major figure in north Monmouthshire, was accused during the 'Popish Plot' of harbouring the priest Francis Dracot. His defence to this charge throws interesting light on the background of a 'church papist'. Having a protestant father and a catholic mother, he was raised a protestant. He attended Abergavenny Grammar School under Morgan Lewis, father of David Lewis, before heading for Brasenose College Oxford and the Inns of Court. His household contained catholics, but he denied that they were 'the greater part'.[42] Accused of refusing a warrant to the priesthunter Arnold of Llanvihangel's henchman Roger Seys, petty constable of Llantilio Crossenny (later to receive a £20 reward for his part in the capture of David Lewis), for the arrest of the priest Walter Price of Clytha, he claimed that Seys had been put up to this by Arnold, a sworn enemy of his. Price later died of exposure and exhaustion as a hunted fugitive in a barn near Raglan.[43]

In 1615, Upper Cwm at Llanrothall, on land belonging to the Earl of Worcester just over the Herefordshire border, was leased for use as a secret Jesuit College. The Cwm had belonged to the Elizabethan recusant William Griffiths and had been a Jesuit base, complete with a substantial library, since the time of Robert Jones, who arrived in the county in 1595 and was made Superior of the Jesuit order in Britain in 1609. The College of St Francis Xavier, one of three in England (the others were in London and Lancashire), housed a number of priests. David Lewis was Rector from 1667–1672 and again from 1674 until his arrest in 1679.[44]

After the civil war, the puritans made vigorous efforts to drain this pool of religious and political disaffection. Seven of the eight Anglican incumbents in Skenfrith Hundred were removed on formulaic charges such as 'malignancy and delinquency' or 'malignancy and drunkenness', and the provision of a new font at Skenfrith in 1661 shows that Lewis Parry, the puritan vicar, was an active Baptist reformer, opposed to infant baptism. Only Thomas Jenkins of

Llanfihangel Ystern Llwyn, accused after the Restoration of maintaining a Quaker conventicle, was allowed to remain.

Gwynllwg

This was the westernmost part of Monmouthshire, bordering on Glamorgan. The two main families were the Morgans of Tredegar and the Kemeyss of Cefn Mably, but cadet branches of the Morgans dominated the area almost in the manner of an Irish or Scottish clan. Of the 13 or 14 gentry families, nine were Morgans, including two absorbed by the family in the late 16th century.[45] Most were minor gentry, often at township rather than parish level. The smallness of their estates encouraged migration or a career in the army, particularly among younger sons. Henry Morgan, the buccaneer, lived at Abergavenny before he went to sea, but married a Morgan of Llanrhymney, possibly a kinswoman, and named his Jamaica estates Llanrhymney and Pen-Carn.[46] Colonel William Pretty of Gwern y Cleppa was a professional soldier who fought on the Continent and in both Scots Wars. Initially a Parliamentarian, he went over to the King on the fall of Bristol in July 1643, only to be cashiered when he was associated with Prince Rupert in the loss of Bristol in September 1645, though the King had stayed with his mother at Gwern Y Cleppa three months earlier.[47] Other Royalist officers from the area included Colonel Myles Morgan, Lieutenant Lewis Morgan, possibly of Pencarn, who presented Prince Charles with a weighty piece of family plate at the outbreak of the war, and Major Lewis Thomas of Peterston Wentloog. In the following century, David Morgan of Coed y Goras was executed as a Jacobite after the 1745 rising.[48] At the time of the Civil War, the head of the clan, William Morgan of Tredegar, was in his 80s, whilst his son, Thomas Morgan of Machen, was a lukewarm Royalist who refused to serve under Edward Herbert on grounds of religion.

In western Monmouthshire, the Elizabethan church settlement met little dissent. Apart from a cluster of catholics in Henllys near Llantarnam, only 14 people in Monmouthshire west of the Afon Llwyd were fined for recusancy in 36 years (1588–1624), whilst the Compton census recorded only 19 catholics in the 17 parishes of Newport Deanery, 14 of them in Newport and Bettws. During the war, the local population were strongly puritan in sympathy. In 1645 locals resisted Royalist efforts to garrison Cardiff Castle, and during the 1647 rising people 'came in freely' to resist the Royalists, one local Parliamentary commander speaking of the 'well affected hundreds' around Cardiff.[49] Earlier, much of the area belonged to religious houses. Nearly all livings were in the hands of the cathedral chapters of Gloucester, Llandaff and Bristol, whilst Bedwas was annexed to the bishopric to augment the revenues of the impoverished see. Only two livings were in lay hands. This explains the high proportion of clergy expelled by the puritans, and how it was possible for the latter to transfer much tithe revenue to their new clergy.

Blaenau Gwent, the high upland of the lordships of Abergavenny and Newport, is divided by deep cut river valleys running south towards Newport like the fingers of a hand. The 19th-century iron and coal industries created a chain of settlements in the valley bottoms, but pre-industrial settlement centred on the upland ridgeways, with isolated churches serving communities living in scattered farms. In the 17th century, Welsh culture remained strong. A book of mid-17th-century Welsh poetry, much of it in the traditional strict metres, collected by Jenkin Richard of Blaenau Gwent (and including several of his own poems), also contains an epitaph in English on 'ould dotard Wroth' (the puritan William Wroth) and a set of accounts of contributions for the Royalist garrisons of north Monmouthshire.[50] However, these scattered pastoral communities, distinctly 'cheese' rather than 'chalk', were to prove fertile soil for the puritan gospel.

Chalk and Cheese: Localism, Religious Allegiance and the War

Catholics were thus numerous in Monmouthshire, but concentrated in particular parts of the county. By the early 17th century there were few in the coastal plains of Gwent Is Coed or in the west near Glamorgan, whilst areas like Skenfrith and Abergavenny were catholic heartland. This can partly be explained by the presence of catholic gentry able to shelter and harbour priests on the one hand, and by the maritime and commercial influence of puritan Bristol and Gloucester on the other. Mark Stoyle has shown how, in the similar terrain of Devonshire, market towns served as focal points for rural communities, an important determinant of the area's religious and social outlook.[51] Seen in this light, Monmouth and Abergavenny, with their hinterlands, were 'catholic' towns (though other religious groups might make good showing), whilst Chepstow, Usk and Newport were 'protestant' towns. Caerleon was a special case, for its catholic community largely depended on the Morgans of Llantarnam. It is clear, however, that people were not simply prepared to take their religious views from the gentry.

One traditional view is that Monmouthshire was a deeply conservative county, loyal to its King and to the catholic Earl of Worcester at Raglan. Many gentry were catholics, or catholic sympathisers, and they and the clergy, linked to the gentry by patronage, and sometimes kinship, were loth to upset the status quo of the county community. This was only de-stabilized by military conquest from outside and by the physical destruction of Raglan Castle. The loyalty of some gentry, like Sir Trevor Williams of Llangibby, was more elastic however. A variant of this view, recognising that few wanted war, was expressed by F.J. Mitchell, sometime secretary of the Monmouthshire and Caerleon Antiquarian Association:

> The chief inhabitants of Monmouthshire seem to have taken the Royal
> side, with the exception of two or three who were, like the majority of the
> commons, only anxious to live at peace, and to save their goods, and for
> that purpose were … to be found first on one side and then on the other.[52]

It is striking how Mitchell at first dismisses the dissident group as insignificant
('two or three') and then says that they shared the viewpoint of the great
majority of the county ('the majority of the commons'), who saw the whole
thing as a disruptive quarrel among their betters.

This concept of a united county society, generally content to follow the lead
of Raglan Castle, can hardly survive the account by Mitchell's namesake,
Julian Mitchell, of the bitter post-war quarrels that followed the Marquis of
Worcester's attempts to enclose and dis-afforest Wentwood. Many courtiers
and future Royalists in various areas of the kingdom were involved in poten-
tially lucrative schemes to drain wetlands and marshes, remove traditional
restraints on the use of woodland, fell profitable timber and reduce customary
tenants to rack-rented tenants at will, whose rents could be raised or tenure
ended at the landlord's wish. They were willing to pay the King large sums for
the right to exploit royal forest land in this way, and the King, desperate for new
sources of revenue that did not need Parliamentary approval, was keen to
encourage them. The large numbers of poor who subsisted on customary rights
to exploit the resources of forest and fen, often without formal tenure, naturally
resisted such moves. This led pre-war to bitter landlord-tenant disputes and
repeated rioting in Somerset, East Anglia and elsewhere. Worcester's activities
in Wentwood, like those of his kinsman, Sir John Wintour, in the Forest of
Dean, led to opposition not simply from poor squatters, but also from neighbouring landowners whose own rights in the Forest were affected. When war
came, areas like the Forest of Dean were noted for their hostility to the King.
Similarly, when we see the people of the county in action, as in Caerleon
churchyard, or in the case of an old puritan soldier from Blaina whom we shall
meet later, they have views on things which they are not necessarily prepared
to take from the gentry.[53]

Two things clear from recent studies are the extreme complexity of regional
reactions to the war, even within individual counties, and that only a small
minority of extremists on both sides sought, or were prepared to risk, war. As
Clarendon wrote of another border county:

> The town of Shrewsbury, and all that good county … he intrusted only
> to that good spirit that then possessed it, and to the legal authority of the
> shirers and justices of the peace. And it fared … as in other parts of the
> kingdom, that the number of those who desired to sit still was greater
> than of those who desired to engage of either party, so that they were
> generally inclined to articles of neutrality.[54]

Even that minority found it difficult to overcome what was not simply inertia or neutralism, but a positive desire to maintain the peace. The county justices were, after all, 'Of the Peace' and sworn to maintain and uphold it against any who might threaten it.

David Underdown's 'Chalk and Cheese' model, developing Joan Thirsk's concept of 'two rural peasant Englands', contrasting conservative arable and sheep farming areas of nucleated villages under close seignurial control (the chalk) with more radical wood-pasture areas with scattered settlement and weaker seigneurial control (the cheese), where Parliamentary support was stronger, was not wholly a new idea. It was expressed succinctly by John Aubrey writing in the time of Charles II:

> In North-wiltshire (a dirty clayey Country) ... Here about is but little Tillage or hard labour, they only milk the Cowes and make Cheese. They feed chiefly on Milke meates, which cooles their Braines too much ... These circumstances make them Melancholy, contemplative ... And by the same reason they are apt to be Fanatiques [puritans] ... On the Downes (sc. The south part) where 'tis all upon Tillage or Shepherds: and labour hard, their bodies strong: being weary after their hard labour, they have not leisure to reade, and contemplate of Religion, but goe to bed to their rest, to rise betimes the next morning to their labour ... So they never troubled their Heads with curious Notions of Religion'.[55]

This distinction of arable areas with closer social control and wood / pasture / maritime areas with a more independent outlook can be seen in various areas of western Europe, but Underwood has himself emphasised that the two should be regarded as 'ideal types' or 'convenient abstractions' and that the reality of settlement geography was more complex.[56] Seen in this light, the concept is useful in analysing cultural patterns within the county, though its settlement and land-use pattern is too complex for a simple chalk/cheese analysis. Aubrey was writing of one county. In Monmouthshire, the puritan Henry Walter was engaged in large scale production of butter and cheese for export, but so was the militant catholic George Langley. Improving landlords of all shades of opinion, in most areas of the county, found themselves in conflict with local people over the enclosure of common land.[57] Only with the Marquis of Worcester did this fester, post-war, into a vicious feud which led to the 'Popish Plot' and the executions of catholic priests in Usk and Cardiff. However the ecology and land use of Stuart Monmouthshire may help us understand its political and religious geography.

Monmouthshire might even seem to turn the 'chalk and cheese' model on its head, for the more arable areas of Gwent Is Coed with more nucleated settlement produced the greater number of puritan gentry and were more solidly protestant, whereas the wood/pasture areas north of Wentwood (save for forest edge Usk) showed more solid support for the King and included the catholic centres. However, the absence of the early Quarter Sessions records and parish documents used so effectively by Underwood and Stoyle make it impossible to quantify this below gentry level. Other factors—religious, economic and social—came into play. The presence of catholic neighbours and kinsfolk in small parish communities dominated by the Herberts of Raglan and their clients north of the Wentwood ridge contrasted with the puritan influence of Bristol, Gloucester and north Devon to the south. On the broader political scene, the southern arable area can be seen as conforming to a puritan central government, whereas the wood/pasture area to the north showed a localism which normally would have aligned it with any radical opposition. The chalk and the cheese were still there, but circumstances reversed the poles of the political magnet.

Abergavenny provides a similar paradox, and shows the limitations of deterministic views of local allegiance. Cloth towns were usually puritan (just as in the 19th century many were Chartist strongholds). There were economic and social reasons for this. In contrast, Abergavenny was a centre of catholicism. Its wartime allegiance was decided, however, not by popular Royalism, but because it was occupied first by part of Hubert Price's Breconshire regiment and then by a garrison regiment commanded by two local catholic courtiers. It was also a deeply divided town. Had it been in the Cotswolds, it might have become a Parliamentary centre.

3 The Great Pyramid:
Grandees, Gentry & Others

When John Edwards, rector of Tredunnock, was expelled from his living by the puritans, he used his enforced leisure to translate Edward Fisher's book *The Marrow of Divinity* into Welsh. His *Madruddyn y Difynyddiaeth Diweddaraf* was dedicated to the main county families 'To the most excellent Herberts, the most kind Morgans, the most noble Kemeyses, the most truly handsome Williamses and other noblemen within the county of Gwent'.[1] This defined the main county families in their generally recognised order of importance as seen by an insider whose father had been curate of Caldicot, and who, after graduating from Jesus College was a pluralist, holding a number of livings in the county. On the ground however, the situation was more complex. Except for the Williamses of Llangibby, who traced their ancestry in fancy from the 5th-century king of Gwent, Caradoc Vreichvras, but more realistically from the Earl of Pembroke's steward, Roger Williams (d.1585), who acquired the lands of the Benedictine nunnery of Usk, and his son, Rowland Williams, a Jacobean property speculator,[2] these were virtual septs or clans, with a bewildering proliferation of cadet branches in various parts of the county. These ranged from the vice-regal Herberts of Raglan to obscure country squires and parochial or sub-parochial gentry. The reason for this luxuriant growth was partly explained, in the case of Rowland Morgan of Machen, by John Leland:

> There is a nother of the Morgans, dwelling by Remny at Maghen, having a fair house. He had bene a man of fair landes, if his father had not devided it partely to other of his sunnes.[3]

The Catholic Magnates: the Earl of Worcester and Sir Edward Morgan

The Herberts had first come into prominence under William ap Thomas, Y Milwr Glas (the Blue Knight), steward of the lordship of Abergavenny, knighted in 1426. His magnificent alabaster tomb still survives in Abergavenny Priory, though without the array of armorial stained glass that existed in the civil war period, including the east window of the Herbert chapel with the kneeling figures of Sir William and his wife and the inscription 'Orate pro a[n]i[m]abus William Thomas militis ux [or] is sue qui istam capellam et fenestram vitrari fecerunt'—Pray for the souls of William Thomas, knight and his wife who had this chapel and glass windows made.[4]

His son, Sir William ap William, was a leading supporter of Richard, Duke of York, lord of Usk and Trellech, whose son became king as Edward IV in 1461. Thereafter the rise of Lord Herbert ap Herbert (as he then became, taking the name of a supposed Norman ancestor), was meteoric. His long catalogue of lordships and royal offices laid the foundations of the family pre-eminence. Created Earl of Pembroke in 1468, even his execution, with his brother Richard Herbert of Coldbrook, after the Yorkist defeat at Edgecote proved only a temporary family setback, although one that can perhaps be traced in the fabric and building history of Raglan Castle. His grand-daughter married Sir Charles Somerset, an illegitimate son of the Duke of Somerset, so bringing the Somerset name into the family. In 1514 Lord Herbert (as Somerset became by right of his wife) was created first Earl of Worcester.[5]

By the time the fifth Earl succeeded to the title in 1628, the Earls of Worcester had been trusted allies and servants of the crown for four generations, closely involved in many of the major events of Tudor history. His father, though a catholic, had been one of the group of four magnates rapidly summoned for the initial interrogation of Guy Fawkes (all happened to be catholics), and was even sent into Wales by the Privy Council to track down Jesuits. In Henry, fifth Earl and first Marquis of Worcester, reputedly the richest man in the kingdom, this family tradition of loyalty to the Crown was to find its most remarkable manifestation.

By contrast, his kinsman by marriage Edward Morgan of Llantarnam, was, until he achieved a modus vivendi with the government in 1612, decidedly the unacceptable face of catholicism. His father, William Morgan of Pentrebach and Llantarnam, bought the lands of the former Cistercian abbey of Llantarnam from the Earl of Pembroke in 1561 and sat in Parliament from 1555 to 1571. He died in 1582.[6] Edward Morgan was M.P. for the county between 1584 and 1587, but was alleged to maintain 60 catholics in his household. He was

> by reason of his greate livinge, power and allegiance in the said county, accompted the chief pillar and only maintayner of the papists and recusants thereabouts, whoe ... are since [the beginning of] your Majesties [James I's] reigne by the countenance and protection of the said Edward Morgan more than doubled, and, thereby ... encouraged in theire superstition that masse is more usually said in the home of the said Edward Morgan and the parishes of Llantarnam aforesaid, Llandenny therunto adoyninge [sic—presumably Llanfrechfa] and other places thereabouts than divine service in the said parish churches.

He took the Jesuit side on the issue of allegiance to James I and refused the Oath of Allegiance. His militant catholicism brought him into conflict with his protestant neighbours, including William Morgan of Machen. In 1603 William Morgan accused Edward Morgan's entire family— Edward Morgan himself, his wife Margery and sons Sir William and George—in the Court of Star Chamber with burial with catholic rites and with affrays in Usk and Abergavenny whilst resisting a court order.[7]

Edward Morgan was an obvious target for the full force of anti-papist legislation. Convicted as a recusant in 1605, two-thirds of his rents were confiscated.

Henry Somerset, first Marquis of Worcester

In all, he paid £7,900 in recusancy fines, possibly the largest amount of any catholic in England or Wales. His monthly fines of £20 for non-attendance at church and failing to take the Oath of Allegiance were matched by the 197 fines for recusancy exacted from Llantarnam people (many of them no doubt his household and clients). He sold some of his estates, but in May 1612, with debts of £2,000, wrote to the Privy Council, pleading his advanced age and ten children to support. He offered £1,000 in cash if he were allowed to take a modified oath swearing obedience to the Crown. The King accepted this.[8]

His son, Sir William Morgan of Penrhos outside Caerleon, was linked with the Jesuits. In 1603 he had been suspected of plotting an armed uprising and in 1605 harboured the Jesuit 'firebrand' Robert Jones. He and his wife, Frances, daughter of the 4th Earl of Worcester, were concerned in the foundation of the secret Jesuit College of St Francis Xavier at Llanrothal. He inherited his father's lands two years before his own death in 1635.[9] Edward Morgan's grandson, Sir Edward Morgan, made a baronet by Charles I in May 1642, gave money and plate to the King and served in arms in 1644–5 at Raglan and Hereford.[10] His grandson and namesake briefly converted to protestantism, but relapsed and was put out of the Commission of the Peace as a recusant in 1672. In 1678 John Arnold told the House of Commons how he had seen in the house of Sir Edward Morgan of Llantarnam 'a Popish chappell with altar and ornament there for the celebration of Mass'.[11]

The Pembroke Connection and the Protestant Gentry

The role of Montague to Worcester's Capulet was played by his kinsman Philip Herbert, fourth Earl of Pembroke by the second creation. His main seat was at Wilton outside Salisbury, whose architectural grandeur was matched by Pembroke's taste for paintings and fine bloodstock. His role within Monmouthshire dated back to the grant by King Edward VI to his father of the lordships of Newport, Cardiff, Usk, Trellech and Caerleon. This may well have been intended as a counterweight to the power of his catholic noble kinsman the Earl of Worcester. His seat in south Wales was at Cardiff Castle, a distant outpost of the Wilton empire. The other castles in his ownership, at Newport, Caerleon and Usk, were largely derelict and played little part in the war.

The Divided Gentry

A contemporary observer described the gentry of Monmouthshire as 'well educated, of great livelyhood and vere potent in the places where they

Wernddu, Llantilio Pertholey, seat of the catholic Prodgers or Prodger-Herberts, who garrisoned and fortified Abergavenny for the King. The existing house is late 17th century, reflecting their position as courtiers under Charles II. (Photograph by Jeremy Knight)

inhabite', which he thought should be conducive to public order and stability. However, the county was 'wholly divided into factions by reason the number of those who, being addicted and misled by Poperie ... so that fewe causes arise ... which is not made a question betwixt the Protestant and the recusant'. One Royalist commander called it 'a countie of great plentie [that] hath never felt the miseryes of war and the gentrie are generallie rich in present monies'. Houses like Treowen, Moynes Court or Llantellen at Skenfrith bear him out, but it was the ready money which interested the cavalier.[12] The catholicism of Worcester, the Morgans of Llantarnam, the Prodgers of Wernddu and, across the Wye, Worcester's cousin Sir John Wintour cut them off from the main-stream of metropolitan political influence in Parliament, though at the same time they were (save for Morgan) powerfully influential at court. Apart from Worcester's long family tradition of service to the Crown, Wintour was secre-tary to Queen Henrietta Maria and the Prodgers were, over several generations, grooms of the bedchamber and the like to three generations of Stuart kings. This group was sharply distinct from the families of protestant gentry who represented the county in Parliament. Under Charles I these included the Morgans of Tredegar; Herbert of Coldbrook; Arnold of Llanvihangel; Kemeys of Llanvair Discoed; Rumsey of Trellech and Williams of Llangibby. Other

Treowen, Wonastow, built for William Jones of Treowen 1615–1627.
Sir Philip Jones of Treowen was a leading Royalist. (© National Monuments
Record for Wales, Royal Commission on the Ancient and Historical
Monuments of Wales)

Sir Nicholas Kemeys, portrait now at Hellens, Much Marcle, Herefordshire. (Photograph, Courtauld Institute of Art, Witt Collection)

families had served in earlier Parliaments: Gunter of Abergavenny Priory; Lewis of Llandewi Rhydderch; Morgan of Machen; Kemeys of Michaelston Y Fedw; Jones of Treowen; and Morgan of Penhow. These dozen or so families represented the core of county society. By 1603, half of the former Crown lands in Monmouthshire were in the hands of the Earls of Pembroke and Worcester, and half the remainder in the hands of four families: the Morgans of Llantarnam, Arnolds of Llanthony, Williamses of Llangibby and the Gunters of Abergavenny. Most of these were neutralist or lukewarm Royalists, Philip Jenkins's 'moderates'.[13]

Only Sir Philip Jones of Treowen, Sir Nicholas Kemeys and his son, Sir Charles Kemeys, can be classed as consistent Royalists, in arms for the King. The Joneses of Treowen claimed descent from a Yorkist killed at the Battle of Edgecote in 1469, fighting alongside the Herberts, and Philip Jones's father inherited a considerable fortune from an uncle, a London merchant venturer, enabling him to built a grand house with a dated screen of 1627. The family regarded themselves as Herbert kin and bore the Herbert arms. Lady Jones, daughter of Edward Morgan of Llantarnam and first cousin of the Earl of Worcester, was an open catholic. It was alleged that her son William Jones 'dyed a Papist' and that the then Lady Jones maintained a priest, Father Sylliard, as tutor to her two sons, who were now 'beyond seas', one of them in a Jesuit College in France. Philip Jones may have been a 'church papist', with only nominal allegiance to the reformed Church. In the 19th century, the Joneses changed their name to Herbert, in what was something of a minor cause célèbre.[14]

Sir Nicholas Kemeys, second son of Rhys Kemeys of Cefn Mably, was M.P. for the county in 1627–9 and Sheriff in 1631–2. The various branches of the Kemeys family were widespread in southern Monmouthshire and Sir Nicholas's first wife had been a Williams of Llangibby. In 1634 he inherited an estate at Llanfair Discoed on the fringes of Wentwood and became steward for the Herberts and Ranger of Wentwood Forest. By 1642 he was a wealthy middle aged man with estates worth £1,800 a year. His son Charles Kemeys (1614–1658), educated at Jesus College and Gray's Inn, like his father a Royalist Commissioner of Array, joined Edward Herbert's army in the spring of 1643 as a Captain. Captured at Highnam, he was exchanged and knighted by the King at Oxford. He was active in both civil wars, down to the siege of Pembroke in 1648. Nicholas Kemeys's main seat at Cefn Mably was on the Glamorganshire border, and Symonds lists him among the principal gentlemen of Glamorgan. He had marriage links with the catholic Stradlings of St Donats, the Bassets of Beaupre and other Royalist families from that county. The family

Sir Nicholas Kemeys's house at Llanvair Discoed, the Court House, was rebuilt by his younger son, George Kemeys, c.1690. Re-set over the porch is a datestone of 1635 from the original house with the Welsh inscription 'Er I Fod yn Ing maen Dda Yn Wng 1635' — 'Though it (the house) is small, it is pleasant to be close together'.
(Photograph by Jeremy Knight)

also had recusant links. David Kemeys O.P. was a Dominican who died in prison at the time of the Titus Oates 'plot'.[15]

Many of the remaining families were lukewarm or inactive Royalists, moderates and crypto-Parliamentarians. William Morgan of Tredegar and Thomas Morgan of Machen were among the 'hinderers' sent for by Parliament for executing the Royalist Commission of Array and disarming 'the well affected party', but, as has been noted, William Morgan was in his 80s and Thomas Morgan refused to serve under Edward Herbert, probably on religious grounds. Neither took any part in the war and Thomas Morgan sat for the county in the Cromwellian Parliament of 1654.[16] He was father-in-law of Sir Trevor Williams of Llangibby who is usually seen, not unjustly, as an ambitious weathercock. He started the war as a Royalist Colonel of infantry at Highnam. Later, he raised a regiment for the King which in the latter stages of the war acted as an almost independent third force. This small private army eventually went over to Parliament on the fall of Bristol in 1645. Equally distrusted by the King and by Cromwell, the key to his allegiance may have been his protestantism, an old fashioned Elizabethan faith with a puritan tinge. In the next reign he was involved with John Arnold and the unsavoury William Bedloe in the paranoia of the 'Popish Plot'.

His father, Sir Charles Williams, was M.P. for the county in 1621, when he was knighted by James 1, and in the 'Short Parliament' of 1640. Sir Charles married a daughter of Sir William Morgan of Tredegar, but Sir Trevor was the child of a second marriage to a daughter of the puritan Sir John Trevor of Flintshire (hence no doubt his Christian name). Sir Charles gave an oak communion table to Llangibby church in 1632, and in the same year presented to Caerwent church a carved Jacobean pulpit with a puritan text and, in case he was taken for a sectary, the view of Llandaff cathedral.[17] Some years later, another of this group, William Baker of Abergavenny (d.1648), made an equally trenchant statement in his will. He was, he said, a protestant 'and against all Papists and Anabaptists'.[18]

Sir Trevor's younger brother, Edward Williams, was a Royalist of a more straightforward kind. Though there are problems with the duplication of names, he initially served as a Major in Sir Richard Herbert's Regiment of Foot, which he may have commanded at Rupert's capture of Bristol in July 1643. At the very time when his brother was raising a new regiment for the King, Edward Williams was one of the officers who signed a petition protesting (in military terms rightly) at the recruitment of such new regiments by prestige conscious gentry, when existing battle hardened units had suffered heavy losses and needed reinforcements. He later transferred to Prince Rupert's Lifeguard of Horse under Lt-Colonel Sir Richard Crane, until Crane's death at the fall of Bristol and Rupert's subsequent disgrace. Thereafter, Williams re-joined his brother, who had declared for Parliament soon after the fall of Bristol, and

Tomb of William Baker (1585–1648), Abergavenny Priory. A Royalist Commissioner of Array for Monmouthshire and 'against all Papists and Anabaptists', his monument proclaims him 'a maintainer of the orthodox faith'. (Photograph by Jeremy Knight)

served as Lt-Colonel in his regiment. He was wounded in the arm in a skirmish at Usk in 1646 before the siege of Raglan.[19]

Other families were represented on both sides. Sir William Herbert of Llangattock nigh Usk was a Royalist Major. His half-brother Sir Henry Herbert of Coldbrook was a Parliamentary Colonel and M.P. for Monmouthshire in the Long Parliament, elected on the death of Sir Charles Williams. He married Mary, daughter of the London grocer John Rudyard, cousin of the opposition member Sir Benjamin Rudyard. As Arthur Dodd pointed out, his metropolitan and opposition links no doubt made him a Roundhead.[20]

The lawyer Thomas Hughes of Moynes Court was appointed Protonotary and Clerk of the Crown in south-east Wales by James I, a profitable legal sinecure. His eldest son and namesake was a Parliamentary Colonel. His younger son, Charles Hughes of Trostrey near Usk, proudly recorded on his memorial stone that he had 'been a MAIOR of a Regiment in King CHARLES ye First's Army against ye rebelles'. He fought in the Earl of Carbery's Redcoats in the Pembrokeshire campaigns of 1643–4 and at the Restoration was rewarded with the family post of Protonotary previously held by his father and brother.[21] We may be seeing again conflicts of interest between periphery and centre, and identification with metropolitan Westminster rather than with the county community, though Clarendon characteristically took a more cynical view, praising the Earl of Northampton, who was 'not like other men, who warily distributed their family to both sides, one son to serve the King, whilst the father or another son engaged for Parliament'. Family ties however were often more important than politics. When the Parliamentarian lawyer Christopher Catchmay of Trellech Court died in the 1650s, his widow married John Catchmay, who had fought in the Royalist army under Gerard.[22]

The neutralist gentry have had a bad press, as 'weathercocks', 'trimmers' or 'mere neuters' (the local term was 'ambidexters'). The sense of opportunism and self advancement was certainly strong in people like Sir Trevor Williams, but they were more numerous than Mitchell's dismissive 'two or three', and often acted as a group, aided by ties of kinship or marriage. One might almost call them the Cousinage or 'The country party', for 'country' was often used for 'county' or 'county community'. We are looking at a group of conservative county gentry, with local perspectives, local loyalties and local feuds, who, like the great majority elsewhere, had not sought war. They were acting, as Woolrych has commented, out of a desire to preserve what they could of local

Coldbrook House near Abergavenny (demolished in 1954), seat of the Herberts of Coldbrook. Sir Henry Herbert of Coldbrook was an M.P. and Parliamentary Colonel. The north front was remodelled in 1746. (Drawing by Sir Richard Colt Hoare)

autonomy and to save the people under their charge from the worst depredations of war. Most were avowed protestants, who no doubt regarded
Archbishop Laud with disquiet. Andriette's comment on the effects of Laud's
appointment as archbishop on their counterparts in puritan Devon is equally apt
in Monmouthshire. With this 'one decisive appointment' and its accompanying
reform from above, 'the moderate puritan movement of reform from below
became automatically ranged on the side of political opposition'.[23] Though
men like Sir Trevor Williams and his son-in-law, Sir Thomas Morgan, initially
remained loyal to the King, their loyalty may have been under strain for religious reasons, and this could explain much.

We first meet this group at the outbreak of the war. In September 1642
Parliament ordered that Sir Thomas Morgan of Machen, Sir William Morgan
of Tredegar, Sir Trevor Williams, Sir Nicholas Kemeys, Philip Jones of
Treowen, and Henry Probert be sent for as delinquents for executing the
Royalist Commission of Array and disarming the 'well affected party'.[24] Most
of these were former M.P.s for the county or their sons — William Morgan and
Trevor Williams's father most recently in the Short Parliament of 1640; Sir
Nicholas Kemeys in 1628 and William Jones of Treowen, father of Philip
Jones, in 1614. The group includes Royalists of varying shades of commitment,
but towards the end of the war the King, like Parliament before him, summoned
a similar group of 'hinderers' before him at Abergavenny. They included Sir
William Morgan; Sir Trevor Williams; Sir William Herbert of Llangattock nigh
Usk; William Baker of Abergavenny and an un-named fifth.[25] To understand
how things had changed in the interim, it will be necessary to follow the course
of the war.

A Papist Fifth Column? Raglan Castle and the Earl of Worcester

In the worsening political climate of the 1630s, catholics in Monmouthshire,
and particularly the Earl of Worcester, were targets for those who saw them as
a dangerous fifth column, plotting armed rebellion. The 1630s also saw severe
outbreaks of plague, which must have increased social anxiety and tension. In
1636 Worcester was deprived of the Lord Lieutenancy, which included
command of the county militia, on religious grounds. Edward Herbert petitioned for his father to be reinstated. Worcester had lent the King £40,000 and
'affronts [were] put on him by the country in consequence of these services'. It
was being claimed that Worcester might use his position to insert fellow
catholics in key positions in the county, particularly in the militia. Whether
anti-papists were reassured by Herbert's double edged rejoinder that this would
be impossible, since they would have to take the Oaths of Allegiance and
Supremacy, is doubtful.[26]

The Earl was plunged into controversy by the King in July 1640 when
Charles wrote to the Deputy Lieutenants of south Wales to say that he had been

'entrusted with some secret service'. This was probably the raising of troops for the Scottish war, but Worcester's catholicism and the paranoia of the times made this 'secret service' deeply suspect. In the following year, during the period of Strafford's trial, when rumours of a 'Popish Plot' abounded, it was claimed that Worcester and Edward Herbert planned to raise troops to join an Irish army raised by Strafford against the King's Scottish or puritan opponents. John Davis, who worked at the George in Ross on Wye, told how he had acted as guide for a mysterious richly dressed stranger en route to Raglan Castle, who had stayed at the Inn. At Raglan, the stranger called for a pewter basin and a 'Venice glass' (wineglass) to wash his hands. The implication may have been that this was a secret sign, perhaps representing a chalice and paten, indicating that he was a catholic priest. A groom took Davis on a tour of the underground stables, where there were a number of light horse and 'great store of match and powder and other ammunition belonging to war' including equipment for five or six score of horse and 2,000 men. The groom claimed that Worcester was secretly recruiting men at 16d. a day and already had 700 in his pay. Later, in London, Davis repeated this tale to Alderman Acton's coachman, who informed his master. Davis gave his evidence to the House of Commons, who ordered that a strict watch be kept on Worcester's London house.[27] On 23 August 1641 Parliament appointed a committee of seven M.P.s for disarming recusants in Monmouthshire.[28] Though such scare stories do not figure among the formal causes of the Civil War, they no doubt had their effect when, in the following spring and early summer, England found itself on the road to the war that had already engulfed Scotland and Ireland. They inflamed public opinion in London and offered a very public insult, amounting to charges of treason, to one of the King's leading supporters. That December, the King wrote to Herbert deploring the 'lying and scandalous Pamflets concerning your father and you.'[29]

4 Community in Conflict: 1642–44

1642-3 'That Mushrump Army'

As in other counties, the first moves, once hostilities were imminent, concerned the raising of troops and custody of the arms of the county militia. The peaceful England of Elizabeth and James had not encouraged private arms, and both sides were anxious to secure what limited supplies were available. Ian Roy has stressed how the King 'possessed, in comparison to other monarchs, a puny military establishment' and how the militia, armouries, coastal defences and town walls were neglected and in decay.[1] The militia was under the command of the Lord Lieutenant, in Monmouthshire the Earl of Worcester until the King dismissed him on religious grounds in 1636. One of the gentry served as Deputy Lieutenant or Captain in each Hundred, with a Lieutenant as his deputy if he was unable to carry out his duties in person. Thus Thomas Morgan of Machen was Lieutenant in Wentloog and Usk Hundreds, since Sir William Morgan and Sir Charles Williams were both elderly. Staff officers comprised a Captain of Horse and a professional Muster Master. A muster in October 1634 showed a strength of 400 Trained Men, 2,000 'Able Men' (Reservists), 50 horse and 60 pioneers. Another muster roll, of 1638, gives a similar figure of 400 foot and 47 horse.[2]

The county armoury was at Monmouth, in the control of the Earl of Worcester, under a deputy keeper appointed by Sir Percy Herbert, son of the catholic Earl of Powys. The main armoury was in 'Monmouth Proper' (the castle), but the powder, lead and match were stored separately in Monmouth town, and in Caerleon, presumably where suitable dry cellars were available. Pre-war there were corslets and pikes for about 160 men, though not all these were serviceable; 130 swords and belts; 80 muskets (ten of them 'oulde'); 20 obsolete calivers (light arquebuses) and a couple of halbards for N.C.O.s. There would have been other arms held privately by individual militiamen. In total, there were 96 barrels of gunpowder, 69 sows of lead and 800 units of match.[3] At one stage, there may have been a subsidiary armoury at Caerleon, at the opposite corner of the county. On the death of Queen Elizabeth, the catholic

Edward Morgan of Llantarnam and his sons had allegedly sent teams of oxen to transport muskets and calivers from the armoury at Caerleon to Llantarnam, but there was still powder stored at Caerleon in 1642.[4]

Early in 1642 the armoury was taken from the control of Sir Percy Herbert and placed under the Mayor of Monmouth. Later that January the future Royalists Thomas Morgan and Nicholas Kemeys wrote to Parliament expressing concern for its safety, indicating that there were many politically ill affected people in the county, puritans hostile to the established church, who might be planning 'some sodaine and unlawfull attempt' on the county magazine. This was a counterblast to the rumour mongerings about ill affected papists in the county. At the end of March, Parliament, following its Militia Ordinance claiming control of the militia and the right to appoint Lords Lieutenant, ordered that the armoury be moved to Newport, where it would be under the control of the Earl of Pembroke. Edward Mason, Mayor of Monmouth, an apothecary, refused to deliver it up, claiming 'it was an ill time to deliver the arms, since there was a difference between the King and Parliament'. As a result he was sent in custody to London. William Gwilym, the deputy Mayor, Edward Taylor, the town Bailiff and Alderman Thomas Packer all in turn denied knowledge of where the keys to the new strong doors of the magazine were kept, and followed the Mayor to London, where they remained in custody for some weeks. Three magistrates—Henry Probert, Nicholas Kemeys and Thomas Lewis—who had resisted the Parliamentary demands, were removed from the Commission of the Peace. The issue of the armoury was becoming a causus belli, challenging Worcester's supporters in the town.[5]

In May 1642, three months after the Militia Ordinance, a petition claiming to be from 'The Knights, Justices of the Peace, and other Gentlemen, Ministers and Freeholders … of the County of Monmouth' was presented to Parliament. Though they claimed to be 'in number many thousands', none were named in the printed text and it was clearly aimed at London public opinion. Most of it is taken up with the Irish rebellion. It claimed that 'we in Wales of all others and in Monmouth Shire above the rest, cannot but be most sensible and suspitious of our owne immediate destruction, as being compassed about with Papists more in number, and stronger in power, Armes Horse and Ammunition than any County … who … to the great terror of the King's faithful subjects … spare no paines or cost to fit and strengthen themselves for their secret designes'. The petition stated that they were taking over the county's great houses for Popish strangers and 'denying the removal of the magazine' contrary to the express orders of Parliament. They could not enjoy security, the petitioners claimed, 'till the magazine be removed to Newport, the county set in a posture of defence, the Papists by some stronger power than ours disarmed, and Ireland relieved'. The Speaker reassured them that orders had been given for removal of the armoury, and took note of their concern about 'the numbers of Papists that flock about the houses of recusants in that county and also of the great numbers of Papists that are inhabitants of that county'. Between December 1641 and May 1642 similar petitions were presented from 37 of the 40 English counties and several Welsh counties, in a concerted campaign. Many were circulated in local churches for signature and carried large numbers of names, but one might feel some scepticism as to whether the Monmouthshire one circulated widely. Its sponsors were probably the M.P.s Henry Herbert of Coldbrook and Thomas Hughes of Moynes Court, both later Parliamentarian Colonels.[6] The Gloucestershire puritan Nathaniel Stephens added fuel to the fire by claiming that inhabitants of Dean had intercepted two cartloads of arms leaving Sir John Wintour s house at Lydney and that the people of Gloucester were apprehensive that Monmouthshire catholics might have designs on their city.[7]

The Earl eventually agreed that the armoury should be moved to Caerleon.[8] Where in Caerleon it was housed is uncertain. The castle was largely ruinous, but the episode could explain the Civil War earthworks around Penrhos outside Caerleon, the home of Sir Edward Morgan's son, where a rectangular fort was strengthened with a series of artillery bastions. Its stay at Caerleon was in any case brief. On 22 August the King raised his standard at Nottingham. In mid September Worcester declared for the King and seized the armoury, which was removed to Raglan Castle. On 3 October, the Royalists seized the Earl of Pembroke's castles at Cardiff, Newport and Caerleon.[9] Sir Edward Stradling's Regiment, raised in Glamorgan and Carmarthen, was briefly stationed in the county at this time. Stradling wrote to William Morgan at Tredegar House, informing him that 500 men of the regiment were to be stationed in the area 'ready to obey Sir William Morgan's commands for the King's and the countrey's service'.[10] Stradling's Regiment suffered severely at Edgehill the following month, when much of the Welsh infantry, including Sir Edward Stradling, was taken prisoner.[11]

The King's response to the Parliamentary Militia Ordinance had been to revive a medieval procedure dating from the time of Edward I, and unused since 1557. Commissions of Array were sent (in Latin) to the leading protestant gentry of a county to summon the county militia and raise and train troops. Catholic gentry were excluded. Those who responded came to form a County Committee to administer the war effort in the county. The first surviving list for Monmouthshire was drawn up on 20 October, three days before Edgehill. On 29 November the formal commission was sealed by the King at Reading, naming 21 Commissioners, plus three *ex officio* members, including Prince Charles. The first name is that of Richard Herbert of St Julians, present with the King, whose local knowledge was probably used in drawing up the circulation list. A supplementary list of nine names omitted in October suggests a second trawl, mostly among lukewarm Royalists or minor gentry, though three names occur in both lists.[12]

Some 30 gentry served as Commissioners of Array for Monmouthshire. They included most prominent gentlemen of the county, (save for Parliamentarians and catholics): Sir Nicholas Kemeys and his son Charles Kemeys; Sir Trevor Williams; Thomas Morgan of Machen; Henry and George Probert of Trellech; Philip Jones of Treowen; John Milborne of Wonastow; John Gainsford of Grosmont; and Thomas Morgan of Llansôr outside Caerleon. Edmund Jones of Llansoy, a Gray's Inn lawyer, became Treasurer. There were a number of lesser gentry and some who took no part in the war for reasons of age, like Sir William Morgan of Tredegar and Nicholas Moore of Crick. The main role of the Commissioners, however, was not command in the field, but administration, recruitment and taxation.[13]

The King's initial choice as commander in the west was not Herbert, in view of his religion, but another grandee, the Marquis of Hertford. Hertford was initially active in south-west England, but in late September was driven out of Somerset, retreated to Minehead, seized some small Welsh coal ships lying at anchor in the harbour and fled to Cardiff by boat with the remnants of his infantry. He was then confronted by the Parliamentarian commander the Earl of Stamford, who had occupied Hereford. Londoners were nervous about the western front and thirsty for news—any news. Journalists cashed in on this with sometimes fraudulent pamphlets recording non-existent events and bogus battles. Nevertheless, Stamford's occupation of Hereford and rumours that he was about to advance on Abergavenny caused the hasty cancellation of a court case at Llanfihangel Crucorney on 24 October. Meanwhile Lord Herbert hastily garrisoned Monmouth with 900 foot and a troop of horse.[14]

On 4 November Hertford and Lord Herbert set out towards Hereford. On the 13th, an advance guard of 350 men were confronted at Pontrilas, on the line of the Roman road from Abergavenny to Hereford, by Stamford's deputy, Robert Kyrle of Ross on Wye, a former professional soldier who had served in the Swedish army and in Holland. Six Royalist soldiers placed outside the village as a guard were shot down. The Royalists retreated to a nearby hill, where Kyrle hesitated to attack, but lost 15 men, one hanged by Kyrle as a notorious plunderer. Such bloodshed was still an unhappy novelty, Walter Powell noting in his diary 'The men slain at Pontrylas'.[15] The following month Stamford withdrew to Gloucester and then to the West Country, leaving his Lt-Colonel, Edward Massey, in command at Gloucester. The Royalists garrisoned Monmouth and Chepstow, and re-occupied Hereford where Fitzwilliam Coningsby was made Governor and set about raising a regiment from the county.

At the time of the Pontrilas episode, Herbert was involved in an acrimonious correspondence with Stamford over the involvement of catholics in the war. An Archenfield man, Thomas Gwithain, was taken from his bed and carried off to Raglan on a charge of treason. Stamford demanded his release, with a provocative reference to 'the war between Protestants and Papists in England'. Herbert (his 'most affectionate cousin and servant') denied that it was any such thing, claiming that catholics and protestants were 'received on both sides'. The war was about the King's demands for obedience to the law 'which Gwithain's trial by the known laws shall confirm'. Parliament was incensed by Herbert's claims that they were recruiting papists, (although they seem to have turned a blind eye to the religion of a number of the professional

Welsh soldiers from the pamphlet The Welsh-Mans Postures, or the true manner how her doe exercise her Company of Souldiers in her own countrey *(January 1643). The coats of arms are those of London livery companies — the Grocers, Mercers, Haberdashers and Spicers. Why these were thought to have a Welsh connotation is not clear. (National Library of Wales)*

soldiers they had recruited). Gwithain was later released, claiming that he was 'carried prisoner to Ragland for no other cause ... but for being a Protestant'.[16]

In January 1643, Edward Herbert of Raglan was made commander-in-chief in south-east Wales and Herefordshire, matched by the Earl of Carbery in west Wales and Lord Capel in north Wales. Clarendon distrusted Herbert, and was critical of his appointment. Without military experience, and 'of that sort of Catholics ' popularly regarded as the 'Most Jesuited', he laid the King open to charges of favouring papists. His appointment would also 'give opportunity and excuse to many persons of quality, and great interest in those counties (between whom and that lord's family there had been perpetual feuds and animosities) to lessen their zeal to the King's cause out of jealousy of religion'.[17] Clarendon was writing well after the war, and he and Herbert had been in opposed factions during the long bitter years of exile. His account of what followed is very much the case for the prosecution.

Herbert raised a regiment of foot, with Howell Gwyn, a Captain in Stradling's Regiment who had been wounded at Edgehill, as Lt-Colonel.[18] Already local rivalries were showing, and Thomas Morgan of Machen refused to serve under him. Herbert planned to advance through the Forest of Dean and besiege Gloucester from the west, whilst Prince Maurice attacked it from the east and a separate force reduced the Parliamentarian outpost at Brampton Bryan in Herefordshire. Money for the campaign was raised through a 'Benevolence' (tax) on local gentry.[19] In mid-February, the army set out, and Herbert wrote confidently to Prince Rupert that he was about to enter the Forest of Dean and 'master the Sevearn'. The Severn river traffic, linking the iron-works and arms factories of the west Midlands with Gloucester was central to the war effort.[20] A professional soldier, Sir Richard Lawdly, was in command as Sergeant Major General with a regiment of dragoons, whilst Herbert's brother, Lord John Somerset, 'a maiden soldier', commanded the horse. The 1,400 foot comprised Colonel Fitzwilliam Coningsby's regiment from Herefordshire and Herbert's own regiment, possibly commanded by another professional soldier, Sir Jerome Brett, although Sir Trevor Williams also held the rank of Colonel of Foot. In what everyone thought would be a short war, there was no shortage of gentleman volunteers, particularly for the cavalry.

The force was drawn from the whole area of Herbert's command, with a number of professional soldiers from further afield. Lawdly himself was an Exeter man. The Lt-Colonels were from Herefordshire and Yorkshire, there were four Sergeant Majors (officers of field rank, usually third in command of a regiment, not to be confused with their present day namesakes), including officers from Shropshire and Herefordshire and a north Welsh recusant. Each regiment would have had the normal complement of six to eight captains, allowing for a few staff posts (there were 17 in all).

*Pewter badge with head of Charles I and the motto 'God Bless The King',
found shortly before 1867 near Woodbank, Llanhennock. Several pounds of
lead bullets were found nearby, under an ancient oak tree known as the
'Caerydor Oak', on the footpath between Pencrug and Llanhennock church.
(Photograph by Department of Archaeology and Numismatics,
National Museums and Galleries of Wales)*

Lord Herbert and his army were entering hostile territory to an extent
perhaps unusual in the Civil War. To the forester's hostility to the Herberts' pre-
war involvement in dis-afforestation projects was added a racial element,
described by Massey's chaplain John Corbet as the 'inveterate hatred, derived
from fabulous tradition ... between the Welch-men and the citizens of
Gloucester'. Lawdly was killed in a skirmish at Coleford, according to local
folklore shot from a window of the King's Head by a silver bullet. His company
commander, Captain Burke, and Randell Wallinger, lieutenant in Captain
Henry's troop of horse, were also killed.[21] Lawdly was replaced by Sir Jerome
Brett. Hutton has shown how Clarendon distorted this episode, for the latter
claims that Herbert's force was opposed only by 'a rabble of country people,
without order or officer of name', when it was in fact a regiment of regular
Parliamentary troops, commanded by Colonel Berrowe, a local gentleman
serving in the Gloucester garrison.[22]

Despite the set back, Herbert's army continued and encamped at Highnam
Court, the house of Sir Robert Cooke, an M.P. and Parliamentary Colonel. This

Edward Herbert, Earl of Glamorgan.
Engraving from a portrait now at Badminton

was across the river from Gloucester, within sight of the cathedral tower, and facing a long bridge over the Severn. Catholics in the Royalist force may have relished the thought that Cooke had been one of the committee appointed by Parliament in 1641 for disarming Monmouthshire papists. After Brett had summoned Gloucester to surrender, they settled behind earthworks and mounted their cannon, waiting for Prince Maurice to arrive. Air-photographs show traces of bastioned works on Ludman Hill, east of Highnam Court, facing towards Over Bridge. Massey occupied Vineyard Hill, north-west of the bridge, a moated episcopal palace of *c*.1400 on the site of the medieval vineyard of Gloucester Abbey. A rectangular earthwork, 'The Mounts', survives.

Massey was safe behind the solid walls of Roman Gloucester across the river, which were successfully to resist the King later in the year. Initially outnumbered, as reinforcements of horse and dragoons arrived from Bristol he was able to go over to the offensive with raids on the Welsh positions. For nearly five weeks there was stalemate. However, once the Parliamentarian Sir William Waller had taken Malmesbury, he took his army, in one of the night marches for which he was famous, over the Cotswolds to Framilode ferry on the Severn. Massey now attacked the Royalist positions with 500 foot, plus horse and artillery, to distract them from Waller's approach. Massey's cannon bombarded the Royalist entrenchments, and a fire fight ensued which lasted until nightfall.

The next morning, Lord Somerset's horse made a sally, and drove back an ill-judged counter-attack by Massey's cavalry. For a while Massey's force was hard pressed, but at Framilode Waller had a number of flat bottomed boats, sent from London on carts, specifically for service on the Severn. Crossing on these, he suddenly appeared to the rear of the Welsh on Rodway Hill, signalling his arrival with a field gun and displaying his colours. Massey then stormed an outpost, taking a number of prisoners. Sir Jerome Brett and his army surrendered on terms on 25 March, after vainly trying to persuade the wet and demoralised infantry to attempt a breakout. Waller captured around 150 officers and 1,444 men, as well as 'seven great horses' and four cannon, which the garrison of Gloucester later put to good use. Much of the cavalry managed to escape, as was common in Civil War battles. The prisoners included three Monmouthshire Commissioners of Array: Sir Trevor Williams, Charles Kemeys and Captain Gainsford, and a contingent of Herefordshire gentlemen that included Henry Lingen, a recusant, whose career as a die-hard Royalist was to last (as Colonel Sir Harry Lingen) to 1648 and beyond.

The regiment of the Mayor of Gloucester, Dennis Wise's Bluecoats, escorted the prisoners into the city. Drawn up in twos, and roped together, the folorn crocodile stretched from the earthworks at Highnam almost as far as the West Gate of the city. The prisoners were held in St Mary de Lode church behind the cathedral and in Holy Trinity church and offered the choice of imprisonment or release on a promise of not fighting again against Parliament. After a few days on stale bread, turnip tops and cabbage leaves, most chose the latter. The officers were taken to Bristol pending exchange or ransom. One veteran of Highnam was interviewed at the age of 90 in 1717. 'Welch Thomas', originally from Carmarthen town, was imprisoned in St Mary Lode, but released on promising to fight for Parliament. He took part in Massey's defence of the city and spent the rest of his days in Gloucester. His career was very similar to that of another rank and file Royalist Welsh soldier, John ap John of Gelli y Crug from the Welsh speaking area of Llanhilleth in Blaenau Gwent. John was taken prisoner, possibly at Edgehill, when large numbers of Welsh prisoners were marched to London and provided with Welsh speaking preachers. This would explain what he was doing in Kent or Essex when he underwent religious conversion. Like 'Welch Thomas' he later served in Massey's garrison at Gloucester, where he got married, and also in the siege of Raglan under his fellow Monmouthshire man Colonel Sir Thomas Morgan, once of Llangattock Lingoed. After the war he settled at Abertillery, where Edmund Jones remembered him in old age as a puritan elder with a long white beard and 'the strictness of the old puritans'.[23]

The Royalist newsletter *Mercurius Aulicus* claimed that Waller lost 400 men in the initial assault and had been repulsed, whereupon Massey attacked the outpost during a truce, forcing the Royalists to surrender with 300 dead and 300 prisoners.[24] Despite this fictitious damage limitation exercise, the military credibility of Lord Herbert had been severely damaged, and the fiasco has usually been laid squarely at his door. Clarendon, who had already distorted the skirmish at Coleford, referred witheringly to '... the end of that That Mushrump [Mushroom] army which grew up and perished so soon that the loss of it was scarce apprehended, because the strength, or rather the number was not apprehended', and implied that Herbert had been grossly negligent in being absent from his army.[25] Rumour on the quays of Bristol (repeated as fact by some modern historians) had the Earl of Worcester and his family fleeing to Swansea, planning to take boat from there if necessary. The Earl of Stamford wrote to the House of Commons on 15 April: 'I was informed from very honest men that came from Wales that the Earl of Worcester with his whole family were come downe with very great haste to … Swansey, there intending to take shipping'. An entry in the Common Attorney's Accounts of Swansea Corporation, sometimes cited as supporting evidence, merely records payments in April 1643 for a group of the Earl of Worcester's servants under Sir Marmaduke Lloyd. Swansea was then building a magazine in the Town Hall and the group's expenses are partly offset against its cost, and it is this construction that evidently brought Lloyd and his party to Swansea.[26] Edward Herbert seems to have been in Oxford at the time of Highnam, and implied that those 'of the King's party' who had detained him there were indirectly responsible for the disaster. He evidently left Oxford on 26 March, immediately after news of Highnam arrived. By the 28th he was at Raglan Castle, coping with the crisis.[27] Around 1860, John Edward Lee, founder of the Monmouthshire Antiquarian Association, found some documents hidden among the slates of his house, The Priory, at Caerleon. Among them was a letter dated 28 March 1643:

> Captaine Thomas Morgan,
> You are to remayne with the Trayne Band under yor Comaund in the Towne of Chepstowe, to secure the said town, and not to permit any of the firearms to go out of the said town; also of the four pieces of ordnance which are there, you are to dispose two of them for the defence of the town of Monmouth : and for so doing this shall be your warrant.
> Dated at Ragland, the 28th day of March 1643. Ed. Herbert.[28]

Lee, by an uncharacteristic error, accepted the identification of the writer by the local historian Thomas Wakeman (who cannot have seen the letter) as the Parliamentarian Edward Herbert of Merthyr Geryn Grange near Magor. The improbability of a local roundhead sitting peacefully writing letters in Raglan Castle at this date is obvious. The writer, the Royalist commander, is where he should be—at Raglan Castle.

Whist Herbert had been absent, the army had been left under the command of a supposedly competent professional soldier. Oddly, some modern historians most critical of Herbert are those who show how much the Royalist war effort suffered from the command of titled grandees rather than competent professional soldiers. Had Herbert been present at Highnam, he would have been criticised for playing soldiers and not leaving command to those with military experience. Ian Roy has emphasised that it was normal practice at this stage of the war to give titular command to a magnate, whilst 'entrusting the real work

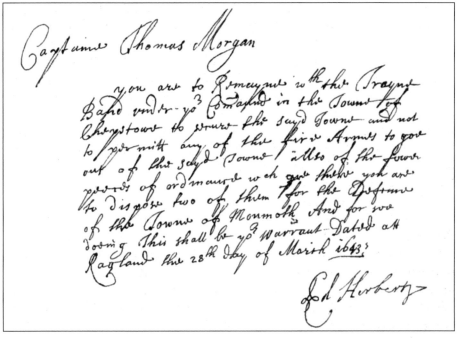

Edward Herbert's letter to Captain Thomas Morgan quoted opposite.
(now Gwent County Record Office Misc MSS 1357)

to a professional second in command'. When a magnate overlooked this convention, and tried to lead in person, the results were often unfortunate.[29]

With his field army gone, Herbert was left with whatever garrison troops were at Raglan and Chepstow, plus the trained bands. Two militia muster rolls give a figure of 400 foot for Monmouthshire, plus 50 horse. The letter shows that these were divided between Chepstow and Monmouth, at the two gateways of the county.[30] Thomas Morgan, of Llansôr outside Caerleon, a Commissioner of Array and Governor of Chepstow Castle, was to guard the river crossings at Chepstow and Monmouth and prevent Waller from advancing into the county.

After Highnam, Waller rested his troops at Gloucester, and then (Thursday 4 April) marched on Monmouth. Its defences were not strong, and his approach caused 'the precipitate flight of his lordship's troops'. With the line of the Wye forced, Thomas Morgan and his Trained Band fell back on the next river line, at Caerleon. Waller noted how 'The Welsh left their garrisons'. The next day, Waller took Usk. There were rumours that some gentry of the anti-Raglan faction, including a son of William Morgan of Tredegar and Sir William Herbert of Coldbrook, had changed sides, whilst Massey's chaplain, John Corbet, claimed that Waller had 'accepted the invitation of a number of resident gentlemen'.[31] The son was possibly Anthony Morgan of Cilfeigan, a man with London links, later involved in a prolonged plot with Sir Trevor Williams to betray the county to Parliament. However, Waller lacked the numbers and the siege train, to attempt Raglan, and on the Saturday fell back on Chepstow 'very weary of the Welsh ways over the mountains'. He rested his troops until Wednesday 10 April, when, in danger of encirclement by Prince Maurice in the Forest of Dean and by Herbert's 'contracted garrisons', he sent his foot and baggage over the Aust Ferry and retreated to Gloucester with his horse via the Forest of Dean. The following day, Sir Richard Cave re-occupied Monmouth for the King with 180 horse and dragoons. The episode had shown the fragility of local defences. Shortly after Highnam, the Breconshire Royalist Hubert Price occupied Abergavenny with two foot companies, soon to be replaced by a locally raised regiment under the 'court papist' James Prodger.[32]

Cave and Herbert had stabilised the situation. However, neutralism in Monmouthshire was already giving concern to the Royalists. Cave was instructed by Prince Maurice to 'persuade or reduce' those in the county 'accused to be averse to His Majesty's service' and other 'suspected persons'. Around 150 men under Howel Gwyn mutinied near Hereford and 'disbanded' themselves, leaving their Commanding Officer to load their abandoned weapons in a cart. Even the citizens of supposedly 'loyal' Hereford ignored Royalist warrants and refused to work on the town's defences. Although these episodes were cited by Cave in his defence at his subsequent court martial for losing Hereford, it is striking to find these symptoms of war weariness not in 1645 but in 1643. Cave called a meeting of the County Commissioners for Herefordshire, Monmouthshire and Gloucestershire at Abergavenny to create a formal association for mutual defence (those of Glamorgan had insufficient notice to attend). On 15 April a Royalist muster at which Lord Herbert was present was held at Hereford.[33] A week later, however, Prince Maurice recalled Cave's troops. With Waller advancing again, Cave was placed in a dilemma. The inexperienced local foot, with little effective leadership, could offer no real resistance. On the 23rd Waller occupied Monmouth for the second time, and two days later Hereford, capturing most of the Herefordshire gentry and commanders, including Cave and Coningsby. Herbert fled to Oxford to seek help. The King promised to send Prince Maurice and wrote to Philip Jones of Treowen, Sheriff of Monmouthshire, instructing him to let the Prince have 20 barrels of powder from the county armoury, with match and bullet proportionable. 'Monmouth taken and a hoohub' recorded Walter Powell 'and Herefford was taken'. On the 28th an attempt was made to take Chepstow by maritime attack from Bristol, then in Parliamentary hands, but the town was quickly re-captured. Cave was court martialled at Oxford for losing Hereford, but exonerated. It was all too obvious that the real blame lay elsewhere.[34]

Herbert felt the need to defend his record, implying that others were to blame for the disaster at Highnam. He had, he claimed, on receiving the Commission of Array, raised six regiments, fortified Monmouth, Chepstow and

Raglan, removed the county magazine to Raglan from 'the Earl of Pembroke's town, Caerleon', leaving a garrison there, fortified other castles in adjacent counties and, at 14 days notice, arrived at the siege of Gloucester with 4,000 foot and 800 horse.[35]

Sidestepping the issue, in June Royalist forces in the area were re-organized. Sir William Vavasour, a Lt-Colonel in the Royal Lifeguards, was made Colonel-General under Lord Herbert. Vavasour had the reputation of being a difficult man, a professional soldier whose relations with local gentry were usually bad. The King himself described him as 'a man that could agree with no one in the kingdom'. Meanwhile, Edward Herbert was busy with advice, writing to Rupert that ships should be sent to reduce Milford Haven, and offering Forest of Dean miners to reduce Bristol Castle if needed. The miners had their own views on the matter. Alienated by the King's interference with their mining and timber rights, they were nowhere to be found when the King sought miners for the siege of Gloucester, and were probably responsible for the mass desertion of the unpopular Wintour's troops the following February. However, they were happy to turn out in force for the Parliamentary sieges of Monmouth and Goodrich later in the war. A number of sources, including the King himself, grumbled that the men of the Forest were ill disposed to the Royalist cause.[36]

The Commissioners of Array were now reconstituted as a 'Committee for the Guarding of the Country' or 'Commission of Safeguard', to defend the area and raise taxes. Henry Lingen and Sir Trevor Williams, both of whom had been taken prisoner at Highnam a few months previously, were authorised to raise new foot regiments for the King, who was besieging Gloucester. Vavasour duly sealed the city off from the west. One factor that may have influenced the King in his fateful decision to besiege the city were the assurances of the south Welsh Royalists that they could support him with troops. When the High Sheriff of Glamorgan, Richard Bassett of Beaupre, arrived with 2,000 reinforcements, the grateful King knighted him on the spot. At the end of August, Walter Powell's son John left to join the Royalist forces around Gloucester and was away with the army until May 1646. In early September the King was forced to abandon the siege, his failure to take the city being one of the major turning points of the war. Vavasour was left to blockade Gloucester during the winter, but Lord Herbert, who resented his appointment, refused his co-operation. Vavasour, hoodwinked by Massey into a long march around the outskirts of Gloucester by a bogus plot to betray the city, was finally discredited, dismissed at Herbert's request, and given no subsequent employment.[37]

At the end of 1643, the King was gathering new forces for what promised to be the decisive campaign in the new year. The truce with the Irish Catholic Confederates made it possible for Ormonde to send over seasoned Irish regiments, mostly protestant and raised in England for service in Ireland. New forces were also being recruited in Wales. As the Venetian Secretary in England reported to the Doge and Senate 'regiments arrive daily from Ireland to serve his Majesty ... Another army is being formed in Wales, to join them, so that the King will soon have 60,000 armed men'.[38]

1644 : The Rise and Fall of Prince Rupert

In January 1644 Prince Rupert was made Captain-General of a new regional command based on Shrewsbury. His main concerns were with the west Midlands, where he re-organized the Royalist war effort and laid the basis of a new regional field army, largely composed of Ormonde's Anglo-Irish regiments. In line with his policy of preferring professional soldiers to local magnates as commanders, Nicholas Mynne was appointed Colonel-General over the area of Edward Herbert's command, although Herbert was allowed to retain Raglan and Goodrich, along with the taxes of neighbouring Hundreds. Herbert's field force included four regiments: the Marquis of Worcester's Horse; the Earl of Glamorgan's Horse; Lord Charles Somerset's Foot; and the Marquis of Worcester's Foot, as well as garrison regiments under Sir Henry Prodger at Abergavenny and Sir Trevor Williams at Llangybi. Proposals were drawn up for raising 2,500 pressed men in Herefordshire and south Wales for the main army, Monmouthshire and Glamorgan both contributing 400. New

The George Hotel and Town Gate, Chepstow. The hotel was garrisoned during the Civil War and the deaths of several soldiers there are recorded. The Gate was forced by Colonel Pride's Cromwellian regiment on 11 May 1648 before the second siege of Chepstow Castle.
(Photograph by Jeremy Knight)

units raised in the area at this time included Sir John Wintour's Regiment at Lydney, for in the autumn of 1643 Wintour had fortified Lydney House against Parliament. During his absence on war service it was held by his wife, Lady Mary Wintour, one of that band of formidable ladies who, on both sides, acted as garrison commanders during their husband's absence.[39]

Rupert may have planned to raise a new regiment at Chepstow under Daniel O'Neill, Lt-Colonel of his Lifeguard of Horse, but on 20 January Massey repeated the amphibious raid on Chepstow of the previous year, this time with greater success. Mooring at the Black Rock, the Parliamentarians transferred to smaller craft, and attacked two or three hours before dawn, killing a Captain Carvine in his chamber at the George Hotel and capturing twelve other officers, and about £300 in cash. They nearly achieved a greater success, for Edward Herbert of Raglan and William Herbert of the Friars at Cardiff had only just left town. Edward Herbert wrote to his brother on the 27th:

> God miraculously defended you in your last journey, for had you stayed till Monday as you were persuaded ... you had been taken that night at Chepstow, for the Gloucester men came by water to the house where you lay, killed a Captain in your chamber, and carried away prisoners all the strange commanders.

Edward Herbert himself had an equally narrow escape, for he took boat from Chepstow and sailed to the Black Rock, quite unaware that the Parliamentary warship was moored there. Massey's intelligence services were usually very good, and the capture of the two Herberts may have been one of the objectives of the raid. The George, which flanks the Town Gate and could have given cover to attackers, was evidently garrisoned, for in the spring two soldiers who 'dyed at the George' were buried at Chepstow Priory.[40] In the following month, another local regiment unravelled when Wintour's troops mutinied and went home. Ostensibly this was for lack of pay, but if they were Forest of Dean men, this could have been from dislike of their unpopular commander. At the same time, O'Neill was at Raglan, engaged on bringing ammunition and horse nails from Ireland for Rupert via Bristol.[41]

In May, Massey took Ross on Wye and advanced on Colonel Nicholas Mynne's garrison at Hereford, sending part of his force to attempt Monmouth. The Royalists got warning of this, and the Monmouth garrison was reinforced by Major-General Scudamore and part of Lord Herbert's Regiment from Raglan. Scudamore, scouting along the Ross road with a young kinsman, Rowland Scudamore, two servants and ten troopers stumbled on the Parliamentary forces drawn up 'within twice musket shot of the town'. A hundred horse and dragoons were advancing through a lane in Dixton, with behind them, drawn up in the river meadows, 400 horse. Scudamore's patrol exchanged shots with the Roundheads, but heavy rain made the pistols on both sides useless. Scudamore sent a trooper back to Monmouth for help. At the gates of the town, he met a Royalist officer, Captain Roberts, who hurried forward to find Scudamore and his little party holding the lane against all comers. A hot half hour skirmish with swords followed before Major Somerset and Lord Herbert's Regiment came to the rescue. With surprise lost, the Parliamentarians retreated towards Ross, leaving three or four of their number dead in the lane and a Quartermaster a prisoner. The Royalists lost four killed, and Scudamore's two servants as prisoners, together with his armour, which one of them was carrying. Massey abandoned Ross.[42]

The main Royalist summer campaign ended in disaster on 2 July on Marston Moor outside York. Rupert retreated via Chester and Monmouth to Bristol. In the same month, Mynne, a professional soldier who had come from Ireland late in 1643 with an Irish brigade, attempted an attack on Gloucester, but was surprised by Massey at Redmarley. Mynne was killed and 500 of his men killed or captured. In September the last Royalist field army in the west was destroyed at the Battle of Montgomery. The luckless Northern Horse, who had formed the Royalist left wing at Marston Moor, only to be swept away by Cromwell's Ironsides, fell back to join Rupert and after an epic cross-country journey through Lancashire and Cheshire, ended up by mid-September in western Herefordshire, plundering the country people and carrying off their cattle. They did little to make the King's cause popular. The north Welsh Royalist Colonel Arthur Trevor wrote to Ormonde from Chester that 'The disorderly retreat, the disasters and the ill discipline used by the Northern Horse when they were here, hath procured some scandal and much prejudice to his Majesty's affairs here, where neutrality is epidemical'. It was no coincidence that this same area of western Herefordshire was soon to become an epicentre of the militarily neutralist Clubmen. Similarly, Sir Michael Ernley told Rupert how 'since the disaster at Montgomery, the edge of the gentry [in mid Wales] is very much blunted—the country's loyalty strangely abated. They begin to warp to the enemy's party'.[43]

From Herefordshire, the Northern Horse moved into Monmouthshire, hoping to cross the Severn and re-join Rupert at Bristol. Sir John Wintour occupied the Peninsula between the Severn and the Wye at Beachley 'a place of exceeding difficult approach', and began fortifying it with an earthwork, hoping that the Northern Horse could embark from there. Two small frigates covered the flanks of the earthwork from the two rivers. Massey arrived on 20 September with his own regiment and four troops of cavalry. He waited until low tide, when the guns of the frigates no longer commanded the earthwork, sent a folorn hope of ten picked musketeers to draw the enemy fire and then stormed the works, taking over a hundred prisoners, whilst a crowd of locals watched from the Monmouthshire bank of the Wye. Corbet gave a spirited account of the assault that did nothing to diminish Massey's part:

The governor gave the signall by the discharge of a pistoll. On went the folorn-hope, and the reserve following, the trumpets sounding and drums beating, run up the works, rushed in among them and fell upon the hack, when the whole and each part of the action was carried on without interruption and the souldiers went up in such a regular march, and so great solemnity, that it seemed more like the pomp of a triumph than the confused face of a fight. Of the enemy, some were killed, and the rest taken prisoners, besides some few that recovered the boats and many of them that took the water were drowned.[44]

The Northern Horse were now marooned in Monmouthshire, where they had outstayed their welcome. The countrymen attacked them when they tried to requisition supplies, and local gentry (including some County Commissioners) refused to intervene. During the summer, Parliamentary sources claimed that 'The Welsh began to entertain better thoughts of the Parliamentary party' and that many Welshmen were 'coming in' to Massey because of his 'liberal carriage', but the activities of the Northern Horse were probably as much responsible for this as any 'liberality' on the part of Massey.[45]

On 19 September one of Rupert's officers, Samuel Tuke, wrote to him asking for boats to be sent to the Usk 'for swift passage' of the Northern Horse, who were in 'a broken condition', many without horses. The following day, they moved to St Pierre near Chepstow, where they rested, fearful of the enemy and 'Jealous of an affront by them'. Tuke's men were quartered in the surrounding villages, in an area whose loyalty was suspect. Tuke continued to bombard Rupert with letters, asking for boats and for warrants for quartering the horse. By the 30th he had moved to Llantarnam, where supplies may have been easier to come by and the river port of Caerleon was close at hand for the evacuation of his troops, but the locals resisted the exactions of the weakened Royalist cavalry by force. Tuke wrote to Rupert that there was 'no trust in the country gentry: the greater part niggling traitors. Their tenants rise, disarm and wound the men for coming to quarters assigned to them'. He proposed a graduated tax from gentry with estates of over £100 a year for maintenance of the horse, optimistically assuring Rupert that this would not hinder other Royalist contributions, whether by the Privy Seal or otherwise. In fact, local opposition meant that the Royalist drive to collect the tax raised only £30 of the projected £1,000.[46]

The resistance to Royalist demands, and the sympathy shown to the resisters by some of the county gentry caused much bitterness among the more committed Royalists. On 17 October Lewis Morgan, Lieutenant in the Marquis of Worcester's Foot in the Raglan garrison, and a local man, wrote to Rupert about an unpleasant encounter he and his men had had with the Breconshire Royalist Colonel Hubert Price, who accused them of being privy to the 'rising' in Monmouthshire. The affair was serious enough for him to ask Rupert for protection against 'this persecution'.[47]

Meanwhile, on 23 September Massey made another attempt on Monmouth. Rupert had appointed a staff officer, Colonel Marmaduke Holtby, a Yorkshire Catholic, as Governor, with Major Robert Kyrle of Walford Court near Ross as his deputy. Kyrle, originally a Parliamentarian and victor of the skirmish at Pontrilas, changed sides after the Royalist capture of Bristol. Now, with the Royalist cause collapsing, Kyrle, fearful of being called to account for his treason, plotted to change sides again, possibly opening negotiations with Massey through his Parliamentarian father James Kyrle, 'old choleric Mr Kyrle', who lived in Gloucester. Kyrle was captured, or feigned capture, and agreed to betray the town. He set out from Monmouth with 30 horse, ostensibly hoping to ambush Massey, but fell into a pre-arranged trap. A junior officer escaped to raise the alarm, but when Kyrle appeared before the Wyebridge Gate at Monmouth with 100 'prisoners', Holtby, after some hesitation, let down the drawbridge. Kyrle and his 'prisoners' then overpowered the guard and admitted Massey. Holtby escaped, but a number of officers and 60 men were taken prisoner. Holtby may have been blamed for the disaster, for he is not known to have held another command. Three soldiers killed in the taking of Monmouth were buried in Monmouth priory.[48]

Massey established an outpost of the Monmouth garrison at Wonastow House, covering the approach from Raglan, with a small garrison of foot and horse under a Captain Bailey of Stroud and a Scots Lieutenant. On 28 September 500 Northern Horse under Sir William Blackiston, with elements of the Chepstow and Raglan garrisons and of Sir Trevor Williams' Regiment, attacked. A Parliamentary news-sheet has a colourful story, possibly even true, of a maidservant who managed to find two bags of gunpowder around the house, and how the garrison melted lead from the windows and from pewter mugs to make bullets. A relief force under Major Backhouse eventually arrived from Monmouth, and the Royalists fled over Wonastow Bridge. Major Somerset and two other officers were killed, Blackiston shot in the thigh, and 40 men taken prisoner.[49] Massey released the prisoners with notes to their masters, or their parishes, claiming that

> the intention of Parliament and himself in coming thither was not to destroy or enslave their persons, or to take away their goods or livelihoods, but to preserve their lives and fortunes, to open the cause of justice and free them from their heavy burdens under the forces of Rupert, a German.

Two days later, the County Commissioners met at Caerleon and drafted a letter to Prince Rupert asking for infantry and ammunition 'in this our great and urgent necessity'. The first signature was that of Sir Trevor Williams. There was a sequel to Blackiston's wounding, for some time later he wrote to the Parliamentary commander Sir William Brereton about a physician, Thomas

Brag, a native of Monmouthshire, who had treated his wound. He asked for a pass for Brag to return home, adding that he had 'previously returned all chirigeons of yours that I have taken, without any exchange'.[50]

Now that Monmouth was taken, the Herefordshire Parliamentarian Colonel Edward Harley of Brampton Bryan planned to raise a regiment of foot to reduce Monmouthshire. Officers were sent to the Forest of Dean and the villages around Gloucester to raise recruits, but Major William Throckmorton wrote from Monmouth that neither Massey nor the Committee for south Wales were offering help or money. Sir Charles Gerard now arrived in Monmouthshire from south-west Wales with 500 men and had occupied Usk Castle and 'other places fitt for garrisons' ('Usk Castle' may have been an error). If Harley's regiment had been ready, they might have done this themselves. The drums, colours and halberds for N.C.O.s had arrived in Gloucester, but there were few men and only 50 firelocks to arm them with. For a change, we hear of the muddle and disagreements of the Roundheads, rather than of their opponents. They could not agree on a Governor for Monmouth and no one knew where Sir Edward Harley's Regiment would be stationed, or who would command it. Local rivalries were showing. The officers, Herefordshire men, were unwilling to serve under anyone save Harley, who was a busy Westminster M.P., or outside the county. His brother wrote to him that if the regiment were stationed in Herefordshire 'you would soon have a gallant regiment', but if elsewhere, and if commanded by others, he feared that the officers and men would desert.[51]

Rupert now devised a plan by which his men would re-occupy Beachley and evacuate the Northern Horse to Bristol, whilst Sir Charles Gerard staged a diversionary attack on Monmouth and Sir John Wintour attacked from Dean. In the second week of October, Rupert landed 100 foot and eight troops of horse at Beachley, whilst Wintour brought 100 of his Lydney men. Wintour brought from Bristol iron shod stakes, which he planted as a palisade outside the thick quickset hedge on the main earthwork. This was flanked at each end by hammer guns and 'murderers' (pivot guns), whilst cannon were mounted across the river at Chepstow to cover the flank.

Massey arrived at Beachley on the night of 13 October, with 100 musketeers and eight troops of horse. His planned night attack had to be postponed when the horse from the Forest of Dean garrisons were late, but he attacked at dawn with 80 musketeers, who broke through the outer defences, but then found themselves trapped between the palisade and the quickset hedge. Massey forced his horse over the hedge, but landed in the middle of the Royalist foot. A musketeer fired at close range, and when the gun mis-fired, knocked off Massey's helmet. He was about to club his unprotected head with the butt when Massey's men broke through the hedge and rescued him. Edward Harley helped Massey to a fresh horse. At this point, Robert Kyrle arrived with the main force and the Royalists broke, having lost 30 killed and 220 taken pris-

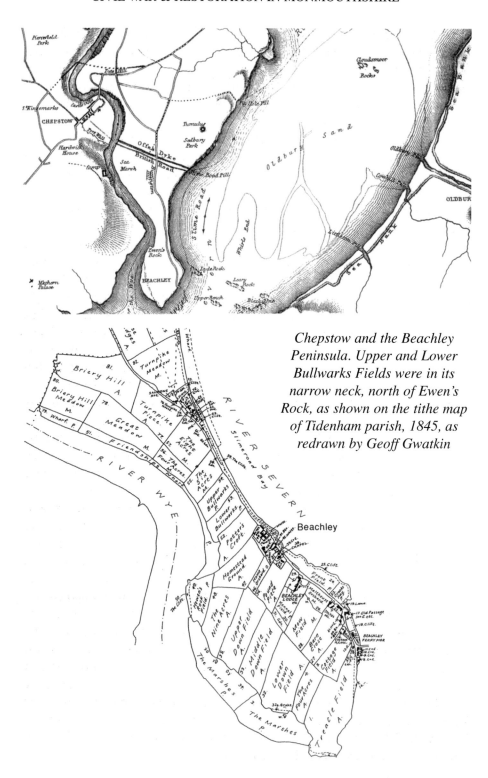

Chepstow and the Beachley Peninsula. Upper and Lower Bullwarks Fields were in its narrow neck, north of Ewen's Rock, as shown on the tithe map of Tidenham parish, 1845, as redrawn by Geoff Gwatkin

oner. Wintour held off his attackers with a pike on the edge of Sedbury cliffs. Kyrle recognised him and called to his men 'That is Wintour, pistol him', but he managed to scramble down the cliff to a waiting boat. Prince Rupert had planned to join the garrison by the next tide, and his bed was ready for him, but he was forced to watch the battle from a boat offshore. The Monmouthshire Royalists were alarmed by the course of events.[52]

Massey was also nervous about Beachley, and wrote to the Committee of Both Kingdoms that the enemy were 'resolved to garrison on Beachley and fortify it as a place without which they cannot maintain convenient intercourse with Wales'. He wished to demolish the 15 or 16 dwelling houses there 'which being destroyed or fired, there will be no shelter for the soldiers this winter'. In 1723 evidence was given in a law suit over Aust ferry that 'during the civil wars the village of Beachley was made a garrison for King Charles 1st by Sir John Winter and … besieged by … Colonel Massey, who took and burnt the said village'. In the 19th century there was antiquarian debate as to whether the stretch of Offa's Dyke across the northern end of the Beachley Peninsula might be a Civil War earthwork dating back to the events of 1644. Mr Alf Webb has now settled this problem by identifying on the tithe map of Beachley two fields, Upper Bullwarks and Lower Bullwarks, across the narrow neck of the peninsular in the area of Beachley army camp. This, some 300m in length, affords a more practicable line of defence and is probably the Civil War earthwork.[53]

The security of Monmouth itself was also a cause for concern for the Parliamentarians. On 15 November Massey wrote to Colonel Edward Harley that it was 'not well fortified, which makes it necessary for you to bring me down money, that it may be provided with ammunition and guns … Good gunners and men skilled in fire works are very requisite here'. Massey carried out some work on the fortifications, but more was needed. His fears were justified, for two days later the Royalists re-took Monmouth in a surprise attack. The governor, Major Throckmorton, had drawn off 300 men for an abortive attack on Chepstow. Royalists at Monmouth sent word to Raglan, whereupon Charles Prodger from Abergavenny, Sir Trevor Williams from Llangybi (who later tried to claim most of the credit), Edward Herbert and Lord Charles Somerset from Raglan rendezvoused near the town. At 5 a.m. they approached 'the higher side of the town that looketh towards Hereford', which was defended only by a 'sloping bank cast up, with a dry graft [ditch] of no depth'. Lord Charles Somerset and 40 horse scaled the defences between the Monnow and the Wye without opposition and reached the Dixton Gate, whose guard of six men fled. Breaking the chain with a crowbar, they let the rest of the force into the town. Several members of the Parliamentary Committee for south Wales were captured, with 200 officers and men, the hammer guns taken by Massey at Beachley, and other arms and ammunition. Edward and Robert Harley's troops of horse both lost their colours.[54]

Remains of Dixton Gate, Monmouth. On the night of 17 November 1644 Royalists under Lord Charles Somerset broke the chain on the gate with a crowbar and re-took the town. (Photograph by Jeremy Knight)

Sir Charles Gerard now began to re-organize local finances. After an initial squabble with Wintour at Chepstow, some progress was made and by 11 December a new financial framework had been drawn up. All arrears were to be remitted on payment of £1,000. Thereafter, a tax of £1,600 was to be raised for four months, half of it in provisions. Free quarter and irregular exactions were to be abolished, though subsequent complaints on both scores were to show that this was an aspiration rather than anything more solid.[55] By March, Sir Thomas Lunsford was in Monmouth as Governor and with Lord Herbert's help the garrison was strengthened to 1,800.[56] The garrisons of Chepstow, Monmouth, Raglan, Abergavenny and Newport were being financed from the taxes of adjoining hundreds, though the revenues and the needs of local garrisons did not always match up. Chepstow had a garrison of 300 men, but the taxes of the hundred were enough to support 500. Similarly, Newport Castle had a garrison of 50, but the hundred paid tax enough for 500. Some money could thus be re-allocated. The taxes of Abergavenny Hundred were topped up from Machen, Bassaleg and Henllys and with cash from Chepstow to meet the costs of its garrison. Raglan had 300 foot, paid by the Earl of Worcester. As Symonds noted in his diary: 'No [tax] contribution and constantly paid'—a reminder that however satisfactory the system looked on paper, it depended on parish officials extracting contributions from unwilling and impoverished taxpayers.[57]

5 The Royalist Ebb, 1644–45

Civilians and the War

The increasing pressure of the war on civilians can be seen in the diary and papers of Walter Powell. Until Waller's incursion of April 1643 he records family affairs and a few national events. He notes a flurry of troop movements after Cave's reoccupation of Monmouth, which was followed by relative quiet at Llantilio until late in 1644 when the Abergavenny garrison was making its presence felt.

After the Royalist recapture of Monmouth in November, the Commission of Safeguard wrote to the Chief Constables and Receivers of each Hundred, including Walter Powell, stressing the need to 'prevent any inroad or violence from the malice or power of the Rebells'. This really meant the urgent need to tighten the tax screw. 'Contributions' (a term introduced from the German wars by Prince Rupert) were to be collected from Skenfrith Hundred, where Powell was Receiver. The two Chief Constables, the petty Parish Constables and their assistants were to deliver £166 13s. 4d. to Powell within 11 days. On Boxing Day, William Lawes, treasurer to Gerard, wrote to Powell reminding him that he was four days late with his payments. In happier times, Lawes had been a composer and musician to the King, writing the music for the first performance of Milton's *Comus*, in which he had also acted. In January 1645 Lawes wrote again. Powell pleaded illness, and sent his son with the money that he had been able to collect. 'Let me sudainly [immediately] hear from you' wrote Lawes 'or else I shall be forct to render [return] you very negligent and backward to the King, the generals, and the countrey's service. If you are not well, employ your sonne or some that may be more active in it, that I suffer noe more delay', Lawes threatening to come with troops if there was more delay. By February, the Hundred was still £65 18s. 4d. in arrears, and Lawes was threatening Powell with Royalist cavalry quartered on the parishes if they did not pay up. On 30 March (Palm Sunday), a troop of 33 horse under Captain Christopher Laythorne duly arrived. Within ten days, they had made their presence sufficiently felt for the 11 parishes to pay up. Despite this, in April Powell received a warrant from Prince Rupert to arrest the two Chief Constables of the Hundred, John Davies of Llangattock Lingoed and Jenkin Scudamore of Llangua. Davies was imprisoned until his arrears were paid.[1] As noted in the previous chapter, Gerard's reorganisation of the finances meant that the contributions were half in cash, half in kind (at a fixed cash equivalent), and Walter Powell's rating documents for Llantilio for 1645 include quantities of bread, cheese, bacon, butter, oats, wheat and straw.

Powell's troubles were only just beginning, however, and the tribulations suffered by his neighbours were multiplied throughout the county. When an elderly Abergavenny recusant was summoned before the County Committee in respect of two small properties after the war, they reported that pre-war they had been worth £10 a year, but now 'in regard of the present distractions' were 'not worth neare so much'.[2]

Other Royalist accounts survive among a collection of Welsh poetry assembled in the mid-17th century by Jenkin Richard of Blaenau Gwent—possibly Llanover—including some of his own poetry. The *Llyfyr Jenkin Richard* includes two anti-puritan poems in Welsh and an English poem 'An epitaph uppon ould dotard Wroth' (William Wroth, d.1641). The accounts, entered in blank spaces in the manuscript, include contributions in kind and in cash during October 1643–October 1644 towards the garrisons of Monmouth, Abergavenny and Raglan and beds for the garrison of Coldbrook (the only evidence for this last garrison). In addition to tax in kind—in beef, mutton, lambs, hay and oats—there were contributions (2s. 4d.) towards the fortification of Monmouth (August 1644); for the buying of muskets, the billeting of soldiers, and towards the cost of arming 1,000 men. The accounts are signed by the two Chief Constables of the Hundred. A second briefer note concerns contributions in April 1646 of oats, barley, wool and money in the period leading up to the siege of Raglan. One striking but perhaps not surprising feature is that in contrast to the official apportionment of taxes from particular hundreds or parishes to specific garrisons, Jenkin Richard was facing demands from four competing garrisons.[3]

In addition to requisitions in cash or kind, there was now forcible recruiting. A 'Commission of Impress ... and the names of persons employed' has a list of 15 county gentlemen, with a note at the side '100 men a Peece'. In April 1645 Lunsford, the Governor of Monmouth, and Marmaduke Langdale with the Northern Horse were ravaging Dean with a force of 2,000 horse and 1,500 foot. They carried off pressed men and brought 3,000 cattle back to Monmouth along with large quantities of leather and wheat seized at Lancaut and Brockweir on the Wye.[4]

Under Gerard, requisitioning sometimes shaded off into simple extortion. Major Roger Whitley, a Flintshire man, sent troops of horse to arrest John Byrd, Edward Rumsey and Edmund Walter to appear before Gerard at Abergavenny.

Instead, they were carried off to the Royalist garrison at Worcester where Whitley extorted £20 a head from them, plus bonds for further payments. George and Roger Whitley had earlier begun a suit in the Court of Common Pleas against Byrd and may have been using his troops of horse in a private quarrel. However, Stephen Roberts has suggested that this was not the whole story. Byrd was a client of the Earl of Pembroke, married into the family of one of his leading supporters, whilst Walter was the brother of the puritan Henry Walter. Moreover, Whitley was no mere freebooting cavalier. Post-war he became a Royalist plotter and intelligence agent. He was one of the architects of Sir George Booth's rising in Cheshire in 1659, the one initially successful element of the planned Royalist risings of that summer, for which he drew up a carefully thought out strategy, though when the time came, this was not followed. Financial gain was always welcome, but there was also a chance to interrogate three men who had links to the opposition. As it turned out, it was their allies that the Royalists had to fear, not neutrals who might be covert enemies.[5]

One paradox of the Civil War is that whereas, in contrast to modern practice, officer prisoners were habitually ransomed or exchanged, often to re-appear in arms after a short interval, the lengthy imprisonment of civilians in castle garrisons was widespread and common. This was almost invariably in order to extort money. At one level this reflects the appearance in English society of a new caste of professional soldiers, trained in the German wars. On another it emphasises the difficulties which these professional soldiers had in keeping the war going, whether in terms of cash or of maintaining an effective officer corps. Many civilians must have wondered for whose benefit the war was being fought.

John Wintour was now Governor of Chepstow, with a headquarters at St Pierre. In October he wrote to Rupert that he was provisioning and fortifying Chepstow, though the meeting of the County Commissioners was 'more like a fair than a rendezvous where enemy is expected'. His wife was still at Lydney

The timber bridge at Chepstow was broken down during the Civil War to prevent surprise attack. It was replaced by the present bridge in 1814–16

'clinging with her children to the mercy of the rebels', for Royalist resistance was collapsing in Gloucestershire also. The following month, with the enemy 'fortified near Chepstow' (at Beachley), he prepared two frigates to defend the river against them.[6]

The towns of Monmouthshire were showing the effects of the war. At Chepstow, the timber bridge over the Wye was broken down as protection against surprise attack. Within the walls, the civilian population was crowded together not only with the castle garrison, but with large numbers of soldiers billeted on the townspeople. Until his death in September 1646 the parish register was kept up by the vicar, Abraham Drew, and thereafter by his curate. In 1644 exactly half the 44 burials in Chepstow Priory were of soldiers. Some were battle casualties, but there were at least as many deaths from disease: 'A souldier dyeing at John Watkins house, his name unknowen'; 'John Thomas, a souldier who died at Wydow Rosser's house'. One train band soldier, again 'his name unknowen' was killed by the fall of a wall. Two women buried on the same day (22 January 1645) 'killed with the fall of a house', suggests a disaster in the overcrowded town. There are also entries on the lines of 'Joane, the daughter of a soldier, his name unknown, but quartered at Edward Phillips's house in Back Lane'. Whether these reflect illegitimate births or the presence of wives, children and camp followers, they show how soldiers and civilians were crowded together within the town. In these conditions, contagious diseases flourished. In Bristol and in Gloucester deaths from the plague and typhus rose alarmingly.[7]

Abergavenny and Monmouth were also garrisoned for the King. At Monmouth, excavations have failed to find any town defences other than the Clawdd Ddu ditch encircling the cross-river suburb of Overmonnow, and the Edwardian town walls. However, a sketch by Symonds of the defences of Borstall House is annotated 'some of thus fashioned palizadoes are upon the old walles at Monmouth'. It shows a section of a wet ditch with a palisade on the counterscarp and rows of sharpened stakes projecting out horizontally from the front face of the rampart. As has been recounted, in November 1644 'the higher side of the town, that looketh towards Hereford' had only 'a sloping bank cast up, with a dry graft [ditch] of no depth'. Monmouth has also produced a Civil War coin hoard. In 1868, a 'considerable number of silver coins' were found in the demolition of an old tan house in Monnow Street, hidden in a roof beam. Of 18 coins recorded, the latest was a shilling of Charles I struck by Parliament in 1643–4. One of the times when Monmouth changed hands in 1644–5 may provide a context.[8]

Abergavenny was fortified for the King by Colonel James Prodger Herbert's Foot and the defences of the Roman fort and medieval town refurbished. In the Flannel Street sector, the town ditch was re-cut to a formidable broad, flat bottomed profile. Post-war this was rapidly infilled by tipping large quantities

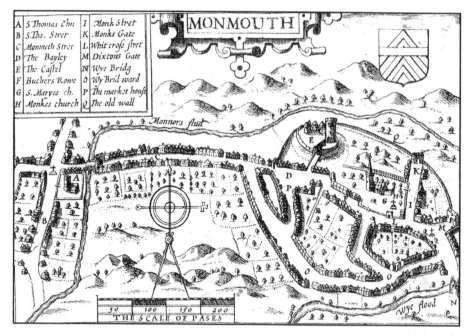

A	S Thomas Chu
B	S.Tho. Strct
C	Monmeth Strct
D	The Bayley
E	The Castel
F	Buchers Rowe
G	S. Maryes ch.
H	Monkes church
I	Monk Stret
K	Monks Gate
L	Whit crofe stret
M	Dixtons Gate
N	Wye Bridg
O	Wy Brid ward
P	The market houfe
Q	The old wall

Monmouth in 1610 from John Speed's Theatre of Great Britain. *The Edwardian defences encircle the higher ground around the castle and church. To the left, Monnow Street runs down towards the defensible Monnow Bridge*

of rubbish, including much late 17th-century pottery and a Monmouth trade token of 1656–72. At the Orchard site near the castle, a four metre wide rubble bank and drystone wall, backed by a soak-away ditch, was built over the medieval defences. A fragmentary rectangular stone setting with a large corner post was interpreted as a Civil War gun emplacement on the analogy of similar Wellingtonian defences in Portugal. Though the castle was partly ruinous, Abergavenny was an important Royalist base. Rupert was there in the following April, and the King in July.[9]

1645 Massey and Morgan

The Gloucester garrison under Massey threatened the lines of communication between Wales and Rupert's headquarters at Bristol. With Chepstow bridge broken down, on 22 February 180 horse and dragoons under Wintour and Colonel Thomas Veale's regiment from Berkeley Castle, supported by one of Wintour's frigates on the river, tried to fortify the crossing of the Wye at Lancaut above Chepstow. This was one of the few remaining routes between Chepstow and the Forest of Dean. Massey's brother, Captain George Massey, governor of Sudeley Castle, attacked them. The Royalists drew up in battle array, but were routed by the Parliamentary foot and encircled on the river edge. Eighty were killed, including Colonel Conrad Gamme, a Swedish profes-

87

sional soldier, Colonel Vangerris and Colonel Poore, governor of Berkeley. Gamme, Poore and two soldiers drowned in the flight from the battle were buried in Chepstow church. Wintour and most of the horse escaped by flight.[10] In April, with their communications cut, and in the face of pressure from Massey, the Royalists abandoned Dean. Sir John Wintour set fire to his own house at Lydney, 'having first spoyled the forest' and retreated to Chepstow.[11]

Exactions against local people continued. In February 1645 John Byrd had his house in Newport looted. Six oxen, six cows and a bull were rustled by Royalist soldiers under Captain John Morgan. A woman named Margaret Rosser was somehow involved and Byrd, a lawyer, tried to initiate proceedings against them. This again suggests that under Gerard, official requisitions were shading off into simple lawlessness.[12] By now, passive resistance to the King's war effort and to his demands for money and supplies from an exhausted country was increasing. In March one of Rupert's officers, Captain Dabridgecourt, wrote to him from St Pierre:

> ... if your Highness shall be pleased to command me to the Turk, or Jew, or Gentile, I will go on my bare feet to serve you; but from the Welsh, good lord deliver me ... send me no more into this country ... without a strong party to compel them, not to entreat them. .... The ammunition is here seven days for want of carriages and I fear shall stay seven more, unless I have some power to force the people. They value neither Sir John Winter's, his warrants, nor mine, nor any. Some say they will not come, the rest come not and say nothing. All are generally disaffected, and the force that is in Chepstow not able to compel them. Here be two or three constables that deserve hanging, and I had done it ere this, if I had but a party to defend me from their Welsh bills.

Lord Herbert did his best to calm the situation by presenting the grievances of the country people over free quarter and irregular exactions directly to the King, but Rupert and other military men were all too ready to see the whole thing as a gigantic conspiracy against the army. The episode recalls Susan Osborne's comment on the West Midlands Clubmen, where 'the military were strong enough to provoke discontent, but not strong enough to deter armed resistance'.[13]

In the same month as Dabridgecourt's letter, a local Royalist assured a friend that although the military situation was deteriorating, the common people 'are yet for the most part loyal'. This optimistically qualified statement was ominous, for also that month the Parliamentarian Committee of Both Kingdoms was informed by a Mrs Morgan

> that Sir Trevor Williams and Captain Anthony Morgan do undertake to deliver the Counties of Monmouth and Glamorgan, with the garrisons

thereof, into the Parliament's power, if they may have some present assistance from you to countenance that work. They also desire that Capt. Anthony Morgan may have a Regt of Horse, and that Sir Trevor have some command of honour and trust in these counties, when they shall be reduced, which, upon the effecting of so great a service, we think very reasonable. We recommend it to you to give them what assistance you can with safety…. if upon intelligence held with these gentlemen you shall find probability of success in so great a design.

Anthony Morgan was Sir Trevor Williams's neighbour at Cilfeigan, Llanbadoc and may have been a Captain in his regiment. A son of William Morgan of Tredegar by a second marriage, he also had kinsfolk and claims to property in Sussex. One of his motives may have been to secure his claim to this land, which lay in Parliamentary territory. His wider horizons may be reflected in the house itself, for Cilfeigan is one of a small group of late 16th-century stone built houses with freestone dressings identified by Fox and Raglan as of 'exotic [lowland] character … in a national rather than a local style'. The land in Sussex belonged to Elizabeth Mansfield, a recusant widow. Since it was common for widows to be referred to by their maiden name, it is possible that she was the mysterious 'Mrs Morgan' of the letter, perhaps a sister-in-law of Anthony Morgan.

Trust was something Williams never achieved, either with Cromwell or the King, but Hutton's verdict on his kind is a fair one:

> They acted as individuals, to salvage their fortunes from the collapse of the royal cause. But they also acted as leaders, to protect their communities from the demands of men who would waste their resources in prolonging a fruitless war and from the destruction consequent upon a hopeless resistance.[14]

One thing that well placed observers on both sides were agreed on was that, just as very few had sought war at the outset, now the overwhelming reaction, particularly below gentry level, was a desire to end its hardships and exactions. Once the Royalist army was too weak to impose its will by force, country people attacked soldiers requisitioning supplies or 'going to quarters assigned to them' and many gentry aided and abetted them. According to the Royalist commander Sir Jacob Astley, the gentry of Glamorgan excused delay in the garrisoning of Cardiff in 1645 'by [the opposition of] the common people, who will not suffer them to do it'. The actions of Sir Trevor Williams and the Glamorgan 'Peaceable Army' have to be seen in this light. Williams referred to 'those that made Rendevouses in the Countrie' and Parliamentary newsletters talked of 'the country Clubmen'. Whether they were directly comparable to the Wessex or Herefordshire Clubmen, or whether journalists were simply bracketing all troublemakers together under a convenient label is uncertain. Townsfolk were equally sick of the war. Astley complained to Lord Digby that Monmouthshire people 'seeing Bristol blocked up' (by the Parliamentary fleet) 'and the river [Severn] trade taken from them do incline to the party of the Parliament, without regard to their oath or allegiance'. From the other camp, Colonel Thomas Morgan, himself a Monmouthshire man, agreed. After capturing Chepstow in the autumn of 1645 he wrote that 'The countrey ... here ... doe much rejoyce at our prosperous proceeding ... By reason of the free traids they are now in hope to enjoy in London, Gloucester and Bristol'. It was not only a matter of trade. In Chepstow, the townsfolk, faced with ruinous tax 'contributions' to the Royalist cause and with soldiers and their families billeted on them, longed for peace.[15]

On 18 July, Massey relinquished command at Gloucester to his deputy, Colonel Thomas Morgan, once of Llangattock Lingoed. At the age of 16 he had joined a regiment of volunteers under the protestant general Bernard of Saxe-Weimer and became a professional soldier, fighting alongside George Monck and Sir Thomas Fairfax. Like many distinguished soldiers, he was small in stature. John Aubrey called him 'Little Sir Thomas Morgan, the great soldier' and described how at the taking of Dunkirk in 1658, when Morgan was fighting for Cromwell's French allies against the Spanish and the English Royalists, Marshal Turenne and Cardinal Mazarin wished to meet him. Expecting to have found 'an Achillean or gigantique person', they saw 'a little man, not many degrees above a dwarfe, sitting in a hutt of Turves, with his fellowe soldiers, smoaking a pipe about 3 inches ... long'.

Massey marched off to join the field army in the west, taking the pick of the Gloucester garrison with him, leaving Morgan with a miscellany of horse and foot, whom Morgan himself described as 'soldiers of fortune', and who gained a reputation as looters and thieves.[16]

The King in Monmouthshire

In the meantime, the King himself had arrived in south Wales, hoping to raise a new army to replace that lost at Naseby on 15 June, where the Northern Horse, having been extricated from Monmouthshire, broke once again before Cromwell's Ironsides. He arrived at Abergavenny on 1 July from Hereford, staying with James Gunter at the Priory. The 'persons of the best quality and largest fortunes of those counties' had in the past sent 'many good regiments to the army' and many of their kin had lost their lives in the King's service. They were now confident of raising 'a good army of foot, with which the King might again look on the enemy'. He issued a proclamation for Rupert to raise 5,000 foot in Herefordshire and south Wales, of which Glamorgan was to provide 1,000 and Monmouthshire 800. Recruiting was badly affected by news of recent Parliamentary successes and by the presence of Gerard, who had 'governed … with extraordinary rigour, and with as little courtesy and civility towards the gentry as towards the common people'. Despite this, the recruiting campaign met with some success, but before Rupert could carry things to completion, he had to leave to defend Bristol against Parliament.[17]

The existing Raglan field regiments were by now much weakened. The Earl of Glamorgan's Horse, originally over 200 strong, had had two troops taken from it for service elsewhere, had lost 60 troopers 'in fight' and was reduced 'by reason of continual duty'. Furthermore, the cost of raising the regiment had not been fully met. On 5 July it was decided to merge it with Colonel Lingen's Regiment until more money was available. Cavalry regiments had a theoretical establishment of 420, and infantry units 1,200, but seldom reached anything like this figure. Joyce Lee Malcolm has shown how Royalist regiments declined in size in the course of the war. At Edgehill, the 16 infantry regiments averaged 500 men, with the two Welsh regiments probably much stronger. By 1644 this average had shrunk to 300, and by Naseby to 200. According to Symonds, by late 1644 Royalist cavalry regiments averaged between 100 and 200, with Prince Rupert's Regiment of Horse and the Northern Brigade much stronger. Generally, the Royalists had less trouble recruiting cavalry (of higher social status) than in filling the ranks of its infantry.[18]

On 3 July, following a meeting with the Commissioners of Array for the county, the King moved on to Raglan, waiting to see the effect of their 'mighty promises'. His guards were quartered between Abergavenny and Raglan at Tregaer, Bryngwyn, Clytha and Bettws Newydd. He left Raglan on the 16th, rode through Usk and Caerleon to Newport, dined with Sir William Morgan at Tredegar House and went on to Cardiff. The next day he met the Commissioners for Glamorgan and instructed them to raise 1,000 men and a tax of £1,250 a month from the county. This was equivalent to Rupert's recruitment target, plus a slightly scaled down version of Gerard's tax assessment, but these unrealistic figures were to have a strange result. By the 19th the King was back at Tredegar House, returning to Raglan the next day. From Raglan he issued almost identical instructions to the County Commissioners for Monmouthshire.[19]

Visitors to Raglan commented on the good order and seemliness which the Marquis and his household maintained there. In particular, no arguments about religion were permitted between its catholic and protestant members. During the King's stay, there was one august exception. Each evening, after the rest of the household had retired, the King and the Marquis would sit late into the night debating their respective Anglican and Catholic faiths, with Dr Bayly, the Marquis's chaplain, on hand to verify biblical references. When Bayly published his account of the conferences in the year of the King's execution, it was he claimed 'published for the world's satisfaction of his Majesties constant affection to the Protestant religion'. At Raglan, the King was also able to indulge his love of bowls, often playing with Walter Pritchard, a local gentleman, though courtiers thought that Pritchard overstepped protocol in pointing out his house to the King. Anecdotes about this were long current locally. Charles Heath, writing in 1829, had spoken to a man who had been told by his grandparents how, as children, they had been taken to the bowling green at the castle to watch the King play.[20]

Charles was by now considering whether to join Rupert at Bristol and link up with his forces in south-west England. He held a Council of War with Rupert (22 July) in the still surviving medieval hall at Crick, the home of the elderly County Commissioner Nicholas Moore, close to the ferry crossing. Fifty men from Raglan and 60 from Chepstow were ordered to guard the Wye crossing at Tintern against surprise attack. Many years later, Giles Gilbert recalled how, as a boy, he had seen the King and his entourage riding through Shirenewton on the way to Crick. His story that Charles was pursued over the Black Rock passage by 'Oliver's soldiers' (who were drowned, like Pharoah's army in the Red Sea), was one of the embroideries which such oral accounts acquire through constant repetition, but there were contemporary rumours that the King had narrowly escaped capture at Black Rock and some of his gentlemen do seem to have been captured whilst carrying money to Bristol.[21]

The Medieval Hall at Crick, home of the elderly Nicholas Moore. Charles I held two Councils of War here in 1645, attended by Prince Rupert and other Royalist Grandees. (Photograph by Jeremy Knight)

One plan discussed was to send all available horse to Bristol, to oppose Fairfax in the south-west, whilst strengthening the Welsh garrisons with the newly raised foot to resist any Parliamentary counter-stroke. Indeed, the King sent reinforcements of horse and newly raised Welsh foot across the Black Rock ferry to Bristol. On the 24th he intended to cross to Bristol to join Rupert and to link up with his forces in Exeter. Ships were ready, but the King was irresolute, influenced, according to Clarendon, by enemies of Rupert, particularly Digby. Then news arrived that Fairfax had crushed the Royalist commander Goring at Langport and taken Bridgwater. The King cancelled his plans and, according to Symonds, the Welsh gentry 'immediately raised the hoop hoop'. What this meant became apparent the next day when he met the Commissioners at Usk to review the troops raised. The Scots army had begun the siege of Hereford and the county gentry, alarmed equally by the Scots and by the cost of the proposed new Royalist army, suggested to the King a sort of Home Guard, a *levée en masse* of the entire male population, under a Commissioner in each Hundred, to harass the Scots should they appear.[22] Charles spent the night at Gwern y Cleppa near Tredegar House, leased to a Mrs Priddy, widow of a former mayor of Newport and mother of the Royalist Colonel William Pretty, before moving on to spend four days with Philip Morgan at Ruperra. It may have been when he was at Ruperra that the medieval castle at Caerphilly was protected by a bastioned earthwork to its rear, denying its use to any hostile force. This may however have been built slightly earlier by Sir Charles Gerard or by Edward Lewis of the Van, whose house is within sight. Early plans by Wyndham (1775) and G.T. Clark (1842) show that the present raised platform behind the castle was surrounded by now vanished bastioned outer works.[23]

Charles had a further meeting with the 'countrymen and inhabitants of Glamorganshire' at Cefn On north of Cardiff on the 29th, but arrived to find not the promised 1,000 men, but 4,000, drawn up in battle array 'The gentlemen of the county in a body on horseback, and the rest drawn up in a battaile, winged with horse and a reserve'. He was forced to listen to complaints about the Governor of Cardiff, James Tyrrell, whom they demanded should be replaced by a local man. The following days saw a series of further demands, including the replacement of commanders by local men, the remission of tax arrears, and a tax level to match ability to pay rather than the needs of the soldiers, before they would agree to march to the relief of Hereford. Clarendon saw that the genii was out of the bottle, for the attempted mobilization had

> raised an unruly spirit, that could not easily be suppressed again, for the discontented gentlemen of those counties, now that they had gotten the people legally together, put them in mind of the injuries they had received from general Gerard, and the intolerable exactions they lay under.

Sir Jacob Astley wrote to Rupert that the county refused to assist the King 'unless they might have [satisfaction on] all unreasonable demands'.[24] The force then chose its own officers out of every Hundred, much as their Monmouthshire counterparts had suggested. On 1 August the force met at Llantrisant and adopted the name 'The Peaceable Army'. Charles replaced Tyrrell with Sir Richard Bassett, a proven local loyalist, whom he had knighted at the siege of Gloucester, but his unrealistic demands for recruits and monthly tax had produced an alarmingly unexpected response, as it had done in Monmouthshire. Astley wrote angrily to Prince Rupert from Cardiff that 'the County of Glamorgan is so unquiet, as there is no good to be expected'. He promised to 'strive as far as I can to put things in order', but he despaired of

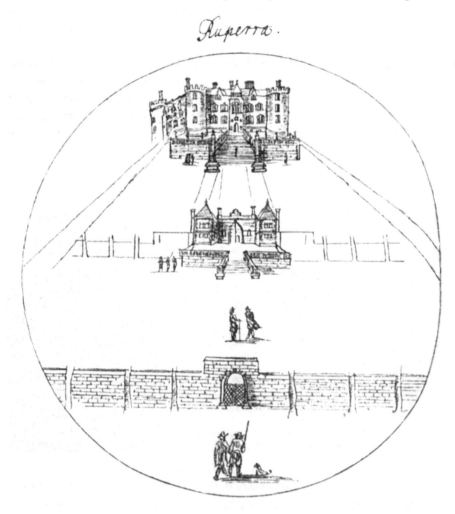

Ruperra Castle in 1684 from Thomas Dineley's
Account of the Official Progress of... the first Duke of Beaufort

the outcome 'because it must be power to rule these people, and not entreaties with cap in hand to such as deserve the halter'. A few days later he wrote in similar vein that he was trying to get the gentlemen of Breconshire to 'engage together to relieve Hereford', but that they were mostly 'inclined to be neutrals, who only wanted to join together with the strongest party'. By now, the Scots were encamped in the Forest of Dean and Lunsford, Governor of Monmouth, was nervous. He wrote to Rupert on 25 July that provided the Scots did not storm him before the promised reinforcements and ammunition arrived, he hoped to give a good account of himself—a tactful way of stressing how urgent the situation was.[25]

Whilst the King was at Ruperra, negotiations were taking place between Charles and the Scots in conditions of clandestine secrecy. The King saw the possibility of dividing the moderate Scots under the Duke of Hamilton from the strict Presbyterians, and enlisting the aid of the former, just as he later sought to exploit the divisions between English Presbyterians and Independents. At the beginning of August the Scots, with 1,000 horse, were encamped at Mitcheldean and about to begin the siege of Hereford. Under examination at Chepstow the following year, William Barry, who lived at Tregate on the Herefordshire bank of the Monnow north-west of Monmouth had a remarkable

Ruperra Castle, built by Sir Thomas Morgan in 1626. Charles I spent four days here as the guest of Philip Morgan in July 1645, in secret contact with the Scots besiegers of Hereford and coping with the Glamorgan 'Peaceable Army'. (Photograph by Alan Nutt, with permission of Ruperra Conservation Trust)

story to tell. Shortly before the siege began, a party of Scots horse came to his house and took him as a prisoner to Lt-General the Earl of Callender at Ross. Callender sent him on to the army commander, Alexander Leslie, Earl of Leven, at Dean, who questioned him about the strength of the King's army, perhaps to gague his loyalties. Thus far, the affair was straightforward, though why Barry had been singled out in this way is unclear. The following day another Scot, Lord Montgomery, had Barry released and asked him to carry a letter signed by himself, and Lords Sinclair and Leveston to Sir William Fleming, who was with the King. Barry reluctantly agreed, and was told that if Fleming was not at court, he was to deliver the letter himself into the hands of the King. At Ruperra, Barry delivered the letter. The King questioned Barry about the strength of the Scots army, and Barry replied that they were 'a Great army, but … His Majesty's faithful servants'. The King agreed.

That night, Fleming and Barry travelled to Caerleon, and the next day to Monmouth, where Fleming met Lord Montgomery in a wood for a secret discussion. Following this, the Scots lords who had signed the letter came to Barry's house at Tregate for a meeting that went on all night. 'The business they were about' said Barry 'was to settle a happy peace'. Two days later, Fleming, who had returned to the King, sent a man to Monmouth with a letter which Barry was to deliver to the Scots lords. Further meetings between Montgomery and Fleming took place at Henllan, seven miles from Hereford, and at New Inn.[26] This was just one of the King's increasingly desperate underhand negotiations with anyone who might give him military aid. This particular one came to nothing, but was to have disastrous consequences for Charles the following May, when he surrendered to the Scots army, hoping for their support. The Scots handed him over to Parliament.

According to Symonds, whilst the King was at Ruperra, on 27 July 1645 'the castle of Aberg'eny burnt, viz the habitable part. Ye garrison drawn out and quitted'. There may have been a fire, but it is clear that it survived as a Royalist garrison until some time that winter. On 8 August, Sir Jacob Astley called a meeting of the county gentry there to plan the relief of Hereford, but Sir Trevor Williams and others of the county party were unwilling to help, fearful lest another Royalist defeat should expose the county to direct attack. At the end of August, Astley wrote to Digby, unburdening himself of the obstructiveness of the County Committee 'who are, the most of them, false'. They had been given too much power and were, he was certain, treating with Parliament. The Parliamentary navy was blockading Bristol, and the country people 'do incline to the part of Parliament, without regard to their oath or allegiance'. The Glamorgan gentry were obstructive, claiming the opposition of the common people as a reason, and had failed to turn up at Abergavenny despite several summonses, whilst the Breconshire gentry had held their own meeting at Crickhowell. Only Monmouthshire people had turned up 'and these not considerable'. Articles of Association had been drawn up, but those present had refused to sign them in the absence of the Glamorgan gentry. He feared that 'each county [will] draw their strength apart, for the defence of their several counties' and saw little hope of them joining together to relieve Hereford. There was a 'Rendezvous' at Penperllini south of Abergavenny on 1 September, but, notes Walter Powell significantly 'I was not there'; once active in Royalist tax collecting, he was now absenting himself from Royalist meetings. Even Walter Pritchard, the King's former bowls partner, was later to claim that he had submitted to Parliament about this time.[27]

In the event Charles relieved Hereford from Oxford without their help the following day and then returned to settle accounts with the dissidents. On 11 September, accompanied by his guards, he rode from Raglan to Abergavenny, where the 'five chief hinderers from relieving Hereford' were summoned before him. They were Sir Trevor Williams, Sir William Morgan of Tredegar, Sir William Herbert of Coldbrook, William Baker of Abergavenny and an un-named fifth. The King was advised to order their immediate trial, but Williams, weeping, protested that 'they were accused by some contrary faction … on old grudges'. This was plausible, but more to the point they were the effective leaders of the county, and Charles, unable to enforce his will, bailed Sir Trevor Williams and eventually pardoned the rest, much to the disgust of the Marquis of Worcester who told the King that he might gain the kingdom of heaven by such doings 'but if you ever get the kingdom of England by such wayes, I will be your bondman'. Charles returned to Raglan the same night.

The Peaceable Army were not a mere collection of countrymen armed with clubs and agricultural implements, but an armed third force. Sir Marmaduke Langdale and Lord Jacob Astley went with a body of horse and foot to negotiate with them. The two armies (so Symonds describes them) met eight miles from Cardiff. After negotiations, the Peaceable Army agreed to provide 1,000 armed men for the King within a month. However they were also in touch with Parliament. John Byrd, the Cardiff Customs Comptroller whose relations with the Royalists had been soured by his experience with Roger Whitley, now used his customs boats for gun running. He received £404 worth of arms from Robert Moulton, the Parliamentary naval commander in the Bristol Channel, and passed them on to a commander in Monmouthshire in league with the Peaceable Army, possibly Sir Trevor Williams, who lived close to Byrd's house at Caerleon. (Byrd was much taken aback six years later, when he received a bill for the arms supplied. He had to contact Moulton in London to sort matters out.) Symonds was aware that the Peaceable Army were receiving arms and ammunition from Parliament, but thought it was via Pembrokeshire. On 17 September they took over Cardiff Castle, to be replaced in the following month by a group of gentry committed to Parliament and radical protestantism. There were rumours that they then had designs on Chepstow Castle. According to a

Parliamentary newsletter, late in October the Royalist horse mustered at Caerleon 'but to as little purpose as our besieging of Hereford', being frightened away by the 'Parliamentary Clubmen', presumably the Peaceable Army, after some fighting.[28]

On the day of the Abergavenny confrontation with the 'hinderers', news arrived at Raglan of a far bigger disaster: Prince Rupert had surrendered Bristol. Rupert's Royalist enemy Lord Digby was with the King at Raglan. The King, his mind poisoned against Rupert by Digby, held him to blame, dismissed him from his service, revoked his commissions and gave him and his companions a pass to go beyond the seas. Charles followed this up with a letter addressed to Rupert at Newark informing him coldly that his remaining in any garrison longer than necessary would be a violation of his pass. On the same day he wrote to Prince Maurice on (as the King was graciously pleased to call it) 'the unpleasant subject of his brother Rupert's present condition' and 'his unhandsome quitting the castle and fort of Bristol'. Charles was confident that this 'great error' arose not from any change of loyalty on Rupert's part, but 'merely by his having his judgement seduced by some rotten hearted villains'. For Charles, loyalty and gratitude for past services was often a one way traffic, as Laud had found to his cost. Charles eventually revoked Rupert's order of banishment, but he ended the war in Oxford, without a commission.[29]

The Floodgates Open

When Astley suspected that some Monmouthshire gentry were treating with Parliament, he was right. Captain Anthony Morgan was still Sir Trevor Williams's go-between and within a month of the fall of Bristol, Williams had thrown in his lot with Parliament. Meanwhile the Glamorgan Peaceable Army 'hearing of the losse of Bristol, joynd with the Pembrokeshire [Parliamentarian] forces'. Clubmen were now appearing in Monmouthshire, as countrymen banded together to resist Royalist exactions. Williams, in a letter to Parliament, claimed that 'the reducing of these parts' was only possible with the help of 'those that made Rendezvouses in the Countrie' ('raised by me' he added), since 'the inclinations of most men were averse, and a malignant [Royalist] party very predominant'. Though he tried to claim personal credit for the activities of the Clubmen, he was equally distrusted by both sides. Colonel Thomas Morgan, Governor of Gloucester, having heard that 'there was some risinge in the counties of Glamorgan and Monmouth under the command of Sir Trevor Williams and Collonell Matthews, with some shewes of being for the Parliament' took 500 horse and 400 foot from Gloucester and marched on Chepstow. Williams had already taken the town after a four day siege and the defenders retreated to the castle. Williams's version was that only after a fortnight's siege, when Royalist forces were massing to relieve Chepstow, did he seek help from Gloucester.[30]

When Morgan arrived he summoned Colonel Fitzmorris, the Governor, to surrender the castle for Parliament's use. Fitzmorris replied that he 'kept it for his master the King'. Morgan sent to Bristol for 300 additional foot and raised a battery within half musket shot (75 yards) of the castle, with two brass culverins and an iron piece. After a three day siege, the walls had been breached. Morgan had intelligence that Royalist troops were advancing from neighbouring garrisons and planned to muster 2,000 horse and foot at Abergavenny that night. He therefore drew out 400 men and formed them up ready for an assault. The Royalists beat a parley and sent out a drummer with a letter offering to negotiate a surrender. Colonel Fitzmorris duly surrendered on the 10th, along with four officers and 106 men. The castle contained 18 pieces of ordnance, great and small, 16 barrels of powder, 'great store of fireworks', 400 barrels of butter, six hogsheads of biscuit and quantities of powdered beef, salt, cheese, oatmeal, peas and beans, metheglin, beer and ale The messenger who brought the news to the House of Commons was rewarded and the House ordered all ministers of religion to give thanks to God. Colonel Thomas Hughes of Moynes Court was installed as Governor.[31]

The Royalist relief force included men from Raglan, Hereford and Monmouth under Sir Thomas Lunsford, and Colonel Henry Washington's dragoons from Worcester. The High Sheriff, Edward Morgan of Pencoed, issued warrants forbidding local people on pain of death from joining the insurgents (Clubmen). Even so, whilst Morgan was besieging the castle, Williams, Kyrle and the Clubmen forced the relief force to retreat. Morgan described how 'Washington, with 1,500 horse and foot fell down into the skirts of Monmouthshire, but by the timely rising of the Glamorgan Clubmen and the happy intervening of the Gloucester forces, were put back and pursued as far as Hereford'. Another source gives most of the credit to Kyrle (who may have had a hand in its writing) and claims that he pursued Washington over the Wye six miles above Hereford. Morgan, echoing Astley's comment earlier in the year that local people were inclining towards Parliament because of the stoppage of trade with Bristol, claimed that: 'The country doe much rejoyce at our prosperous proceeding ... by reason of the free traids they are now in hope to enjoy to London, Gloucester, Bristoll and other parts of the kingdome'. Resistance to the Royalist soldiery was not confined to Gwent, for the Foresters of Dean set up turnpikes and barricades on the roads and forest rides to resist parties of foraging troops. 'The Parliament soldjers cap in hand for a night's quarter' notes Symonds, though the Foresters were happy to turn out for the Parliamentary sieges of Monmouth and of Goodrich the following year.[32]

Parliament was also apprehensive about the Clubmen, some 6,000 of whom still remained in the field, and about semi-autonomous local commanders like Williams at Llangibby, Colonel Matthews in Glamorgan and Colonel John Poyer at Pembroke Castle. Robert Moulton feared that 'the multitude of general persons in those counties, each commanding in chief and absolutely, as in Gloucestershire, Monmouthshire, Brecon, Glamorgan, Pembrokeshire may in time cause some confusion if not prevented'. He suggested a Commander in Chief, appointed by Parliament 'over all those counties' with 500 commanded men, strangers to the place, in each county. This was prophetic, for it was the attempt to replace Poyer with Fairfax's nominee Colonel Fleming in February 1648 that triggered the outbreak of the Second Civil War in Pembrokeshire.[33]

Morgan and Williams now rendezvoused between Chepstow and Monmouth and marched on Monmouth, with Morgan's 1,500 regulars from Gloucester; the 200 cavalry of Sir Trevor Williams's horse and a troop of horse under Colonel Kyrle. Of the foot, Williams's regiment was swollen to around 1,500 with 'the Monmouth and Glamorgan Clubmen' and a detachment of sappers recruited from Forest of Dean miners. The Royalist Governor, Thomas Lunsford, had left two days before and the acting Governor, Captain Price, without enough men to man the town walls, pulled back into the castle. The townsfolk lowered the drawbridge to admit the Parliamentarians, mostly local men, into the town. Colonel Morgan summoned the castle to surrender, but Price refused. The country people were summoned to bring in shovels, spades and pick-axes to assist the siege, and according to a Parliamentary newsletter soon turned up in large numbers. The Forest men mined the walls in several places. With the mines ready to be sprung, Monmouth Castle surrendered on the 24th after a six day siege. Morgan's booty included seven cannon, four sling pieces, 300 muskets, 600 pikes and large quantities of powder.[34] The gates of Monmouthshire were now open. Morgan returned to Gloucester, leaving 100 men in Monmouth Castle under Captain Foster, with the town in the charge of Trevor Williams and his local levies. Williams's men complained that 'they did come to keep garrisons' and returned 'every man to his own home', leaving the town defenceless. Williams blamed this on local Royalists, and fearing attack from Raglan, sent for help to Gloucester and Ross on Wye. Lt-Colonel Kyrle and Captain Gainsford reached Monmouth next day with 700 men, who guarded the town until 200 of the Gloucester garrison returned. Williams and Kyrle then issued a proclamation ordering suspected persons to leave the town upon pain of death, whereupon ' divers families of malignants were put out'.[35]

The desertion of Williams' forces was just one case where the privately raised units proved of doubtful reliability. In February 1644 Wintour's newly raised regiment of Forest of Dean troops had mutinied at Chepstow and gone home, ostensibly for lack of pay, but perhaps also because they did not wish to serve under such a locally unpopular commander. On another occasion, the historian Webb recounts a family tradition of the Herefordshire Royalist, Captain Wathen. Escorting a force of raw recruits to Monmouth, Wathen and his men, whilst climbing Llanlawdy Hill beyond St Weonards, heard a jingling of horse harness 'coming down upon them through the hollow road'. Expecting to be charged by Roundhead cavalry, the recruits fled. Wathen prepared himself for a hopeless fight, calling to one of his officers 'If I fall, search my pockets'. At that moment, the 'cavalry' revealed themselves as a train of charcoal burners on their way to the Forest. Even Rowland Laugharne's men, veterans of several victorious battles in south-west Wales, tired of the siege of Raglan and returned home to Pembrokeshire.[36]

Early in November, the Venetian Ambassador in France reported the changed situation in Wales to the Doge and Senate:

> The province of Wales, which at first followed the King, is now coming over to Parliament, the majority having accepted the conditions granted them to escape the calamities of war, not finding the King's forces strong enough there to support his interests. Mainmuth has surrendered to Parliament, with other places of less importance.[37]

Morgan, with 600 men, now made an attempt on Abergavenny. He left Colonel Hopton there with a small force of cavalry, but they were driven out by 400 foot from Raglan and Hereford, who seized five leading citizens as hostages.[38] Yet the strains of defeat were now showing among the Royalists. A fortnight before Colonels Birch and Morgan finally took Hereford at the end of November, Sir Nicholas Throckmorton, the deputy Governor, accused Sir Thomas Lunsford of losing Monmouth 'basely', by being absent from his post. They were only prevented from fighting a duel by the guards. After a committee of six gentlemen had failed to calm matters, the two had to be locked up. The prisoners taken at Hereford included several important Royalists: Sir Thomas Lunsford, Sir Richard Bassett of Beaupre, Sir Philip Jones of Llanarth and the High Sheriff of Monmouthshire, Edward Morgan of Pencoed. Some were exchanged, for Jones and his wife were at Raglan during the siege and Lunsford was to take an active part in the Second Civil War.[39]

After the fall of Hereford, the gentry of Breconshire, previously lukewarm Royalists, declared for Parliament.[40] Some Monmouthshire Royalists were also making their peace. Herbert Vaughan of Oldcastle, who had served as a Captain in Lord Hopton's Regiment of Horse in the west country, submitted to Parliament in November and claimed to have subsequently been 'in special service' for Parliament and to have 'suffered very much in his estate by the enemy at Raglan Castle' in consequence.[41] In the meantime Parliament were continuing negotiations with Sir Trevor Williams, now their open ally, and Anthony Morgan over their role in reducing the county.[42]

Despite the fall of Hereford, Parliamentarian control of Monmouthshire was still not secure. Trevor Williams complained that the Royalists were 'plundering all the well-affected Countreymen', inflicting unheard of cruelties and making it impossible for him to raise money from them to pay his troops. Similarly, Thomas Herbert reported that:

the enemy has raged more than ever and so overpowre the county with their horse that they … raise their contributions at leisure, to the terror of our friends, and the daily hazard of Monmouth and Chepstow-the two keys and most considerable garrisons of south Wales, which are likely to fall … if such a number of false hearted cavaliers be contynued there.

On 5 December, the Royalists beat up Parliamentarian garrisons at Abergavenny and Ross. There were rumours that they had taken Monmouth. The Governor of Chepstow pulled back his garrison of 100 foot into the castle, leaving the town defenceless and Royalist spies there were suspected of being in touch with Raglan on a daily basis.[43]

6 End Game;
Raglan and Chepstow 1646–48

In this final stage of the war, Lord Charles Somerset at Raglan and Sir Michael Woodhouse at Ludlow were raiding newly won Parliamentary territory with bodies of horse in an attempt to regain the initiative. In the short term, this was successful. About 22 January, the Raglan horse surprised a newly raised Parliamentary force of 200 infantry and 80 horse under Bussey Mansell and Captain Bowen at Caerleon, killing 40 and taking 140 prisoners. According to one account, the Royalists threw some prisoners in the Usk and drowned them, though Bowen and a lieutenant were taken to Raglan and exchanged. Mansell sent a plea for help to Rowland Laugharne. Sir Trevor Williams gave a different version, claiming that these were his men, in winter quarters at Caerleon, surprised whilst he was away in Cardiff raising money for pay. He blamed the disaster on 'ill affected townsmen' in Caerleon (which had a large recusant community) who had sent news to Raglan, and on lax sentry duty by the horse. Two days later, the Royalists raided Newport, which Thomas Morgan of Machen had occupied for Parliament. Williams claimed that the town was gallantly, but unsuccessfully defended, but the account of a mythical 'battle of Newport', with 200 killed and the explosion of a powder magazine, is journalistic fiction intended to 'sex up' an otherwise unexciting newsletter by a postscript allegedly from Raglan. There may also have been confusion between the two Thomas Morgans. A few days later, Somerset attacked Abergavenny, taking 50 prisoners.[1] Sir Thomas Morgan put a garrison of 200 foot and 100 horse into Llanarth, between Raglan and Abergavenny, to prevent further raids. Captain Edward Wakeman and some of the Marquis of Worcester's horse were sent to dislodge them, but whether this met with any success is unknown.[2]

The Royalists also made a final attempt to re-take Monmouth, seizing the fortified medieval gateway of Monnow Bridge at the bottom of Monnow Street. Kyrle counter-attacked, but another company of Raglan troops waded across the shallow river upstream of the bridge and reached Monnow Street, taking Kyrle in the rear. He managed to get back to the castle at the top of the hill and assembled 100 of its garrison in the Market Place (now Agincourt

Square), raising the castle drawbridge to prevent them retreating. Attacking down Monnow Street, he routed the Royalists after a violent battle, killing eight and capturing five more. The expulsion of more 'malignant' townspeople and the arrest of officers believed unreliable followed. Shortly afterwards a small party of Royalists tried to enter the town across the now frozen Wye, but were repulsed.[3]

On 6 February, Edward Carne of Ewenni, High Sheriff of Glamorgan, and Sir Charles Kemeys of Cefn Mably attacked Cardiff, now ruled by a group of religious and politically hard line Parliamentarians. Carne, a devout Anglican, feared that they were about to impose the Solemn League and Covenant on Glamorgan. Fearing, they claimed, both for their souls and their estates, the Prayer Book rebels forced the Parliamentarians to seek refuge in the castle. From Raglan, Lord Charles Somerset wrote that he had heard from Sir Charles Kemeys that the county of Glamorgan had risen for the King. The Parliamentarians in Cardiff were short of ammunition but John Crowther, Captain of the ship *Entrance*, ran in a supply from Bristol, and managed to reach the castle garrison with it (the Taff then ran roughly along the line of the present Westgate Street, hard outside the castle walls). The Royalists offered quarter to all save members of the County Committee and Crowther's men, who had brought six cannon from their ships. A sally from the castle ended in disaster, with half the garrison taken prisoner. The situation was serious, but Parliamentary troops were converging on Cardiff. Laugharne advanced from the west, Sir Philip Skippon from Bristol and Morgan, Williams and Kyrle came down from Monmouth. Skippon and Morgan duly routed the Royalists in a battle at the Heath north of Cardiff, whilst Laugharne attacked from the west, lifting the siege. The besieging Royalists, trapped in the town, were forced to surrender. Allowed to march out with the honours of war, they were then attacked by Laugharne's dragoons, many killed and Carne and Kemeys captured. Carne's force was dismissed as 'that Runnagado crew, to whom many Clubmen were joined'. 'Clubmen' may have been simply a journalistic cliché, but elements of the old Peaceable Army, disillusioned with the County Committee, may have been involved. There may also have been an element of the populist defence of traditional Prayer Book religion that sometimes surfaced in other Club risings. Many Anglican clergy were involved with the Clubmen in Shropshire (where the parson of Bishops Castle was among the leaders) and in southern England. Later, a number of Glamorgan clergy were active in the 1647 rising there.[4]

A disaster of a quite different kind now afflicted the Royalists, putting the relationship of the King and the Marquis of Worcester under severe strain. Edward Herbert's disastrous negotiations with the Irish catholic Confederacy are only marginally relevant to the progress of the war in Monmouthshire, but their repercussions were strongly felt at Raglan. Ireland had a complicated civil war of its own, involving the catholic Confederation of Kilkenny; the English protestant Royalists of Dublin under Ormonde and the feuding Scots/Irish clans of east Ulster and the western Isles. Ormonde had sent mostly protestant Anglo-Irish regiments to aid the King, but these were destroyed at Nantwich and Montgomery in the autumn of 1644. Ormonde secured a truce with the Confederates, but, faced with the King's increasingly desperate wish to negotiate with the catholic rebels for military aid, by November 1644 he was seeking to resign.

How much the King or Ormonde knew of Lord Herbert's plan for secret negotiations is unclear, though the King's reputation for duplicity was well deserved. In December Charles wrote to Ormonde, with a postscript in cipher:

> Ormonde
> My lord Herbert having business of his own in Ireland (wherin I desire you to do him all lawful favour and furthurence), I have thought good to use the power I have both in his affection and duty to engage him in all possible ways to further the peace there; which he hath promised to do. Wherefore (as you find occasion) you may confidently use and trust him in this, or in any other thing he shall propound to you for my service; there being none in whose honesty and zeal to my person and crown I have more confidence. So I rest,
> Your most assured constant friend
> Oxford 27 Dec 1644. Charles R
> (in cipher) His honesty or affection to my service will not deceive you; but I will not answer for his judgement.[5]

Edward Herbert, Earl of Glamorgan was well placed to negotiate with the Irish, for his second wife was Margaret O'Brien, daughter of Lord Thomond. He and his brother Lord John Somerset (who had commanded the horse at Highnam) set out on their quixotic mission in March 1645. After an adventurous crossing which included shipwreck on the Cumberland coast, they finally arrived in Ireland at the end of June. Herbert's negotiations resulted in a secret draft treaty of 25 August 1645. An Irish catholic army of 10,000 men would land at Chester to assist the King, in return for Charles granting liberty of conscience, repealing the penal laws against catholics and allowing the Irish rebels to retain the churches and land that they occupied. Whether the King knew of its terms is debatable, but if not, he must have been remarkably ill informed. Copies had been printed and circulated, and its content was common knowledge, both to Ormonde and in London, even before a copy was captured at Sligo in October, when Malachy O'Queely, archbishop of Tuam, was killed and his carriage, containing his papers, captured. When the storm broke, Charles repudiated the negotiations and Ormonde imprisoned the Earl, though he later released him on the orders of the King. The affair was a disaster for the Royal cause. Not only did the treaty confirm the very fears that the King's enemies had worked on since before the war, but the King's repudiation of Glamorgan created a breach with the Marquis of Worcester. When, shortly afterwards, Charles sent a trusted messenger to Raglan with a letter explaining his actions, the angry Marquis at first refused to receive the letter. Despite this, Glamorgan continued his intrigues in Ireland, in alliance with the Papal Nuncio Rinuccini, who hoped to make him Lord Lieutenant in place of Ormonde. The only effects were to fatally divide the Irish Confederates and to drive Ormonde into the hands of the English Parliament. The affair also had other consequences. Suspicions of Charles's connivance in the Irish rebellion of 1641 and the subsequent massacres, and of his later negotiations with the rebels were a major component of his 'blood guilt' in the eyes of the Parliamentary radicals who were to put him on trial.[6]

Late in the same month, another episode showed the rifts opening in the King's cause. A petitioner turned up at Sir Thomas Fairfax's headquarters with a letter from the Committee of Both Kingdoms. This was Captain Anthony Morgan, Sir Trevor Williams's go-between in his negotiations with Parliament. 'There hath been some service undertaken by the bearer' the Committee told Fairfax 'about the reducing of Cos. Monmouth and Glamorgan to the obiedence of Parliament'. Now that Chepstow and Monmouth were taken, Morgan was seeking his reward, command of a regiment. The House of Commons 'ordered that he should have a regiment speedily'—or when one became available. Fairfax was to allow him to serve under him 'and give him such encouragement and respect as he may deserve'. Whether this was deliberately ambiguous or no, it is doubtful if Morgan got his regiment, though sequestration of his estate was lifted in the following November. He later served in Ireland under Cromwell. Following his role in the relief of Cardiff, Sir Trevor Williams had been made Commander in Monmouthshire, but by May had lost his place. Late in 1646 he had ambitions to enter Parliament for Monmouth Boroughs, but he lacked the political patronage, and probably the trust, of the local power brokers. He was pushed aside by Thomas Pury the younger of Gloucester, whose father had played a leading role in the siege of Gloucester and in the creation of the New Model Army.[7] These frustrations may help to explain why this perennially restless man became involved in the Royalist plot to seize Chepstow Castle two years later.

A lively account of conditions in southern Monmouthshire in late February 1646, in the aftermath of the relief of Cardiff, and of the straits to which Royalist communications had by then been reduced, is given by the adventures of Alan Boteler, a former cup bearer of the King, who left Oxford on the 22nd with secret despatches for Raglan. The Marquis had been incensed at Charles's repudiation of his son's mission to Ireland and his imprisonment by Ormonde, and the letter was an attempt by the King to pacify him. In his report to Ormonde, Boteler told how he reached Acton Court in Gloucestershire, seat of

Sudbrook church in 1798. Alan Boteler concealed himself and his horse in the
porch (right), with his despatches hidden in the rocks.
(Drawn by Sir Richard Colt Hoare)

the Poyntz family, and after hiding for five days, crossed by the Black Rock
ferry disguised as a grazier, with a friend who knew the area dressed as a
farmer. The area was full of Parliamentary soldiers rounding up fugitives from
Cardiff. With the help of the 'farmer', he hid with his horse in the porch of
Sudbrook church, concealing his despatches in the nearby rocks. Hoping to
reach Sir Richard Herbert at St Julians, Boteler moved westward through the
Gwent levels with a guide, avoiding the main roads. Boteler now claimed to be
a butcher from Bristol, making for Caerleon. Near Goldcliff, he ran into three
Parliamentarian officers who had landed there from Bristol. Questioned,
Boteler claimed that 'by his being there, they might easily judge who he was
for', adding that a friend had told him that Charles Somerset was close at hand
with 300 horse. Hearing this, the roundheads galloped back into the moors in
haste. After these adventures, he reached Sir Richard Herbert at St Julians
safely.

Boteler was able to send a messenger to Lord Charles Somerset at Raglan.
Lady Mary Herbert concealed the dispatches in her bed at St Julians for later
recovery and Boteler set out. He had been warned of the garrison at Llangibby
and of soldiers quartered in the villages. Making for a rendezvous with an
escort from Charles Somerset at a windmill on Christchurch Hill, he encoun-
tered a troop of roundhead horse and foot and hid in the woods before returning

St Julians near Caerleon (now demolished), seat of the Herberts of Pembroke and Montgomery. Alan Boteler was hidden here by Sir Richard Herbert whilst trying to reach Raglan Castle. (Drawn by Sir Richard Colt Hoare)

to St Julians. He eventually managed to make his way to Raglan with one of Sir Richard Herbert's servants. Worcester, still angry, refused to send to St Julians for the despatches, but after a fortnight relented. The news of Glamorgan's mission to the Irish Catholics had however caused such divisions between the protestant and catholic officers at Raglan that a number of the former quitted the castle.[8]

Raglan Besieged

In the meantime, the remaining Royalist garrisons and field forces in the west of England were being eliminated. Chester surrendered on 1 February, Sir Ralph Hopton in Cornwall on 14 March and on the 22nd the King's last field army, under Sir Jacob Astley, surrendered to Brereton at Stow on the Wold. In the words of Josuah Sprigge the 'Oxford Garrison … being now reduced, many other Garrisons that attended its fate fell with it, even like ripe fruit, with an easie touch : But … Ragland and Pendennis, like winter fruit, hung long on'.[9]

As the Parliamentary forces closed in on Raglan, many Monmouthshire gentlemen made their peace with Parliament. Major Charles Hughes of Trostrey had 'come in' in January and in March the County Committee issued a proclamation calling on remaining Royalist officers to submit. Colonel William Pretty and 'divers other chief commanders' did so. Walter Powell had moved to Penrhos the previous November, and his diary now records the frequent tribulations of himself and his neighbours. In December one of these neighbours, Valentine Jones Lewis, was carried off to prison in Raglan. In January Thomas Lewis, the father of his servant Andrew Lewis, was slain—presumably by soldiers. On 14 March Lt-Colonel Charles Prodger was 'at Llanvapley to burn my hay'. Over the next fortnight his hay at Llantilio was burnt by the garrison of Monmouth whilst another neighbour, Mistress Nelson, had her oxen plundered. Meanwhile, the decreasing area under Royalist control put greater financial pressures on those which remained. In February and March 1646, the cash 'contributions' of the parish of Llantilio Crossenny towards the garrison of Raglan amounted to £53 15s. 0d. The two divisions of the parish, 'About ye church' and 'Whitecastle', corresponding to the medieval manors of Llantilio Episcopi and Llantilio Regis, each had their own collector, who reported to Walter Powell as Head Constable of the parish. Eventually, on 25 May, Powell himself was imprisoned at Raglan, probably for having failed to raise the taxes demanded from his hard pressed and impoverished neighbours.[10]

Powell made his first acquaintance with the new administration in July 1646, only a month after his release from Raglan, where on 6 June he had been

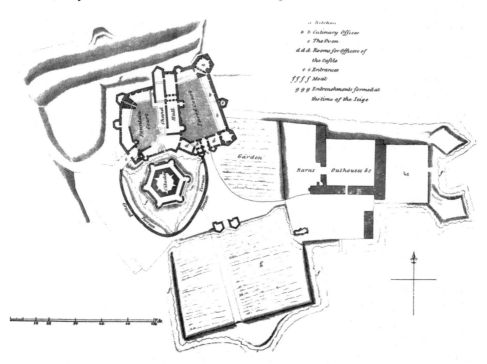

Plan of Raglan Castle of 1798 by Thomas Morrice. Two large bastions are shown east of the (later) farm buildings. The area west of the 'Grand Terrace' was the bowling green, where Charles I played

allowed to pass through the siege lines then in place. His note to the Parliamentary commander has been preserved among his papers:

> Sr
> It has pleased my lord in regard of my age and infirmities of body to give me (that now am a prison'r) leave upon my par[o]ll[e] to goe home to my wief and children to my house at Penros, and therefor I humbly desire you would be pleased to graunt me a passe to goe freely throughe yo'r army w'thout lett or molestac'on and I shall remayne
> Yr humble servant
> W.P.

His new house at Penrhos had been plundered by Parliamentary troops, ironically whilst he was a Royalist prisoner. Now the Parliamentary commissioner William Loup arrived to discuss contributions (the monthly assessment) and free quarter, but Powell only notes that he negotiated a concession of some sort for Andrew Lewis and his son, whose taxes may have been part of the assessment from Powell's estate. In November there were further meetings at Penrhos with William Loup. Again, he obtained concessions for Lewis and

Raglan Castle and its gardens, c.1620. The Parliamentary siege works were concentrated on the higher ground beyond the castle. (Artist's impression by Ivan Lapper, 2003, © Cadw)

another man, but Loup 'denied me, because my bill did treble the rent', Powell's assessment being two thirds of the whole.[11]

The story of the siege of the castle has frequently been told, yet one of the most striking features about it, and one that accords ill with the idea of Monmouthshire as a staunchly loyal Royalist county, is that until the arrival of Sir Thomas Fairfax late on in the siege, it was conducted by two Monmouthshire gentlemen belonging to the opposing faction within the county—Thomas Morgan, once of Llangattock Lingoed, and Sir Trevor Williams of Llangibby. In February, Morgan had installed a garrison of 200 foot and 100 horse at Llanarth, between Raglan and Abergavenny. The Raglan garrison could still prove troublesome, and raided Monmouth carrying away 'many well affected people prisoners to Raglan', but another raid on 13 April ended in disaster when Trevor Williams skirmished with a force of 100 men, killing or capturing 60. Abergavenny was still in Royalist hands in the early months of 1646, when Alan Boteler was there, but in April Charles Prodger, its Royalist commander submitted to Sir Thomas Morgan.[12]

At Raglan the castle began to prepare for siege and a number of people left, partly because of divisions within the garrison between catholics and non-catholics. Tenants promised supplies of corn 'as each tenant shall subscribe herewith to give'. The first signatory, Henry Milborne of Wonastow, promised 20 bushels of wheat and 20 of oats. At Llanover, Jenkin Richard was busy during April collecting oats, barley and wool to supply Raglan. However, the options for loyal Royalists were narrowing and deft footwork was necessary for economic survival. It was normal Royalist practice before a siege to destroy any neighbouring houses that might give shelter to attackers. Walter Pritchard of Tre-Worgan, the King's former bowls partner had (so he later claimed) surrendered to Parliament the previous autumn, and his house was burnt and his stock and goods plundered by the Royalists. He later used this destruction to evade payment of a fine for delinquency on the grounds of poverty, but his poverty did not prevent him from sending a substantial sum of money to the Earl of Glamorgan in Ireland.[13]

During late April and early May, Parliament also made preparations. Morgan was made commander in Monmouthshire and William Herbert of Coldbrook High Sheriff, with his brother Henry Herbert commanding a troop of horse. They were given £3,000 from the sale of woods belonging to the Marquis of Worcester. The preliminaries of the siege are recounted in lively detail by 'M.P.', the author of *The Gallant Siege of Parliament's Forces before Ragland*. This was almost certainly the Monmouth Parliamentarian clergyman and schoolmaster the Revd. More Pye. The author is a soldier and eyewitness resident in Monmouth, able to drop Latin phrases into his text, and the style of the pamphlet is similar to that of Pye's diary. Late in April Sir Trevor Williams mustered at Usk 80 horse and foot from Llangibby; a similar number from

Pencoed and 150 from Chepstow. The Raglan garrison tried to dislodge them, but were repulsed with 16 killed and 20 taken prisoner. Of the roundheads, Sir Trevor's brother, Lt-Colonel Williams, was wounded in the arm and an unfortunate corporal captured; since the latter proved to be a deserter from the Royalist army, he was shot. Lt-Colonel Williams was presumably the former Royalist Major Edward Williams.[14]

Laugharne's forces were now at Abergavenny and Llanarth and Kyrle's close to Raglan. Laugharne, Williams and Morgan rendezvoused at Gwehelog Common and set up their headquarters at Llandenny, 'two Welsh miles and a half from the castle'. On 20 May a party under Major Thomas Lewis and Captain Evan Harris entered Raglan village under cover of darkness. They seized horses grazing in the fields between village and castle, brought from Goodrich, where John Birch had destroyed the stabling in a raid. In the words of Pye they were 'so bold as to borrow three score and ten ... belonging to Goodrich Castle, whence they came but the night before'. A Royalist posse attacked the raiders and there were casualties on both sides, but Lewis and Harris got away with the horses. Four days later, a group of roundhead soldiers were drinking in an ale-house in the village 'within a little of the castle' late at night. Since the enemy were quiet 'they began to refresh themselves with such things as the house afforded', but the Royalists were told of the revellers and 60 or 80 horse made a sortie, capturing several horses, though the drinkers managed to hide in a nearby cornfield and to capture two of the Royalists. Another sortie by 150 cavalry the next day was 'disputed a long time', but the days when Charles Somerset had been able to raid far and wide with his cavalry were over. The garrison set fire to the houses in the village and retired to the castle.[15]

The siege began on 25 May. Morgan, Williams and Laugharne had 1,500 men to oppose the castle's 800, and the services of an experienced engineer and gunner, Captain Hooper, 'a very ingenious person ... who ... understood all kinds of operations, in almost all things imaginable'. He had assisted Colonel John Hutchinson in the defence of Nottingham, siting and building earthwork defences, manufacturing powder and match and even casting mortar pieces. Later, he served under Cromwell and Fairfax at various sieges, most recently at Oxford and Banbury. He began to draw his siege lines around the castle and 'as soon as he could get spades and shovels, he went most dexterously to work against this Castle of Ragland'. Rowland Laugharne was at Abergavenny with 600 horse and foot, but by 5 June, mutinous for want of pay, they wanted to return home. The Usk Committee raised £200 to pay them off. They returned to Pembrokeshire.[16]

Hooper sent in a demand for surrender, which the Marquis rejected. A month later, on 28 June Morgan sent in a second summons, announcing that Fairfax was marching on the castle with a siege train, and a message that other garrisons had already surrendered on the orders of the King. Charles, without an army and a prisoner of the Scots, had, on 10 June indeed ordered his garrison commanders to lay down their arms. Worcester refused both summonses, on the grounds that the King's orders made no specific reference to Raglan.[17]

On 23 July Morgan reported to Parliament that he had raised a battery, opened fire on the guns on the castle's battlements, and silenced them. Traces of both the Parliamentary and Royalist siege lines survive. By a fortunate chance, William Coxe, author of *An Historical Tour in Monmouthshire* (1801) was able to employ a professional surveyor, Thomas Morrice, whose usual job was the survey of tramroads and canals. Morrice's plan of Raglan shows a number of Civil War earthworks, and this, with surviving traces on the ground and the evidence of air photographs, enabled John R. Kenyon to produce an account of both sets of siege lines.[18]

The Royalist defences were concentrated around the southern and eastern sectors, since to the north and west were steep slopes with formal gardens, terraces and large fishponds. There was a rectangular outer ward between the extant White Gate and the Red Gate, in the area of the present car park. At its south-west corner, right of the car park entry, an angled bastion is visible as a substantial earthwork. The corresponding south-east bastion is largely within the orchard of the present farm, and is again visible on the ground, close to the angle of the car park. The Red Gate lay midway between the two. From this outer ward, the Royalist defences went through two right angled turns to a small square enclosure east of the present farm, with two large angled bastions whose eroded remains survive in a clump of trees. From here, the line ran back to the east face of the castle along a natural slope on the northern flank of the present farm buildings.

The clearest trace of the Parliamentary siege lines is on the rising ground east of the castle. The battery raised by Captain Hooper is visible, conveniently marked by a square concrete water tank. Its arrowhead form points at a substantial gap in the east curtain which may be its work. Air photographs and traces on the ground show that it stood at an angle of the siege lines, with trenches running along the slope to the north-west and north-east. The site of the besiegers camp was still known in the 19th century: 'The large piece of old pasture land (on the left) is called the Leaguer Field, being the camp of Sir Thomas Fairfax. The Forest Field, with finds of bullets and coins adjoins it'.[19]

At this stage the garrison were still able to harass the besiegers. In one sally they captured a Parliamentary colour and killed the Cornet who was defending it, though a Royalist Major and Captain were also killed. The Marquis remarked sadly that the colours 'were but borrowed'. With the arrival of 2,000 more Parliamentary troops after the fall of Oxford, the defenders 'were reduced to more caution and taught to lie closer'. Through the summer, more Parliamentary troops arrived: 400 from Bristol; Colonel Birch, fresh from the capture of Ludlow and Goodrich; and Colonel Rainsborough from newly captured Worcester.[20]

On 7 August, Fairfax himself arrived, and sent in a third summons to the Marquis, demanding that he deliver up the castle for Parliament's use since it obstructed the kingdom's universal peace. Worcester, dating his note from 'my poor cottage at Ragland' refused to be turned out of 'the only house now in my possession to cover my head in' and asked leave to send to the King to know his will. Fairfax replied that if the Marquis had not fortified his house, he would not have been troubled. Fairfax's disciplined New Model Army, in the new red coats (with blue facings and grey breeches) that were to characterise the British army for the next two hundred years, may have contrasted with Williams's levies or Morgan's 'soldiers of fortune' from the Gloucester garrison. By now Worcester was prepared to discuss terms, and was perhaps more prepared to surrender to Fairfax whose 'noble grandfather at York' he had known, than to two members of the county gentry (one very minor and no longer resident), belonging to the faction who had long been his enemies. A lengthy exchange of letters followed. He would be happy to dismiss his garrison, he told Fairfax, for its presence gave him little pleasure, if he could be allowed to live quietly

'Roaring Meg', a mortar piece probably used in the siege of Raglan in 1646, now at Goodrich Castle

with sufficient for his maintenance, at peace with Parliament 'and in no danger from the malice of the gentlemen of the Parliamentary Committee for the county'. Fairfax re-assured the Marquis that he had nothing to fear from the Committee since 'I shall easily reconcile that party' and they would do nothing save on the orders of Parliament. He advised the Marquis to accept the terms on offer rather than hazard his own safety, that of his family, and 'the spoil of the castle'.[21]

Hooper had now driven his trenches within 60 yards of the castle, and expected in a few days to be just ten yards away. Two batteries, one with four great mortars, one with two, capable of firing grenades of 12 inch calibre, had been set up, some on the battery visible north-east of the castle. The mortars, including 'Roaring Meg', now preserved at Goodrich, were morale sapping weapons, not least because of the unpredictability of where their explosive shells would fall within the castle, rather as the unpredictability of German V.1 flying bombs tried the nerves of wartime Londoners. An eyewitness of the siege of Lathom House in 1644 commented that even 'the little ladyes' (the Countess of Derby's two small daughters) 'had stomack to digest canon, but the stoutest souldiers had noe hearts for granadoes'. At Raglan, heavy cannon had breached the castle wall and everyone in the castle must have been very aware that, under the laws of war, if the attackers were put to the trouble and bloodshed of storming the breach, no quarter could be expected.[22]

On 14 August Fairfax, who was 'every day in the trenches' set Captain Hooper to work on a new line of siegeworks a hundred yards in circuit 'as if they were works against a storm'. Next day the Marquis sent out a

Cannon shot mould from Raglan Castle.
(National Museums and Galleries of Wales)

drum, and agreed to meet the Parliamentary Commissioners (who included a future Leveller spokesman and a prominent Baptist republican) at Roger Oates' house, Cefn Tilla, at 2 p.m. next day. During the truce, soldiers of both sides mingled freely outside the stockades and trenches and chatted. After negotiations lasting several days, the Marquis agreed to surrender on terms on 19 August.[23]

At ten o'clock on the morning of the 19th, the castle gates opened and the garrison marched out, with the usual honours of war, with horses and arms, colours flying, drums beating, trumpet sounding, matches lit and each soldier with powder, match and bullets. It was usual for surrendered troops to be given leave to go to the nearest remaining garrison, but in the present case this was impossible, and 'in respect his majesty hath no garrison in England, nor army anywhere within the Kingdom', arms were to be given up and the soldiers disbanded. The sick and wounded, together with any exempt from pardon, including the Marquis, were to remain in the castle. Otherwise, officers and gentlemen were to be given passes to go to their homes, or those of friends, with horses, arms and baggage, without molestation. Any wishing to go overseas were to be given passes to any sea port, or to London, to arrange passage.[24]

Fairfax's chaplain, Josuah Sprigge, described the sequel: 'The enemy were no sooner marched forth than [Fairfax] entered the castle, took a view of it, and had some conference with the Marquess'. Worcester received him leaning on the arm of his chaplain, Dr Bayly, and accompanied by his servant, James Redman. He told Fairfax that he had heard that he he was a man of his word 'otherwise, had you never been so tall a man … you should have stay'd a little longer before we had bid you welcome.' Fairfax replied curtly that he would see him fairly treated according to the terms of the articles. Fairfax moved to Chepstow, and a few days later to Bath for his health.[25] Nearly 500 officers, soldiers and gentlemen surrendered, but many local people refused passes, saying they did not need them (passes were only needed to move outside one's county) and so were not included in the list. Even so, the list included the Marquis himself; his son Lord Charles Somerset; Sir Philip and Lady Jones; the Countess of Glamorgan (whose husband was still in Ireland); and over a hundred officers and commanders, of whom 68 are listed by W.C. (almost certainly Walter Cradock) in *A Letter from his Excellencies Quarters*. According to Sprigge there were four Colonels; 82 Captains (though the surrender list names only 21), 16 Lieutenants, six Cornets, four Ensigns and four Quartermasters. There were nearly 70 'Esquires and persons of quality' (Sprigge says 52) and a number of ladies. There were also 300 soldiers (we know the name of only one) and many servants.[26]

The castle contained 20 pieces of ordinance, but only three barrels of powder. A gunpowder mill was capable of making a barrel a day, although they probably lacked the raw materials (saltpetre was always particularly hard to come by). There was 'great store of corn and mault, wine of all sorts and beere', but the few horses were starved for want of hay and oats were running out. The fittings and furniture were handed over to Thomas Herbert.

On 25 August Parliament ordered that all papers and letters at Raglan were to be delivered by Herbert to the Committee of the Army and

> That the castle of Raglan, the works about it, and the house and build-
> ings thereof, be forthwith pulled down and demolished [and] that it be
> referred to the Committee of the County of Monmouth, to take care that
> the same may be totally demolished, and all the materials thereof sold
> and disposed of for the best advantage of the State, deducting the charges
> for pulling it down, and a due account rendered for the same.

The rental of the Marquis's estates was computed at £20,000 a year, those from Monmouthshire alone totalling £4,631. Parts of these were granted to Cromwell, to the Marquis's two granddaughters and for 'preachers in the county and south Wales', the preacher and future regicide Hugh Peters receiving £200 a year. Some people who had taken goods into the castle before the siege now tried to get them back. Thomas Lewis of St Pierre petitioned Fairfax for the return of his writings, household goods and apparel. He received a curt reply worthy of the Duke of Wellington, referring him to the Commissioners for the disposal of malignant's goods at Raglan, as the petitioner was a stranger to him.[27]

Walter Cradock's metaphor of the fall of Raglan being as if a floodgate had been opened was all too apt. A now lost manuscript account of the castle seen by Charles Heath describes the slighting in detail. After the surrender, 'the country people were summoned to rendez-vous' with pick-axes, spades and shovels and set to work to drain the moat in hope of finding treasure, 'but being disappointed ... they were sent to cut the stanks of the great fish ponds, where they had store of very large carp and other fish'. The lead and timber were carried to Monmouth and thence by water to Bristol, where it was used to rebuild the bridge after a fire, but the oak roof of the hall was too massive to be taken down and remained in place for some 20 years after the siege. The demolition of the Great Tower presented similar problems. After 'tedious battering the top therof with pick-axes' it was undermined on two of its six faces and propped with timber. When the foundations were cut away, the timbers were fired, and the two faces 'fell down in a lump' where they remained until cleared away in about 1760–65. Heath in 1820 spoke of finds of bullets and coins in and around the castle, and more relics of the siege came to light during conservation work in the 1950s. A number of cannon shot were found embedded in he north-east curtain between the Closet and Kitchen towers and a shot mould for balls of 3 inch calibre was found at about the same time. Minions or light culverins of this type may have been mounted on the towers of the castle and,

*The Great Tower being partially demolished, 1646.
(Artist's impression by Roger Jones, 1988. © Cadw)*

*The 15th-century Great Gatehouse at Raglan Castle. The defences in front of
its central arch have been demolished, probably in the 1646 slighting,
rendering the gatehouse indefensible. (Photograph by Jeremy Knight)*

The Great Tower at Raglan Castle showing the face brought down by
Parliamentary slighting. (Photograph by Jeremy Knight)

as has been noted, Morgan recorded that he fired on guns mounted on the
battlements and silenced them.[28]

In October, orders were given that the Marquis was to be taken up to
London 'in a horse litter or some other way as he shall be able to endure the
journey', with an allowance befitting his quality and accompanied by his physician and servants.[29] His arrival in London was duly reported to the Doge in
Venice: 'The Earl of Uster [Worcester], a Catholic, has been brought prisoner
to London, having been taken in a strong castle of his' . He was put in the
custody of Black Rod, but by December was seriously ill. His response when
told that he was to be buried at Windsor is well known 'God bless us all! Why
then, I shall have a better castle when I am dead than they took from me when
I was alive'. He died on 18 December and was buried on Christmas Day 1646
in the Beaufort Chapel at Windsor Castle by his chaplain, Dr Bayly.[30]

Ancient Malignants of a Deep Stain : The Glamorgan Rising of 1647

The defeat and capture of the King did not solve the political dilemma. Charles
began negotiations with Parliament and the Scots in June 1646, but used
delaying tactics to exploit divisions among his enemies. By the early summer
of 1647, it seemed to hopeful Royalists that the Parliamentary cause was about

to dissolve in anarchy, with enmity between Presbyterians and Independents; conflict between Parliament and its army and radical agitation within the army. The summers of 1646 and 1647 saw mutinies over pay arrears, with troops sometimes seizing local committeemen and holding them prisoner until they paid up. Parliament hoped to send much of the army to Ireland, under Presbyterian commanders rather than Independents like Cromwell and Ireton, and disband the rest, but the army demanded to stay under its own officers, with arrears of pay and indemnity from prosecution for any wartime acts. On 5 June Cornet Joyce seized the King at Holmby House and placed him (not unwillingly) under the protection of the army. In response to an attempted coup by the Presbyterians, the army marched on London, demanding impeachment of the coup leaders, including Massey and Waller. The Royalists who rose in revolt in Glamorgan in June 1647 claimed to do so on behalf of the King and Fairfax. In the circumstances of the time, this was not unrealistic. The King was in negotiations with Fairfax and Ireton on the 'Heads of the Proposals', as the basis for a political settlement and his own re-instatement. These came close to success and only the King's habitual deviousness and bad faith (which were soon to cost him his life) prevented this. Rumours abounded that the King and the New Model Army had allied against the Presbyterians and the Glamorgan Royalists decided to seize their opportunity, claiming that 'it hath pleased God to make Sir Thomas Fairfax's army a miraculous means of the King's restitution'.

The Glamorgan rising was an affair of diehard Royalists, 'ancient malignants of a deep stain' as Rowland Laugharne called them: Stradlings of St Donats, Bassetts of Beaupre, Thomases and Kemeyses—indeed it was almost a family affair. Sir Edward Stradling's Regiment had fought from Edgehill in 1643 (where they took heavy casualties) to Naseby in 1645. Sir Edward was taken prisoner at Edgehill in 1643, was released on exchange the following May, but died of fever in Oxford a month later. His son John Stradling then assumed command, with his brother Thomas as Lt-Colonel. John and Thomas Stradling were out in rebellion in 1647, along with Sir Henry Stradling, a former Royalist governor of Carlisle, and Major Edward Stradling of Roath in Cardiff. Richard Bassett of Beaupre, knighted by Charles I in 1643 for bringing the Glamorgan militia to the siege of Gloucester, had been the King's choice to replace the unpopular Tyrell as its commander in 1645. Five members of his family were involved in the rising, including Henry Bassett, whose wife Catherine Morgan of Llanrhymney was the widow of Sir Nicholas Kemeys's brother. Both her sisters were married to leaders of the rising, Blanche to Major Edward Stradling and Mary to Sir Charles Kemeys.[31] Stephen Roberts has suggested that the rising may also have had elements of a 'Prayer Book Rebellion', in reaction to the banning of the Book of Common Prayer and the expulsions of Anglican parish clergy. This might account for the muster taking place at Llandaff and that at least ten Glamorgan incumbents were actively involved, including two Llandaff clergy—a Canon and a future Bishop.[32]

The rebels sent warrants to the Constables of every Hundred, calling on them to assemble with their men at Cowbridge, where the county armoury was situated. On Sunday 15 June a force of 1,000 foot and 300 horse appeared, led by Sir Edward Thomas, Sir Richard Bassett, Sir Thomas Nott and several Stradlings—'the arch-delinquents of our county'. Here they issued a proclamation setting out their grievances over the arbitrary and illegal acts of the County Committee, in the names of the King, Parliament, Sir Thomas Fairfax and the army. They promised to disperse on redress of their grievances, hoping for 'An agreement between the King and his Parliament whereby the kingdom and people may be happy in their Religion and Laws'.[33] On 17 June they marched to Llandaff and sent messages to the governor of Cardiff, Colonel Pritchard, calling on him to surrender the castle. A note delivered by a gentlewoman, Mrs Oldisworth, the wife of one of Pembroke's servants, (with no return address complained Pritchard) was followed by a drummer demanding an answer. Pritchard in turn demanded by what authority they had disturbed the peace of the county and assembled its inhabitants in a warlike manner.[34] They also wrote to Rowland Laugharne at Carmarthen, claiming to be allied with the King and Fairfax and that they had risen only to save themselves from the County Committee. They offered Laugharne £1,300 a month to pay his troops, but his only response was to imprison the messenger, Major Weekes.[35]

The rebels declaration—*The Heads of the Present Grievances*—was 'for the satisfaction of all other counties of England and Wales, who groane under the same or like burthens of Oppression and Tyrannie'. The rising was 'only for the vindication of our estates and liberties from the unjust and arbitrary disposition of the Committee here', who had made 'all men of considerable estate' delinquents. Since the Committee for South Wales included both Monmouthshire and Glamorgan they were accused of 'bringing men out of other Countreys' to outvote the gentlemen of Glamorgan. Attempts to seek accounts for money raised had been voted 'scandalous and malignant' and those asking for them were declared delinquents. Garrisons and 'Contributions' had been continued for their own private ends and if the rents of those sequestrated were not punctually paid, musketeers would be lodged on them at free quarter until they paid up. Ironically, 'Contributions', with soldiers at free quarter to enforce them, had been Royalist innovations, brought in by Rupert and others from the German wars, but the Committee had proved apt pupils. It was propounded that money intended for the relief of Ireland had been embezzled. The Committeemen had not only enriched themselves, but their servants and retainers, who 'insult over the gentry'. On the list of grievances went: they were ejecting and imprisoning clergymen for refusing oaths, failing to appoint others in their place and had taken bribes from a clergyman and the wife of a lunatic gentleman to save them from being declared delinquents. A man who muttered 'I pray God mend these times' was threatened with the same fate. The Committee threatened that in the event of unrest, suspect gentry would be held 'a Ship-Board'. Several gentlemen 'of fortune and integritie' had been imprisoned, with the aid of bodies of foot and horse—a proceeding which will surprise no one familiar with the activities of the Somerset Committee under John Pyne, as described by David Underdown.[36] Committee men were notoriously minor gentry who would not have gained access to the county élite pre-war. They were frequently suspected of lining their pockets from public funds and from the proceeds of sequestrated estates and of coercion and physical violence towards any who resisted them.[37]

Pritchard meantime sent to Monmouthshire for help. The County Committee called an urgent meeting at Usk, claiming that the rebels planned to 'seize on all faithful religious people … and particularly such … as acted most eminently for Parliament'. There was talk of raising the *posse comitatus*, but the Sheriff had a body of horse, Colonel Birch was on his way and Robert Kyrle was to protect Monmouth. The rebels, 1,500 or 2,000 strong, had seized the county armoury and were drawn up on St Lythans Down, but when Laugharne appeared with his troops, the largely unarmed rebels scattered. The leaders, to the number of 50, all well mounted, fled to Breconshire, where there was further unrest the following year. Two days later the County Committee for Monmouthshire decreed that papists and delinquents be disarmed, suspects arrested, places of strength secured, and suspected houses searched. It was hoped that the Sheriff's troop of horse would be brought up to a strength of 100 within a few days.[38]

Popular support for the rising had been limited around Cardiff. Two years earlier the inhabitants had resisted Royalist efforts to garrison Cardiff Castle, and during the rising people from the surrounding area, who had probably formed the core of the Peaceable Army, 'came in freelie' to resist the cavaliers. The western fringes of Gwent and east Glamorgan had few Catholic recusants and after the Restoration there were puritan conventicles in most parishes. In reporting their own good services to Parliament, the Cardiff leaders made two pleas. One, heard everywhere in that post-war summer, was for the soldiers' arrears of pay—in this case amounting to 30 weeks. The other was that the people of the 'well affected Hundreds' should be given some relief from the burdens of taxation and quartering.[39]

Aftershock: The Second Civil War, 1647–8

The continued political uncertainty, and difficulties in disbanding the army, meant that the country remained on a war footing. Complaints about tax and the cost of the army continued. Even before the Glamorgan rising, Parliament decided to reduce the dangers of Royalist unrest. Monmouth was a post-war town, where an errant boarder from Monmouth School could spend his time at the Leaguer—a Civil War earthwork—drinking with a gang of 'rougish boys'. On 1 March, the House of Commons gave orders that Monmouth should be dis-garrisoned and the works slighted and two days later that Abergavenny should be 'disgarrisoned and made indefensible'. On 30 March Kyrle arrived and began slighting the defences and disbanding the garrison. More Pye, Usher of Monmouth School, noted how 'Ye townsmen and soldiers began to pull down ye Round Tower of ye castle, and to demolish ye works'. Less welcome was a 'loan' of £100 imposed on the town by Kyrle to pay off his soldiers. The work continued for much of the year. In July Parliament found it necessary to repeat its orders, with specific instructions that 'works made since the troubles' at Monmouth were to be slighted. There may have been some disagreement locally regarding the extent of demolition necessary. On 22 December the sermon in St Mary's church was rudely interrupted when 'about 12 o'clock, ye Tower of ye Castle of Monmouth fell downe upon one side whilst we were at sermon'.

There were still the periodic burden of quartering soldiers and paying for their keep. In October a troop of 60 horse returning from Wales passed through Monmouth. Pye's share of their entertainment was 14d. The following month quartermasters arrived with 30 dragoons 'out of Wales'. Pye, with the vicar and headmaster, had to maintain two troopers and their horses for three days. The former Parliamentarian seems to have been disillusioned by this time, for when the King escaped from the army at Hampton Court on 11 November, he wrote in his diary 'Vivat, Vivat, Vivat in Aeternam'. On 27 December the garrison of Monmouth stood down: 'Ye soldiers all marched from Monmouth'—no doubt to the great relief of the inhabitants.[40]

By the spring of 1648, a few fragile green shoots of peace were beginning to appear. The historian Ian Roy has noted a short lived economic revival in the Severn region in the immediate post-war period, though it was hardly enough to make good the damage of the war years. One of the Usk Committee claimed that the Glamorgan rising had had little popular support 'the common people ... having had a sweet taste of peace already'. The soldiers had left Monmouth and an official order was given to fell timber to repair Chepstow bridge, broken down during the war. Before peace finally came to Chepstow however, there was a violent aftershock to be endured.[41]

At this volatile time, Fairfax was nervous of local commanders acting as independent forces. If the army was to be disbanded, an obvious place to start was with these local irregulars. In January 1648 he sought to replace Colonel John Poyer, Governor of Pembroke Castle, with his own nominee, Colonel Fleming. Poyer refused to surrender the castle, demanded the repayment of money spent on it and on payment of his soldiers' arrears. He arrested the mayor of Pembroke and built up a garrison of 200 men with which he plundered the surrounding countryside. The mutiny quickly spread. Major-General Rowland Laugharne had played an important role at Raglan and Cardiff in 1646 and in the suppression of the Glamorgan rising but, like Poyer, he was now faced with disbandment. By March his troops, who had shown a mutinous streak when they quitted the siege of Raglan and returned home, were resisting this and many were defecting to Poyer. At the end of April Laugharne, politically marginalised by the New Model Army and its Independent allies, threw in his lot with Poyer and with Colonel Powell in Carmarthen, calling among other things for the restoration of the Book of Common Prayer and a treaty with the King. In Brecon, neutralist gentry were garrisoning the town for the King: 'malignant gentlemen [who] wore Blew Ribbonds in their hats with the motto I long to see his Majestie C.R.'[42]

The rising in Pembrokeshire on 23 March marked the opening of the Second Civil War. It was hoped to co-ordinate risings throughout England and Wales with invasion by a Scots army, but on the very day that the Scots crossed the border the Welsh Royalists were crushed at the Battle of St Fagans. Cromwell left London for south Wales on 1 May with two regiments of horse and three of foot. In the meantime (5 April 1648), the estates of the Earl of Worcester, including Chepstow Castle, had been made over to him. At Gloucester on 9 May he was greeted with the news that the Glamorgan Royalists had been defeated the previous day at St Fagans by Colonel Horton, but next day at Monmouth he learnt that Chepstow Castle had been betrayed by one of the garrison during the absence of the governor, Colonel Thomas Hughes of Moynes Court. Sir Nicholas Kemeys had collected 40 horse 'gentlemen and others' and 100 foot, hoping that other local Royalists would join them.[43] Sir Nicholas, a middle aged man, had been a Commissioner of Array for Monmouthshire and Treasurer of the Glamorgan Arraymen. By 1644 he was already sufficiently obnoxious to Parliament to be included (with Henry Lingen) in the list of Royalists to be surrendered to Parliament by the King under the abortive peace negotiations at Uxbridge. In prison in London since May 1646, he had been unable to negotiate with the Committee for Compounding, or to sell land in order to pay his fine. He may have been in touch with plotters in the capital or with Scottish emissaries. In 1647 he obtained leave from Parliament to go to Bath for his health, and then slipped across the Bristol Channel to Llanvair Discoed to join Sir Trevor Williams and the other plotters. When the Royalists seized the castle, a Parliamentary officer named Cantrill retreated to one of the towers (probably Marten's Tower) with a few soldiers, but had to surrender. Williams was not present at Chepstow, but (hedging his bets as usual) evidently planned to declare for the King should the rising succeed. There was a clear danger that the revolt would spread, and waiting for Cromwell at Monmouth were two Somerset Parliamentarians, Alexander Popham and John Pyne, seeking his help with troops to secure their own restive county.[44]

Cromwell's force marched on Chepstow from Monmouth on 11 May to find the town walls 'well lined with musquetiers'. Colonel Pride's Regiment attacked and after a sharp engagement managed to force the town gate and took the town together with a number of prisoners. Sir Nicholas Kemeys withdrew to the castle with about 150 men. Cromwell sent in a summons to surrender, but the Royalists fired on the drummer who accompanied it and hung out their flag of defiance. A sharp fire fight followed. That night Pride's Regiment attempted to storm the castle gatehouse in pouring rain, but Major Grigson was mortally injured by a stone dropped on his head from above, and four or five soldiers killed. Cromwell, anxious to reach Pembroke with the least possible delay, left Colonel Ewer to complete the task.[45]

Ewer sent for two siege guns from Gloucester, and took two more from a ship, planting them across The Dell from the south face of the castle, where the curtain west of Marten's tower had to be substantially rebuilt after the war. We 'raised [razed] the battlements of their towers with our great guns' reported Ewer, 'and made their guns unuseful to them', at the same time bombarding the interior of the castle with mortars: 'One fell in the Governor's chamber, which caused him to remove his lodging to the other end of the castle'. After this initial bombardment they set up their guns in siege batteries and all morning 'played … with our great guns very hot'. By noon they had breached the medieval curtain wall 'so low that a man might walk into it'. According to one source, the Royalists had a boat moored in the small rocky inlet in the river cliffs used to haul supplies up to the cellar below the Great Hall. They hoped to escape in this, but a Parliamentary soldier spotted the boat, swam the river with a knife between his teeth, cut the boat's painter or mooring rope and swam back, with the end of the painter between his teeth. When the Royalists looked for the boat during the final assault, it was no longer there.[46]

Some of the garrison tried to surrender, but Ewer's men fired on them. When 'Esquire Lewis' of St Pierre called from the battlements to some friends of his among the besiegers, offering to surrender at mercy, Ewer replied that he was not interested in individuals, but only in the surrender of Nicholas Kemeys and his officers. There was now dissension between the Governor and Lewis on terms of surrender. The Governor asked to speak with Ewer at the drawbridge. Ewer refused, since the Governor had rejected Cromwell's summons, but 'being over-persuaded by some gentlemen of the country who

ON THE 25TH DAY OF MAY 1648
NEAR THIS SPOT WAS SLAIN
SIR NICHOLAS KEMEYS
KNIGHT AND BARONET OF
CEFN MABLY AND LLANVAIR ISCOED
MEMBER OF PARLIAMENT AND
HIGH SHERIFF FOR THE COUNTIES
OF MONMOUTH AND GLAMORGAN
WHILST DEFENDING THIS CASTLE
FOR KING CHARLES THE FIRST
AGAINST THE FORCES OF
OLIVER CROMWELL.

ERECTED BY MEMBERS
OF THE KEMEYS FAMILY 1935

Plaque to Nicholas Kemeys at Chepstow Castle, probably on the site of the breach stormed by Parliamentary troops in 1648. Sir Nicholas was shot out of hand after the fall of the castle. (Photograph by Jeremy Knight)

were there', Ewer dismounted from his horse and spoke to the Governor at the drawbridge through a port hole. The latter asked that the officers and men should be allowed to march out without having anything taken from them, but Ewer demanded that they surrender at mercy. Ewer ordered his men to stand by for an assault. When some of the garrison ran out through the breach and surrendered, the Parliamentarians 'ran in at the same place' and stormed the castle, shooting Sir Nicholas Kemeys out of hand and 'he that betrayed the castle'. The prisoners were locked up in Chepstow church to await Cromwell's decision on what should be done with them.[47] Despite the death of Sir Nicholas Kemeys there were rumours that he had escaped and reached a castle in Carmarthenshire, but this was confusion with his son Sir

Charles Kemeys, who was in Pembroke Castle. After the Restoration, Nicholas Kemeys' daughter, Florence Button, claimed she had been left portionless by the murder of her father and bracketed his death with that of Colonel John Poyer, executed in London after the fall of Pembroke, he having 'surrendered it and afterwards murdered'.[48]

Papers seized by Ewer at the castle implicated Sir Trevor Williams and Thomas Morgan of Machen in the plot. On 17 June Cromwell wrote to Major Thomas Saunders at Brecon from before Pembroke, giving him detailed instructions for their arrest. Saunders was to move from Brecon to Glamorgan adjoining Monmouthshire, since 'We have plain discoveries that Sir Trevor Williams of Llangibby … was very deep in the plot of betraying Chepstow Castle, so that we are out of doubt of his guiltyness thereof'. William Morgan the High Sheriff, was also to be arrested, but Williams was

The most dangerous by far ... seize him first.. He is a man, as I am informed, full of craft and subtlety, very bold and resolute, hath a house at Llangibby well stored with arms and very strong. [His neighbours there were] very malignant and much for him [and] apt to rescue him if apprehended ... He is full of jealousy, partly out of guilt, but much more because he doubts [suspects] that some that were in the business have discovered [informed on] him, which indeed they have, and ... he knows that his servant is brought hither, and a minister ... who are able to disclose the whole plot.

If you march directly into that county ... it's odds he either fortify his house or give you the slip. So also, if you should go to his house and not find him there, or if you should attempt to take him and miss ... or if you make any known inquiry after him, it will be discovered. [Therefore go] out of Breconshire to quarter about Newport and Caerleon, four or five miles from his house. You may send to Colonel Herbert, whose house lieth in Monmouthshire, who will certainly acquaint you where he is.

You are also to send to Captain Nicholas, who is at Chepstow, to ... assist you, if he should get into his house and stand upon his guard ....
Capt. Burgess's troop quarters between Newport and Chepstow.

Williams was to be sent under a strong guard to Cromwell and Llangibby disarmed, and Saunders was to make sure that the arms there were not 'embezzled'.[49] Next day Cromwell wrote to the former Royalist Colonel Richard Herbert at St Julian's warning him 'I have good report of your secret practices ... by means of which that arch-traitor Sir Nicholas Kemeys with his horse did surprise the Castle of Chepstow', but Cromwell regarded Trevor Williams as 'the malignant that set on foot the plot'. 'I give you plain warning' he wrote to Richard Herbert 'by Capt Nicholas and Captain Burges, that if you harbour or conceal either of the parties, I will cause your treasonable nest to be burnt about your ears'.[50] Pembroke Castle surrendered on 11 July. Laugharne, Poyer and Powell were sent to London for trial, though eventually only John Poyer, chosen by lot, was executed. The remainder of the leaders, including Sir Charles Kemeys, were exiled. Cromwell hurried north from Pembroke and on 17 August destroyed the invading Scots army at Preston.

The fall of Chepstow did not end the miseries of war. In August Monmouthshire and other counties were ordered to collect what forces they could against yet another rising, this time by the Hereford Royalist Sir Henry Lingen. That October Walter Powell had two troops of horse billeted on him at Llanarth and next month three troopers were at Llantilio Crossenny for 14 days at his cost. The following February he was 'disarmed of the peece and searched'.[51] The Pembrokeshire rising resulted in more levies towards the cost of the campaign. Monmouthshire's share, the largest, was £192 9s. This was in addition to the monthly assessments, equivalent to an income tax of 2s. to 2s.

6d. (10-12.5p) in the pound; free quarter; and the hated excise. To make matters worse, in the following year Monmouthshire was fined £3,000 for its 'delinquency'. For its war-weary inhabitants, peace had brought little relief.[52]

7 A Reformation Too Far?

The French political thinker Alexis de Tocqueville wrote in 1848 that 'In a revolution, as in a novel, the most difficult part to invent is the end'. In contrast to France, those in England who sought to change society radically were few in number, without effective power, and were rapidly marginalized by Cromwell. The word 'Revolution' in anything like the modern sense only appeared in English after the events of 1688, whilst the term 'English Revolution' was coined by the French historian Guizot in 1826 on analogy with the French Revolution. Even the radicals of 1648 would not have understood the term 'The English Revolution'. They spoke instead of 'Reformation'. To a great extent, the disputes that preceded the war were between those who saw the Tudor Reformation, which created a gentry fattened with monastic lands and a Church under gentry control, as a finished process and those who sought further reformation, and the eradication of 'Popish' survivals.[1]

The County Committees of the new regime had grown up piecemeal, partly from the Deputy Lieutenants who replaced the Royalist Lords Lieutenant, partly from various *ad hoc* local committees dealing with such matters as taxation, the sequestration of Royalist property, the militia and the reform of the clergy. Usually these functions were united under a single Committee, often made up of minor gentry previously unimportant outside their own parish. For most of the war, the Parliamentary Committee for South Wales, based on Gloucester, was a committee in exile, an offshoot of the Gloucestershire Committee, responsible for Herefordshire Monmouthshire, Glamorgan, Brecon and Radnor. In 1644 it included Colonels Broughton and Stephens, and two civilians: the lawyer Christopher Catchmay of Trellech Court who was a minor member of a family whose head, Sir William Catchmay of Bigsweir, was a Royalist, and William Jones of Usk Priory who was a distant kinsman of Sir Trevor Williams and Sequestrator-General for the county.[2] Later members included John Walter of Piercefield (nephew of the puritan Henry Walter) and William Blethyn of Dinham. All were from the forest-edge area of central Monmouthshire, where Pembroke influence, early puritanism and opposition to Worcester's activities in Wentwood had created an opposition party by the 1630s. Two Parliamentary Colonels and M.P.s, Henry Herbert of Coldbrook and Thomas Hughes of Moynes Court, were probably *ex-officio* members.[3] In 1647, the Commission of the Peace, depleted by the exile or exclusion of many of its Royalist members, had its numbers made up with puritan gentry, none of whom had been judged to be of sufficient status to serve as J.P.s before the war.[4]

'Scandalous and insufficient Ministers'

The Committee's functions included raising the weekly (later monthly) assessment tax and the hated excise; sequestration of the estates of Royalists and papists and raising revenue from them, and the purge of Anglican clergy considered unsatisfactory or unreliable by the new regime. The 'Act for the Better Propagation and Preaching of the Gospel in Wales', passed in February 1650 was followed by the 'Ordinance for ejecting scandalous, ignorant and insufficient ministers and schoolmasters' of August 1654. In England and Wales, a little over 2,000 clergy, 'scandalous either in life or doctrine' were eventually expelled from their livings. Madeleine Gray estimates that 65 out of a total of about 90 Monmouthshire clergy were expelled. In Gloucestershire only 22 were expelled in a county of 237 parishes. In Somerset there were just over 100 expulsions from about 500 parishes. Herefordshire saw about 50 evictions in the first year alone, so that the county's final total may have been similar to Monmouthshire. There was also considerable variation in numbers of expulsions across Monmouthshire. In Abergavenny Hundred, of 15 beneficed clergymen serving the 24 parishes, seven were ejected (at least five lived to be restored). These included parishes with concentrations of Catholics — Abergavenny, Llanarth, Llanfoist and Llanelen, but not John Arnold's parish of Llanfihangel Crucorney, where the rector, John Quarrell, was a kinsman of Thomas Quarrell, a leading Monmouthshire puritan of the 1670s. Skenfrith Hundred, with its many catholics, had ten beneficed clergymen serving its 12 parishes. At least eight were expelled.[5]

When expulsion was proposed, clergy were summoned before a county committee of lay 'ejectors' and clerical advisers at Chepstow or Usk and confronted with witnesses from their parish, usually a small group of 'godly' activists. There was a long list of offences meriting expulsion, but clergy with wives and small children were allowed to retain a fifth of their stipend for their maintenance. No provision was made however for single men or for cathedral clergy.[6] Some of those expelled had been active Royalists. Walter Harris of Wolvesnewton had been 'in arms against the Parliament'. Michael Hughes of Usk had 'promoted the late tyrant's service' as well as using the Book of Common Prayer and 'publishing the declarations of the late king'. Henry Vaughan, vicar of Panteg, recorded in his parish register that he had been 'away at Oxford and elsewhere', but did not add that his duties at Oxford had included preaching before Charles I. Other clergy had made themselves unacceptable to the 'godly' for other reasons. In June 1641 Sir Robert Harley had presented a petition to Parliament by Walter Cradock of Llanvaches and Henry Walter of Piercefield on behalf of the godly in south Wales, who were being arrested and 'molested by mulcts' (fined) for hearing sermons outside their parish. John Edwards, vicar of four Gwent Is Coed parishes, plus Tredunnock, was expelled for 'malignancy and the persecution of the godly in his neighbourhood', some of whom no doubt testified against him at Chepstow. Similar activities may account for the high proportion of expelled clergy in Gwent Is Coed. John Clegge, archdeacon of Llandaff and vicar of Llangybi and Llansoy would have been involved in proceedings against separatists by reason of his office. His lengthy charge sheet included 'sending to the bishops in prosecution of godly people, being an officer under them'.[7]

Elsewhere, a glance at the reasons given for ejection is enough to show their stereotyped nature: 'inability to preach and reading the Book of Common Prayer' (John Dobbins, Llangattock vibion Avel); 'tippling and swearing and reading the Book of Common Prayer' (Edward Williams, Gwernesney); 'malignancy and delinquency' (Robert Brabone, Monmouth); 'malignancy and drunkenness' (William Clarke, Dixton); 'drunkenness and being an ignorant reader' (William Jones, Dingestow). John Clegge was deprived for not being able to preach in Welsh and for (perhaps sensibly) 'quitting his habitation ... whenever the Parliament forces came near', as well as 'betaking himself to the late tyrant's service against the state' and being involved, as Archdeacon, in the persecution of sectaries. He was at least more fortunate than Charles Lewis of Llanllowell, who was deprived for alleged drunkenness, but also put in the stocks at Chepstow. In other counties, where Laudian reforms had made a deeper impact, and the religious conservatism evidenced in Monmouthshire less marked, the formulaic charges differed—use of altar rails or bowing at the name of Jesus.[8]

The few charges of being unable to preach in Welsh imply that most Gwent clergy were able to preach, or converse with their flock, in Welsh. Many were local men, one the translator of a theological work into Welsh, whilst others came from Welsh speaking areas like Merioneth. In the next generation, the catholic priests of the 'Popish plot' are routinely described as preaching in English and Welsh. Robert Frampton, vicar of Bryngwyn, a Dorset man, claimed to be fluent in Greek, Latin, Hebrew and Welsh. He took refuge in Raglan Castle, with his parish register, before the siege. In the confusion of the surrender, the register got left behind and 'was all torne in pieces' by Parliamentary troops. Part of it was rescued by the Parliamentary County Commissioner William Jones of Usk, who passed it to his kinsman, David Pritchard of Bryngwyn. Eventually 'one poore leafe' was returned to the vicar.

Frampton was examined by the County Committee at Usk in October 1649. Despite his presence at Raglan during the siege, he was approved and initially allowed to remain at Bryngwyn. However, in 1654 his living and rents were confiscated as part of the estates of the Marquis of Worcester, and granted to John Games, a former County Sequestrator. Four years later, Frampton became headmaster of Monmouth Grammar School, but was restored to Bryngwyn at the Restoration. In 1664 he bought a new parish register, in which he carefully preserved the remaining leaf of the previous one with a note explaining its adventures. He died in 1685 at the age of 83.[9]

The catalogues of Oxford and Cambridge graduates often give the parentage and the place of residence of the father, though the information is incomplete and there is the usual problem of the duplication of names. It is impossible to be certain which of the two Richard Heaths (if either) became vicar of Grosmont or which Walter Evans became vicar of Kemeys Inferior. With 'John Jones of Jesus College', the problem is even worse.[10]

One clergyman with a more varied career was Revd. More Pye, a Parliamentary officer, possibly a regimental chaplain, who may have held a pre-war curacy. He was a university graduate, but does not appear in *Alumni Oxoniensis*. The Pyes were a Herefordshire family whose head was the Royalist Sir Walter Pye of the Mynde in Dewchurch. More Pye's unusual Christian name presumably derived from a marriage alliance, possibly with the puritan Moores of Bishops Castle in Shropshire, clients of the Harleys of Brampton Bryan. He had connections with Walford on Wye, between Monmouth and Ross, and his wife and family were living in Monmouth in 1647. Pye was at the relief of Cardiff in March 1646 and was chosen to carry the dispatches to London, customarily a reward for an officer 'mentioned in dispatches' for gallant service, and was rewarded with a gift of £20. He may also have acted as an emissary between Sir Trevor Williams and Parliament, and later served under Williams, if the pamphlet *The Gallant Siege of Parliament's Forces* of May 1646 is by him. In the following month Pye was appointed Usher (deputy headmaster) at Monmouth School. In January 1647 he bought a copy of William Lilley's almanac *Merlini Anglicae Ephemeris* and used the blank spaces for a private diary, much as Walter Powell's diary was based on longer contemporary entries in old almanacs. (In the early 19th century, extracts were made by the local historian-printer Charles Heath and in 1859 a transcript was printed in the *Monmouth Beacon* by W.H. Greene 'copied from a curious old pocket book lent me by Mr John Baker of Overmonnow, Monmouth'. The section from February to October was already missing, and by the time W.M. Warlow reprinted Greene's version in 1899, the book itself had been lost.) In 1649 Pye was approved as Minister of Llanvapley by the Committee for Plundered Ministers, only to be ejected the following year by the Committee for the Propagation of the Gospel in Wales. In March 1653 he became a schoolmaster in Swansea and in January 1655 parson of Bishopston in Gower. Although he petitioned for restitution to Llanvapley in 1660, he remained at Bishopston until his death.[11]

Churches and Preachers: The Gwent Parishes in the Interregnum

A number of the new puritan clergy were Baptists, opposed to the baptism of infants, and in consequence some churches had to replace their fonts at the Restoration, the medieval fonts having been removed or broken up. These included Llangibby, Skenfrith, Penallt, Llandenny and Tredunnock. The puritan incumbent of Tredunnock, Walter Prosser, became minister of a Baptist congregation at Hay on Wye in his native Breconshire at the Restoration. At Bedwas, Rees Davies, having failed to break up the very solid font, relegated it to the status of a horse trough under a yew tree in the churchyard.[12] Sadly, the finer and more elaborate the font, the more likely it was to attract the enmity of the iconoclasts. Raglan church was sacked during the siege. The octagonal 15th-century font of which a fragment survives, with demi-angels carrying shields, no doubt once with painted heraldry, would have particularly offended puritan susceptibilities. At St Gwynllywy's, Newport, the puritan vicar, Henry Walter, must have put a lot of effort into breaking up the Romanesque font, with elaborate sculpture of the Gloucester school; the surviving fragment, dug up in St Mary's chapel in 1854, shows that it was a very solid piece of stone. Less theologically elevated were the motives of the men who sold off the bells of Mynyddislwyn and of Merthyr Tydfil and Gelligaer across the border in Glamorgan.[13]

In 1646, Parliament sent Walter Cradock, Henry Walter and Richard Symonds as itinerant preachers to south Wales, each receiving £100 a year out of the sequestrated revenues of the Church. Building on this, the puritan strategy was to establish a centralised ministry for the former Deaneries of Netherwent, Usk, Abergavenny and Newport, with stipends of £100 a year from former ecclesiastical revenues. The four ministers, who presumably exercised similar functions to an Anglican archdeacon were Francis Symes (Netherwent); Walter Cradock (Usk); George Abbott (Abergavenny) and Henry Walter (Newport). Symes was later translated to Trellech, his place at Chepstow being taken by Richard Blindman, a Chepstow born 'minister of God's word' from Bristol, and an associate of Cradock, William Wroth and the Harleys of Brampton Bryan. In 1638 he had been a witness of Wroth's will.[14]

When William Wroth died in 1641, he was succeeded at Llanvaches by a man from Llangwm in the forested area east of Usk, Walter Cradock of Trevela (c.1606–1659). Cradock had been curate to William Erbury, the vicar of Cardiff expelled under Laud, and was later curate at Wrexham before returning to Llanvaches. In 1642 he led his flock into exile, first in Bristol and then in London before serving with Fairfax's army as a chaplain. He was almost certainly the 'W.C.' who wrote *A Letter from His Excellencies Quarters* describing the siege of Raglan, for it was normal for army chaplains to act as war correspondents. Minister in Usk in place of the Royalist Michael Hughes, when Charles II and the Scots invaded in 1651 he reverted temporarily to his military persona. He assembled 6,000 horse and foot in Chepstow, but in the event Cromwell's victory at Worcester made them unnecessary.

In 1658 Cradock retired to his native Llangwm. His daughter Lois had married Major Richard Creed, secretary to Admirals Blake and Sandwich and brother of Pepys's colleague and friend John Creed, who appears frequently in his diary. Creed had acquired a lease of the tithes at Llangwm, but agreed to surrender them for the benefit of the minister. In exchange Cradock was granted £80 a year from a sequestrated estate. He died in December 1659 and was buried in St Jerome's church Llangwm, which preserves one of the finest roodscreens in Wales and a little medieval glass. The second Llangwm church, Llangwm Isaf, kept its screen and medieval altars until the 19th century. Like Cromwell, Cradock was a believer in liberty of conscience and religious toleration. He was involved in the re-admission of the Jews to Britain and was wary of over rigid church government. His lack of puritan iconoclasm may still be reflected in the church of his native parish.[15]

In one Monmouthshire parish we can see the new order of things working in practice. In May 1650, a few months after the Act for the Propagation of the Gospel in Wales, which envisaged six itinerant preachers in each county, Walter Powell noted that the 'new preachers' had begun work in Llantilio Crossenny. Over the following months various puritans, including Henry Walter, preached there, even though the Anglican incumbent, Owen Rogers, remained in post. Lieutenant Hopkin Rogers of Caldicot was there in September, with the 'smyth of Malpas' expounding the scriptures. The following May, John Morgan and Revd. Robinson were 'preaching damnation' to the people of Llantilio. In March 1654, shortly before the Ordnance, Owen Rogers was finally removed for alleged drunkenness and malignancy. On his tombstone he claimed to be 'A shepheard late of Christ his sheepe / From sheep-clothed wolves his lambes did keepe'.[16] In Bedwellty, the curate Lewis James remained in his parish, supported by his parishioners, despite his eviction. He continued to baptize (his successor Edmund Rosser, an Independent, may not have been a believer in infant baptism), though performing marriages and burials presented more problems.[17]

Claims that a number of Monmouthshire churches were 'pulled or let fall down' in the Interregnum are dubious. Raglan church and its Herbert memorials suffered damage in the siege, but the patently untrue claim in a Parliamentary newsletter that the defenders of the castle had 'levelled that stately steeple with the earth' is in a postscript added by a London propagandist.[18] In Herefordshire and Gloucestershire, damaged churches were rebuilt or repaired during the Commonwealth, Llantrithyd in Glamorgan acquired a new chancel in 1656 and Montgomery church underwent extensive repairs in the mid-1650s. At Panteg, where the fabric had been neglected in the war years, the Parliamentary Commissioners abated £1 from the parish rent to pay for repairs. The bells may have been sold off for the same purpose, for three new ones were provided in 1661.[19]

The continuation of parish administration during the Commonwealth and the continued upkeep of churches is shown by surviving church bells. Puritans had no ideological objection to bells, which served useful social and religious functions, as the inscription on the sermon bell of 1640 at Monmouth reminds us: 'When I call, then come to hear God's word'.[20] The addition of a new bell to an existing peal, or the re-casting of a worn or damaged bell was not a simple matter. Funds had to be collected, as bequests or gifts from wealthy parishioners, or by wider communal effort, as the people of Abergavenny had done in the 15th century. An order had to be placed with bellfounders in Gloucester or Bristol, usually at this date John Palmer of Gloucester. The finished bell had to be shipped to Chepstow or Caerleon and transport arranged to the parish. The carpentry of the bell frame might need to be adjusted or repaired before the bell could be hung.

Trellech acquired a new bell in 1642. Thereafter there is, unsurprisingly, a gap, but by the later 1650s the economic and social damage of the war had been sufficiently overcome for the sequence to resume. Wartime destruction, labour shortages due to army recruitment and the burning of crops almost doubled the price of wheat by 1650, but by 1653–5, things were getting back to normal.[21] Rockfield acquired two new bells (complete with Latin inscriptions) in January 1656 (1657 new style) and Dingestow, Mitchel Troy and Henllys in the same year. Llanelen followed in 1658. All were by John Palmer II and carried the names of the churchwardens.[22] The sequence continued after the Restoration. Some bells now carried loyal mottos like 'Feare God, Honnor the King' or the impression of a coin of Charles I pressed into the mould, as at Llanwenarth or Llangwm. Llanelen may have been saving for a further addition to its peal since 1658, but significantly, there were a new pair of churchwardens.[23]

The extent to which parish administration continued is shown in the parish registers that survived. At Llandewi Rhydderch, the new register of 1670 includes lists of overseers of the poor (1647–1660) and parish constables (1652 on), perhaps copied from loose sheets that were all that remained of earlier registers. At Panteg, where there was a gap from 1640 to 1646, Henry Vaughan inserted a note explaining that this was

> partly by negligence and carelessness of curates while the rectors were living away at Oxford or elsewhere, partly by the fact that the register was removed from the chest ... and deposited elsewhere, that it might not become the prey of the soldiery who had burst open the doors and torn away the tapestry.[24]

As ever, Abergavenny was the epicentre of religious dispute. At the time of Charles I's visit, St Mary's Priory still had its gilt rood loft and pair of organs, whilst the Herbert Chapel, as well as its medieval tomb monuments, had an array of stained glass, with coats of arms and kneeling figures in armour. Save for the tomb monuments and the 15th-century choir stalls (used by the boys of the Grammar School for their weekly Welsh language service), these did not survive the puritans, though much of the armorial glass was still in place in 1683.[25] The vicar of Abergavenny was replaced by a London open communion Baptist—in which communion services were open to all believers, not just those who had received adult baptism—named James Abbot. Views on infant baptism were still fluid among the puritan devout, as can be seen by Lucy Hutchinson's (the wife of a leading Nottingham Parliamentarian and army colonel) hesitations about the baptism of her own children. Two of Abbot's own children were baptized in Abergavenny Priory.[26] In August 1652 about a dozen men and women separated off on the issue of open or closed communion and began a closed communion cause in private houses in Abergavenny, Llanvihangel Crucorney and Llanwenarth. On 4 September, John Tombes, the puritan minister of Leominster, preached at St Mary's. Tombes was a Baptist of Calvinistic views who founded separated churches in Herefordshire and Worcestershire but also held parochial cures in Leominster and Bewdley. His subject was infant baptism. After the sermon he was followed to his lodging by the vicar of Llanwenarth and Aberystruth, Anthony Bonner. They agreed to debate the issue publicly and returned to St Mary's church to do so, the debate lasting from 1 p.m. to 6 p.m.[27] Tombes and Abbot were seconded by Christopher Price, an apothecary, Baptist preacher and coal lessee, who had served as clerk to the Monmouthshire section of the Committee for the Propagation of the Gospel in Wales. Bonner was supported by John Cragge, vicar of Llantilio Pertholey and Henry Vaughan, the former Laudian vicar of Panteg, now headmaster of Abergavenny Grammar School.[28]

'Insulting over the Gentry'—Sequestration and the County Committee

One major role of the County Committee was raising money by the fining of former Royalists, and the sequestration of their estates. Anyone who had assisted the King, whether in arms or with money, even under compulsion, had to submit particulars of his estate to the County Committee. If they accepted the valuation (and there were plenty of sharp eyed puritans watching for under estimates), this was forwarded to the Committee for Compounding which met in Goldsmiths Hall, London. They would determine the culprit's composition fine, usually a tenth, sixth or third of his estate, the estate being confiscated until half the fine was paid. The principle behind this was, in theory, a positive one. The repentant Royalist attended at Goldsmith's Hall, admitted his errors, took the requisite oath and was restored to his estate. Estates worth under £200 a year were exempt. Catholics, or, worse still 'papists in arms', were unable to compound and faced loss of their property, without any lower limit of annual value. Many Monmouthshire cases were therefore concerned with the very modest properties of local catholics.

In practice, it would have been impossible for any landowner in Royalist areas to have gone through the war years without substantial contributions, voluntary or involuntary, to the Royalist war chest. Even a prominent Shropshire puritan like Humphrey Walcott, of Walcott near Clun, a friend and neighbour of Sir Robert and Lady Harley and patron of Clun and Llanvair Waterdine churches, to the latter of which he had presented Walter Cradock, could not escape sequestration. He had been imprisoned by the Royalists in Ludlow Castle until he ransomed himself with 'a great sum of money' in order 'to save his estate from utter ruin'. He then faced a second heavy fine as a 'delinquent' who had assisted the King. Here, enmity between the Presbyterian Harley faction and the Independents on the local committee may have been involved. The possibilities for corruption and peculation are obvious, since the profits of the sequestrated estate were paid to the County Committee until half the fine was paid, after which they had no further claim on it. Thus it was to the Committee's financial advantage to prolong the sequestration proceedings for as long as possible. Often there was bargaining between the committee and its victim, which did little to allay suspicion that the main purpose was not to punish 'delinquents', but to extort money. Humphrey Walcott's fine, originally £947, was reduced to £500 on condition that he paid £40 towards the stipends of each of four ministers in Clun parish, and the committee eventually settled for a payment of £170. To make matters worse, the County Committee were mostly minor gentry, suspected, not always unjustly, of enriching themselves in land and in money at the expense of their less fortunate neighbours. It is not surprising that they were loathed and feared by the Glamorgan gentry who rose against them in 1647, and accused them of 'insulting over the gentry', or by the Monmouthshire Royalists. The sequestrations, as might be expected, led to a plethora of claims and counter-claims to properties inherited, leased out or given as marriage portions. The bulky files which often accumulated in such cases, with repeated hearings of appeals and witnesses, give a more positive view of the conscientiousness of the Committee, particularly since its members were not full time civil servants. Many, however, were lawyers, for whom such attention to detail was normal. To add to the confusion, the Commissioners sometimes admitted themselves unsure which Charles Somerset or Thomas Veale they had sequestrated. Nor were such problems confined to gentry. The tiny estate of an ex-recusant, Edward George ap Howell of Llanhennock, with its half dozen stock, was seized in mistake for that of another ap Howell, of Llanfrechfa, leaving him, his old wife and seven children with no means of support. Happily, in this case, the Committee soon admitted their mistake, but often when appeals were made they were unable to provide details of particular cases, from genuine muddle rather than corruption.[29]

It was not only Royalists who were concerned about Committeemen lining their pockets. In November 1644, Massey wrote to his fellow Presbyterian Edward Harley: 'The Committee dispose of all the malignant's estates very strangely, taking the benefit of them and disposing it not so much to your garrison [at Monmouth] as they should do'. Nor were members of the Committee the only ones who hoped to profit. Following a long standing practice, individuals denounced ('presented' or 'discovered') the 'concealed lands' of former Royalists and papists in the hope of obtaining some of the spoils. Such estates of 'delinquents' were confiscated, half going to the state, half to the discoverer, with any arrears owed him by Parliament being paid out of the proceeds. The Parliamentarian Lucy Hutchinson explained 'There were clerks and solicitors, who in those days made a trade of hunting out such discoveries, and making them known to such as had any arrears due to them'. The widow of the Roundhead Colonel Rainsborough 'presented' Thomas Morgan of Llansôr, former Governor of Chepstow Castle and Howell Gwyn of Hay, sometime Lt-Colonel of Lord Herbert's foot, whilst William Harris of Llandenny 'discovered' some alleged concealed lands of the Marquis of Worcester.[30] When a catholic priest, William Gwynn, alias Powell, died in December 1650, 15 people were accused of owing money to his estate (pursuing the debts of 'delinquents' was a major concern of the Committee for the Advance of Money). These claimed that they were only executors of Gwynn's estate and that their accuser, Captain Philip Nicholas of Skenfrith, made his living by threatening vexatious lawsuits and forcing people to purchase their peace, by pursuit of non-existent debts.[31]

It was not only Royalists who suffered at the hands of the sequestrators. Catholics, particularly 'papists in arms', were not allowed to compound with a fine, but suffered confiscation and whilst Royalists with estates worth less than £200 a year were exempt from sequestration, no such lower limit applied to Catholics. Appeals were allowed, but often took several years to be heard. Even though it was often claimed that cases had been initiated by personal enemies to settle old scores, or by persons hoping to profit from sequestrated lands, a reluctance to push matters to harsh extremes was sometimes apparent.

William Jones of the Hardwick was from a recusant family of minor gentry, kinsmen of the Prodgers of Wenddu, with a small estate outside Abergavenny worth £300 in goods and cattle. He lost half his cattle during the war 'partly by soldiery, partly by murrain'. Worse was to follow. In 1648 he was arraigned before the County Committee and deprived of his family estate as a papist in arms. He had paid what he claimed was an innocent social call on his cousin Colonel James Prodger, governor of Abergavenny, and in January 1646 had fled from his house to escape Rowland Laugharne's soldiers who had killed

The Hardwick, Abergavenny seat of the catholic gentry family, Jones of the Hardwick, sequestrated after the Civil War. Their chaplain, Father Thomas Andrews, died of exposure and privation whilst hiding in a barn during the 'Popish plot'. (Photograph by Jeremy Knight)

one of his neighbours, and threatened him. After going to his mother-in-law's, he ended up in Raglan Castle, but produced witnesses to show that he had left before the siege, and had never borne arms. The allegations were the 'malicious pretences of some who intended his utter ruin'. On appeal, he was granted a fifth of his estate, and his house, until proved a papist in arms.[32] Eventually in 1653 he was allowed to compound for £172 17s. A few months later, with half the fine paid, his sequestration was discharged. His son's widow was still there in 1717, and still a catholic.[33]

Thomas Gunter senior of Abergavenny had similar troubles. His house was sequestrated for recusancy in 1648, though he was allowed to remain in it as a tenant. 'Tho' Gunter dismissed because he had no good lease' noted Walter Powell. In arrears with his rent, he appealed in July 1655 on the grounds that the house was not his own, and that he was 86 years old and poor. The Committee eventually discharged him after he had sworn an oath that he had no other house. He also appeared before the Committee in respect of two small properties in Abergavenny and Penrhos. Before the war these had been worth £10 a year, but 'in regard of the present distractions' they were now 'not worth neare so much' and Gunter could, under the sequestration regulations, retain a third. The matter was thought not worth pursuing. The case of another Abergavenny catholic, the Haberdasher Nathaniel Pritchard, shows the London Committee, that subsequently replaced the local County Committee, in a more favourable light. Pritchard, a Capital Burgess of Abergavenny, was originally sequestrated as a Royalist and a recusant. He appealed against the former charge, claiming, like William Jones, that he had taken no part in the war. The local committee were ordered to search the books of their predecessor, the old County Committee, to see what the evidence was. Pritchard was cleared of being a papist in arms, though still sequestrated as a recusant.[34]

One particularly contentious issue was that of standing timber on sequestrated estates. Monmouthshire is a well wooded county, its primary oakwoods supplemented by beechwoods, secondary woodland from re-growth during the later Medieval population decline. The Elizabethan blast furnaces and forges established by the Hanburys in central Monmouthshire and the iron industry of the Wye Valley consumed huge amounts of coppiced timber, which fetched a high price. The County Committee had only temporary enjoyment of the profits of sequestered estates and sought to maximise these by leasing standing timber to contractors for felling. On the other hand, both the owners and the London Committee had longer term interests in maintaining the value of the estates. When the owners of estates appealed to the latter against this asset stripping, the County Committee were usually ordered to preserve the timber.[35]

Allegations of mis-administration and corruption became so widespread that early in 1650 the committees were virtually abolished. The new Sequestration Committee was controlled from Goldsmith's Hall in London, with the local committee acting as its agents, though residual bodies still dealt with tax assessments and the militia. 'The Committee for taking the accounts of the kingdom' audited the accounts of the previous County Committee and the creation of what Ashton has called 'Committees to control Committees' led to confusion, resentment, and passive resistance. The sequestrators of Skenfrith and Abergavenny Hundreds petitioned the new body that they had delivered up their books, papers and accounts to 'the late committee'. Its successor was now asking for fresh accounts, which they were unable to provide. In 1655 John Ward of Newport asked that Judith Evans, widow of Thomas Evans of Trellech, be ordered to surrender the books of the Sequestration Committee, of which her husband had been a member. She had been repeatedly asked to do this. The following March he wrote that he was unable to complete a questionnaire on local papists and delinquents since Judith Evans still had the relevant papers and he had surrendered the rent rolls and leases that he had held as a Committeeman to John Nicholas, the Governor of Chepstow Castle.[36]

Whilst most of our sources see the Usk Committee from below, from the standpoint of its victims, one shows that sometimes the tables were turned. In the winter of 1646–7 an Irishman, Richard Fitzgerald, arrived in Hereford to oversee the collection of taxes for the English army in Ireland. Brecon, Radnor and Glamorgan paid up, albeit reluctantly, but Monmouthshire was more recalcitrant. Fitzgerald moved to Usk to confront the Committee, only to be told that they had no plans to meet for several weeks. Frustrated, he went to Abergavenny to see Henry Herbert of Coldbrook, the High Sheriff, 'who commands in chief now in that county'. Herbert proved 'very reserved in my business'. Eventually the Usk Committee met 'all the prime gentlemen of the county then sitting'. The order for collection had been sent in October; it was now mid-January and nothing had been done. Eventually, warrants were drawn up, but the Sheriff and others initially refused to sign them, hoping, as the Herefordshire gentry had done, for a countermanding order from London. The only Committeeman to support Fitzgerald was Sir Trevor Williams. The warrants were finally signed in time for a meeting of Quarter Sessions, but some time later all the money was still not in, as some constables were in gaol for non-payment and others sent for 'which revives the languishing state of the collection'.

Eventually, £390 was raised and lodged in the house of William Jones in Usk Priory. Fitzgerald now faced the problem of getting the bulky cash to Bristol for shipment to Ireland. No military escort was available, so he loaded the money on a pack-horse and set off for Chepstow with a nervous soldier, plus a 'stout fellow on foot with a long staff and a pistol' and a boy to drive the horse. At Chepstow, no boat was available, and he had to hire one. Such almost ritual delays and negotiations were normal at the time. Fitzgerald's experiences can be matched by those of Cervantes in his role as a tax collector for the king of Spain before the 1588 Armada.[37]

They Were Defeated. Royalists and Others Under the Commonwealth

Some Royalists made their peace with Parliament fairly quickly. Sir Richard Bassett of Beaupre surrendered Cardiff Castle without bloodshed on 20 August 1645. He compounded for his estate and was fined £753. Although he was active in the Glamorgan rising of 1647, within two years his fine was paid and his estate discharged. Edmund Jones of Llansoy, former treasurer of the Commission of Array, was Attorney General for south Wales in the early 1650s and M.P. for Brecon in 1654. Two years later, he was excused the decimation tax on former Royalists as since the mid 1640s he had 'shown himself very affectionate to the good people and uppon several occasions hath been very sevicable to them and given good testimony of deserting the late King's interest'. Walter Pritchard, the King's former bowls partner, claimed that he had submitted before 1 September 1645 (Royalists who submitted before certain specified dates received preferential treatment). Since Trewogan is within sight of Raglan Castle, this is suspiciously early. He claimed that as a result his house had been burnt and his goods and stock plundered by its garrison. In 1655 he was still successfully pleading poverty to avoid payment of his fine of £186, a sixth of his estate. Presumably the sequestrators were unaware that in 1648 he had sent £3,000 to Edward Herbert in Ireland via his daughter.[38]

In Monmouthshire there was no shortage of gentry willing to serve the new regime. The Commissioners for the Militia in 1648 (or at least those nominated) included surviving members of the 'country' party, all active Whigs in the next reign, along with longer established Parliamentary supporters. The gentry saw the militia as insurance against unrest, whether from Royalists or Parliamentary radicals. Such support suggests a potential solid foundation for the Parliamentary government if political troubles could be overcome In contrast, unreconstructed former Royalists and 'Raglanders' faced a bleak future.[39]

Edward Herbert, Earl of Glamorgan, inherited his father's title on the first Marquis's death. He was in Ireland until at least 1648 and remained in exile until 1652, when he was forced home by poverty. Imprisoned in the Tower from July 1652 until October 1654, he was nevertheless granted a pension of £3 a week from his confiscated Raglan estates.[40] His younger brother, Lord Charles Somerset, also went into exile. In 1647 his wife Elizabeth received news that he had been drowned 'by the miscarrying of a ship in France'. This seems to have been only a rumour, however, and he later became a priest, ending his days as a Canon of Cambrai in Flanders.[41] Sir John Wintour was exempted from pardon and banished as a traitor. He returned to London in 1649, but was recognized, sent to the Tower and arraigned for high treason. The case was not proceeded with, but he remained in the Tower for the next ten years. Whilst he was there, his wife Mary, who had held Lydney for the King, was forced to sell much of his land in Dean, including the Gunn's Mill iron furnace, to two Parliamentary Majors, John Brown and the ex-Leveller John Wildman, so as to provide marriage portions for her daughters. After the Restoration, Wintour sold the land he had purchased pre-war in the Forest of Dean back to the crown for £30,000. However, he kept up his interest in the iron industry, experimenting with a new type of coking oven for the 'charking and calcining of pit coals'. This foreshadowed the process of smelting iron with coke eventually achieved by Abraham Darby at Colebrookdale.[42] He shared his interest in iron technology with another former Royalist catholic, Colonel James Prodger, who in 1661 was one of the petitioners for a patent in a similar scheme to 'melt down metals with coal instead of wood'.[43]

Sir Charles Kemeys had been besieged in Pembroke Castle at the time of his father's death at Chepstow. When Pembroke surrendered, he was exiled from the realm for two years. He was fined a third of his estate (£4,600) in respect of his and his father's delinquency.[44] Later re-arrested, he was in prison in Cardiff Castle until December 1651. On release he took the oath of loyalty to the Commonwealth and retired to Cefn Mably. He died in 1658, still a suspect

Royalist.[45] He was at least more fortunate than John Gainsford, Lt-Colonel of the Marquis of Worcester's Foot, who died in prison for his loyalty.[46]

At the Restoration Sir Charles's brother, Nicholas Kemeys, petitioned Charles II for command of a foot company at Dunkirk, or a recommendation to Lord Albermarle, as General Monck had by then become, reminding the new king that his ancestors had fought and some had died for his father. He mentioned that he had been 'trained in the service', served under the Duke of York in Flanders during the Interregnum and in the Guards until their establishment had been reduced. The King duly recommended Kemeys to Monck for the first vacant Colonelcy on account of his loyalty and 'present distressed condition'.[47] He might have met another Monmouthshire soldier in Flanders, though on the opposite side. Thomas Morgan was by 1652 a Major-General and Colonel of Dragoons in Cromwell's army in Scotland, commanding one column whilst George Monck led the other. In 1657 he was Second in Command of the British Expeditionary Force in Flanders and in the following year fought in the Battle of the Dunes outside Dunkirk for Cromwell's French allies under Turenne against the Spanish, whose regiments of English and Irish Royalists included the Duke of York and (probably) Nicholas Kemeys. Morgan has left a lively account of the battle, written for a friend.[48] Fought in the dunes from which a later British Expeditionary Force was evacuated in 1940, the battle resulted in the capture of Dunkirk and Ypres. Morgan then helped Monck re-organize the Scottish army, which Monck realized would be a powerful force in establishing a stable regime after Cromwell's death. When that time came, the divisions between Monck and the radicals in his army led to many officers leaving him, but 'that little man' wrote Monck 'was of more worth than the 17 score officers who had deserted the service'. When in 1660 he marched south over Coldstream Bridge to the political settlement that restored Charles II to the throne, Morgan was left in command in Scotland. He subsequently became Governor of Jersey, where he died in 1670.

Another ex-Royalist soldier, Captain John Poyntz, had been an officer in James Prodger Herbert's Foot. When Abergavenny was abandoned in the winter of 1645, Poyntz joined the garrison of Raglan, where he was present during the siege. Perhaps kin to the Poyntz family of Iron Acton in Gloucestershire, he had links with the recusants of Caerleon, possibly as a kinsman of Sir Edward Poynes of Caerleon, fined as a recusant in 1613. His own religious affiliations are not known, though he chose to serve in a regiment whose commanding officer was a well known papist. After the war, he and his three sons enlisted in the Parliamentary army and served in Colonel Ingoldsby's regiment for ten years. In 1655, owed £240 in arrears of pay, he petitioned Cromwell, citing his ten years' faithful service and offering to inform on a number of papists in the Caerleon area, including the late Jennet Poyntz of Penrhos whose estates had escaped sequestration, in return for payment of his arrears out of the proceeds. It is doubtful if Poyntz ever received his money. After the Restoration, he served in Ireland in the garrison of Dublin Castle under Ormonde.[49]

Several Catholic priests of the next generation were called 'Captain Pugh' or 'Captain Evans'. In some cases this may be explained by priests dressing as an officer as cover when moving between houses. However, Captain William Pugh, surgeon to Lord Charles Somerset's foot, was a catholic from Gwynedd, a bard and collector of Welsh catholic poetry. After the fall of Raglan he went abroad. He spent from 1670 to 1677 in Valladolid in Spain where he became a Benedictine monk and was ordained as a priest. In 1677 Gwilym Pue returned to Gwent, where he was priest at Blackbrook in Skenfrith. Tried at Monmouth assizes at the same time as David Lewis, he was acquitted for lack of the second witness needed in cases of capital treason. Similarly, Lieutenant Sylliard of the Marquis of Worcester's Horse may later have been Sir Philip and Lady Jones's priest at Llanarth.[50]

'Vice Abounding, and Magistrates Fast Asleep'—Monmouthshire Towns under the Major Generals

Unable to produce a stable political settlement, the 'Barebones' Parliament, which had replaced the 'Rump' six months earlier, dissolved itself on 12 December 1653. Four days later, Oliver Cromwell was installed as Lord Protector. The first Protectorate Parliament, elected the following July under the new Articles of Government, contained many members of the traditional governing elite prepared to cooperate with the Cromwellian regime. For Monmouthshire Colonel Henry Herbert of Coldbrook (who had sat for the county since the death of Sir Charles Williams in 1642) and Colonel Thomas Hughes of Moynes Court were joined by the borough member, the neutralist Thomas Morgan of Machen. However, Penruddock's rising in March 1655 persuaded Cromwell that he could no longer rule with the assent of former Royalists.

That August he devised a new system of Godly rule. Eleven Major-Generals were to govern through specially appointed Commissioners, separate from the Justices of the Peace. A new cavalry militia, paid for with a 10% 'decimation' tax on Royalists, was to act as a mounted gendarmerie responsible for public order and the 'reformation of manners'. James Berry, Major General for Wales and the Marches appointed Lt-Colonel John Nicholas, Governor of Chepstow Castle, as Deputy Major-General for Monmouthshire, with Colonel Wroth Rogers, father of Nathan Rogers, in a similar post in Herefordshire. Nicholas's militia troop had Francis Blethyn, younger brother of William Blethyn of Dinham, as Lieutenant, plus a Cornet, quartermaster, three corporals, a trumpeter and 76 troopers.[51]

Even more unpopular than the decimation tax was the 'reformation of manners' and the social control that went with it. Blood sports and other pastimes were to be suppressed, public morals regulated and alehouses shut down.[52] The government was also nervous of fairs, markets and fox hunts which might serve Royalist gentry as cover for disorders or plotting. The fringes of Glamorgan above Cardiff had been the centre of the 'Peaceable Army' of 1645, and there were still suspect former Royalists around, including the Kemeyses of Cefn Mably. Caerphilly market was important locally for the sale of cheese and knitted stockings made in the surrounding countryside, but the castle had been in ruins for centuries and the market and fair lacked a formal charter. 'People out of severall parts doe frequently assemble unlawfully at Caerphilly' it was reported in 1656, 'under colour of holding a market and fair, though without any authority for the same, at which meetings manie disorders are Comitted'. The deputy Major-General for Glamorgan was ordered to 'learn their nature' and suppress them to prevent disorders. However, the real motive became apparent after the Restoration, when Cardiff Corporation lobbied Charles II claiming that the city was being reduced to poverty by competition from Caerphilly fair. Evidently Cardiff feared that it was losing trade to its neighbour.[53]

In February 1656, James Berry arrived in Monmouth on a tour of inspection and met the gentlemen of the county, 'these inconstant people who had played with both hands'. Sir Trevor Williams hoped to lobby Secretary of State Thurlow for a personal favour, though Berry warned Thurlow that 'with those that know him in these partes he hath no argument that will prevaile'. Berry wrote 'I am much troubled with these markett townes, every where vice abounding and magistrates fast asleep'. He put pressure on the Corporation of Monmouth to take action against unlicensed beer sellers, as a result of which a number of disorderly alehouses in the town were shut down and some of the bailiffs, who ran the alehouses concerned, fined or imprisoned. The affair caused a great stir locally, not least among the godly 'who are in this place a pittiful people'.[54]

In reforming local government in the towns, one strategy was to encourage the 'godly' inhabitants to petition for a new municipal charter. This would reduce the numbers of burgesses, making possible a quorum of the same godly, who were often short of suitable candidates for office. In Abergavenny, the 'well affected' sought to consolidate their power in this often turbulent town in this way. The original borough charter of Henry VIII had been replaced in 1638 with one giving power to a Chief Steward and 25 capital and inferior burgesses. The steward was Sir William Morgan of Tredegar, with the brothers William and Henry Baker serving as his deputies. Capital burgesses included the wealthy catholic haberdasher, Nathaniel Pritchard, and Richard Gunter, brother of the recusant Thomas Gunter. In November 1656 the inhabitants (no doubt the 'well affected' ones) petitioned for a new charter. The timing suggests that James Berry was the motivating force. This was not a unique case, for in many towns the new regime was busy revising the terms of local government, as the government of Charles II was to do on an even larger scale later. In Glamorgan, the puritan lawyer Evan Seys of Boverton was scrutinising borough charters with the intention of similar reform. If the new charter had been accepted, Abergavenny would have been governed by a Mayor and 12 burgesses. The list omitted leading members of the old order, Nathaniel Pritchard and Thomas Gunter had by now had their estates sequestrated in any event. A few names were carried over for continuity. Two former capital burgesses, John Rogers and James Harris, would have become Mayor and Bailiff, but the other bailiff was to be the apothecary Christopher Price, a leading figure in the Baptist cause in the town. The petition was considered by the Lord Protector's Council in January, but nothing further is heard of it, and it seems to have been lost when the Major-Generals fell from power.[55]

The experiment of ruling through the Major-Generals lasted barely a year. By the end of 1656 Cromwell, who needed money, was forced to call a Parliament in which John Nicholas, along with the other Major-Generals, took his seat. Neither of the two county members in this Second Protectorate Parliament were significant landowners in the county. Edward Herbert's

Merthyr Geryn (or Moor) Grange near Magor. A former grange of Tintern Abbey, leased during the Interregnum by Edward Herbert, 'Cromwell's right hand, talked of for a knighthood' and M.P. for the county in the Second Protectorate Parliament. At the Restoration, the Marquis of Worcester reclaimed his former property, and Herbert withdrew to Bristol. (Photograph by Jeremy Knight)

family, descended from an illegitimate son of Sir Richard Herbert of Coldbrook, had been settled around Magor and Undy since early Tudor times, when his ancestor Thomas Morgan was steward of Tintern Abbey's Moor Grange (Merthyr Geryn). This, with Tintern's other possessions, passed to the Earl of Worcester at the Dissolution and under the Commonwealth was granted to Cromwell, from whom Herbert leased it. He also held tenancies from the Earl of Pembroke in Caerleon. A Commissioner for the Propagation of the Gospel in Wales, a member of Cromwell's High Court of Justice, and in religion an Independent, he was described by a hostile source as 'Cromwell's right hand, talked of for a knighthood'. When Worcester recovered his lands at the Restoration, Herbert retired to Bristol. He was arrested in 1662, suspected of being 'an instrument of new mischief' and in correspondence with Welsh malcontents and nonconformists.[56]

The second county member was John Nicholas, the younger brother of Edward Nicholas of Trellech Grange and third son of Philip Nicholas of Lanpill in Llanfihangel-Tor-Y-Mynydd. The family claimed descent from Brychan Brycheiniog, but also had links with the local puritan establishment. Edward Nicholas married the widow of Thomas Evans of Trellech, a member of the county Sequestration Committee and his son married a daughter of William Jones of Usk, the County Sequestrator. Like other local puritans, Nicholas left Monmouthshire at the outbreak of war. He joined the Parliamentarian army and distinguished himself sufficiently to be marked out for promotion. At the Battle of St Fagans in May 1648, he was Captain-Lieutenant of Colonel John Okey's Regiment of Dragoons. A Captain-Lieutenant was an experienced junior officer marked out for 'fast track' promotion, in command of the Colonel's own troop of horse in order to free the latter for wider duties, and with first claim on the next vacant Captaincy. Shot through his hat, but otherwise unhurt, Nicholas got his promotion shortly after the battle, when Cromwell refers to 'Captain Nicholas' as a trusted aide in several letters.[57] At the Reformation, Nicholas fled abroad, but was pardoned by the King. David Underwood has noted how the Protectorate relied heavily on a few key men in the counties, often outsiders. In Herefordshire, for example, the moderate Parliamentarian Harleys had been eclipsed by the military governor, the radical Independent Wroth Rogers. In Monmouthshire, Cromwell's men were John Nicholas and Edward Herbert.[58]

Even though Raglan and Monmouth castles had been slighted, Chepstow was kept up as a fortress, important for the supply of naval timber from the Forest of Dean and for holding state prisoners. In 1649, the mayor of Bristol wrote to John Nicholas complaining of the 'great waste of timber in the Forest of Dean, the only place in those parts where there is timber for shipping'. Wood was being destroyed for iron making with no thought of coppicing to ensure future supplies. Forest officials were ordered to stop offenders cutting wood or carrying it away. Nicholas also found himself involved in a complicated dispute over standing timber, characteristic of the Interregnum. The timber on the sequestrated estate of Sir Edward Morgan of Llantarnam was sold to one Samuel Jones for £600. Nicholas was to have £300 of this for the repair of war damage at Chepstow Castle. He had spent most of this when Morgan intervened with the London Committee to stop the asset stripping of his estate. The Committee then demanded the £300 from Nicholas and forced him to give a bond for its payment. He petitioned for the cancelling of the bond or (he added hopefully) for himself to be admitted as tenant of the land. Eventually, he was forced to write to Cromwell in an attempt to settle the matter. The castle was also still important as a fortress, and In 1651 Walter Cradock assembled a body of foot and horse there when the future Charles II's invasion had reached Worcester.[59]

8 Restoration and Reaction 1660–90. Plus ça Change

'The more things change, the more they stay the same' is not a bad motto for Restoration Monmouthshire. Henry Herbert, eldest son of Edward Herbert, Earl of Glamorgan, aged 13 when the war started, was sent abroad for his education and safety. On his return in 1650 he announced his conversion to protestantism and made peace with Cromwell, who in 1654 returned to him some of the family lands in Chepstow, Magor and Caldicot which Parliament had granted to the Lord Protector. Henry Herbert then sat in the Cromwellian Parliament as M.P. for Brecon. The period between the death of Oliver Cromwell in September 1658 and the Restoration saw some strange bedfellows. Edward Massey, the professional soldier who had defended Gloucester against the King, was now an ally of the conservative Presbyterians and Royalists against the Independents and their army allies, and threw in his lot with those plotting to overthrow the regime. Herbert was involved in Massey's plot of July 1659 for a rising in the Forest of Dean, aimed at seizing Bristol and Gloucester for Charles II. Many principal players of 1642–3 were involved, including Colonel Berrowe of Awre, who had fought against Edward Herbert's 'Mushrump army' at Coleford, and in whose house the conspirators met; Colonel Thomas Veale of Alveston and John Gainsford of Awre. The most obvious absentee, Sir John Wintour, was still in the Tower of London.[1]

This was part of a plan to seize various cities whilst Charles II and the Duke of York waited at Calais and Boulogne with an invasion force, though for most of those involved, the restoration of the king was one option among a number. Booth's rising, named after its one initially successful leader, Sir George Booth in Cheshire, was quickly suppressed. The Royal cause now seemed more hopeless than ever. Arrests followed. At Chepstow John Nicholas, the Governor, raised 40 recruits to strengthen the garrison. Orders were given that prisoners there should be questioned, and their written examinations sent up to London, with any additional information available on them and (ominously) the value of each man's estate.[2]

Within six months, the political situation had changed again. A power struggle between the Rump Parliament and the army under Lambert culminated in the army physically barring the former from the House of Commons. General Monck, commanding the army in Scotland, concerned at the slide into anarchy, declared for the Rump. Over 90 officers whose loyalty lay with Lambert left his army. On his own initiative, his second-in-command, Major-General Thomas Morgan, visited his old comrade from Raglan days, Sir Thomas Fairfax, in his retirement at Nun Appleton in Yorkshire. Fairfax had kept clear of politics since the King's trial but told Morgan that many Yorkshire gentlemen would support Monck, though he personally favoured the restoration of the Long Parliament. Monck was playing his cards close to his chest, but on 1 January 1660, he moved his troops across Coldstream bridge into England. In November, Thomas Veale's son had told the sequestration agent that his uncle, Nicholas Veale, was about to be released from Hurst Castle (where Charles I had been imprisoned for a while), adding 'Now you rogue, now Monck is a-coming' whilst Mary Veale added that 'she hoped the English army and Monck's army out of Scotland would neither eat nor drink until they had fought'. Fairfax seized York in support of Monck, and at the beginning of February Monck's troops entered London amid popular rejoicing and calls for a free Parliament. There was still work to be done, however, in neutralizing the old Commonwealthmen and their allies. Sir Trevor Williams was made Colonel of the county militia and joined with the Gloucestershire Royalist Baynham Throckmorton of Clowerwell in Newland, to disarm radicals and others in Dean who might oppose a Restoration settlement.[3]

At first Monck kept his own counsel, and his intentions were unclear, but after discreet negotiations with the Rump Parliament and those moderate M.P.s excluded from it by Pride's Purge, the Long Parliament re-convened itself on 21 February amid bonfires and popular rejoicing. There were still dangers of a counter-revolution by army republicans from the left, or of an uncontrolled reactionary Restoration from the right, but the Long Parliament finally dissolved itself. A General Election followed in April resulting in the Convention Parliament that was dominated by moderates and ex-Royalists. Three days after it sat, a declaration signed by the king was laid before it. The Declaration of Breda promised a free pardon to former enemies, save for those excluded from it by Parliament, a 'liberty to tender consciences' on matters of religion and that Parliament should settle disputes over claims to the confiscated estates of former Royalists. On 1 May the Lords and Commons voted for the Restoration of the monarchy. On 29 May the king entered London.

Henry Herbert had acquired the Wiltshire property of Badminton from a half cousin and moved there in 1660, in place of the bombed out Raglan. He sat for Monmouthshire in the Cavalier Parliament of 1661, alongside William Morgan of Tredegar, son of the former neutralist Thomas Morgan of Machen. His father,

Edward Herbert, Earl of Glamorgan, had 'contracted great debts in lending vast sums to the late king'. He paid off £50,000, but at one stage his estates were seized by creditors and shortly before his death was still being pursued for £6,000 borrowed in 1642. Henry Herbert, now a protestant, became Lord Lieutenant of Gloucestershire, Herefordshire and Monmouthshire, the link between the Royal administration and the counties. When his father died in 1667, he became third Marquis of Worcester. In the resulting by-election, his candidate, James Herbert of Coldbrook, was defeated by Sir Trevor Williams, despite Henry Herbert's attempts to overawe the electors with files of musketeers from Chepstow Castle. Williams then made a name for himself in the House on a series of anti-popery committees. When the M.P. for Monmouth Borough, Sir George Probert of Penallt (who happened to be Williams's brother-in-law) died in 1677, his son, Henry Probert, was passed over for the seat in favour of Worcester's son. Resentment at this slight may have contributed to Probert's involvement with Arnold and Williams in the subsequent anti-papist agitation.

In 1682 Worcester was created Duke of Beaufort, fulfilling Charles I's promise to his father, though the dukedom seems to have been a riposte by the king to an attempt by Arnold and Williams to abolish the Council in the Marches at Ludlow, of which the Marquis was Lord President. His role as the representative of central government brought him into conflict with the local gentry who dominated county politics. Whig opposition to the Tory Beauforts centred on the Berkeleys in Gloucestershire and the Morgans of Tredegar in Monmouthshire. The old hatreds between 'Raglanders' and others continued unabated.[4]

Herbert needed a new seat of power in the county to replace Raglan. As there was talk of Chepstow Castle being 'dismantled', Herbert wrote to the king pointing out that it was 'the key to the four adjoining Welsh Counties, remote from all other garrisons, a bridle to the ill affected, who abound in those parts'. He was anxious to install his own men in the castle, and told the king that it was 'not fit to be trusted to the militia, who are so few that Monmouthshire cannot afford 15 men on constant duty. 'Instead he proposed that the garrison should be reduced from 100 men to 60 and that he should pay the salaries of the Captain or governor, the lieutenant and the ensign, so putting the force under his direct control. The events of the next decade were to show that Herbert was prepared to use files of musketeers, whether to overawe the electors of Monmouth or to protect his enclosures in Wentwood Forest, as well as using Chepstow Castle as a convenient prison for those who opposed him. At the same time, Chepstow remained a Royal castle, important for the supply of timber for shipbuilding, and in the Dutch wars as a prisoner-of-war camp and hospital for sick and wounded soldiers.[5]

Chepstow's most famous prisoner was the radical republican Henry Marten, a signatory of Charles I's death warrant. His radical politics and sexual procliv-

*Henry Marten, the regicide, from a painting once in the possession of the Lewis family of St Pierre. According to John Aubrey (*Brief Lives*) he was 'a great lover of pretty girles ... as far from a Puritane as light from darkness'*

ities both earned him Cromwell's dislike. John Aubrey described him as 'a great lover of pretty girls, to whom he was so liberal that he spent a great part of his estate' and 'as far from a Puritaine as light from darkness'. This may have saved his life at the Restoration, for Lord Falkland reminded the House of Commons of the Old Testament rule that sacrifices were to be without spot or blemish whereas the House proposed 'to make this old Rotten Rascal a sacrifice'. He had also intervened to save several Royalists on trial for their lives under Cromwell. Initially imprisoned in Windsor Castle, he was removed to Chepstow as 'an eyesore to His Majesty'. He lived there, in comfortable imprisonment in the tower which now bears his name, with his wife and two maidservants, until his death in 1680.

Monmouth Castle, dominating the county town, had, like Raglan, been slighted at the end of the civil war, though it was still central to such events as county elections and the Assizes. These were held in the surviving medieval Great Hall until they were transferred to Great Castle House around 1700. Castle House had been built by Worcester in 1673. Facing on to the spacious inner ward of the castle, it is 'a house of splendid swagger, outside and in ... intended for official and ceremonial purposes', with elaborate chimneypieces, carpentry and plasterwork. Its façade is dominated by a large Italianate central first-floor window, with a carved pediment above, where the Marquis could display himself to the crowds below on great occasions. Faced with such a powerful opponent, it was not surprising that men like Arnold and Sir Trevor Williams felt that they could only fight fire with fire.[6]

The Anglican Restoration

In May 1660, Lewis James, the expelled curate of Bedwellty, wrote in the parish register that he had bought in Bristol in happier pre-war days how 'Our most gracious Soveraigne Lord Charles the Second ... Came from beyond sea, first to London. Vivat Rex. Exurgat Deus et dissipentur inimici' (Long Live the King, Let God arise, and his enemies be scattered). Later, he added a note:

> Be it remembered that the twentieth day of June Lewis James cler'[icus], then curate of Bedwelltie, was ejected at Chepstol and after his tenne yeares ejectm't He began (againe) to read & preach in Bedwelltie church aforesaid uppon Sunday being the twentieth day of May 1660, Edmund Rosser having given over the place ye Sunday before ye 13th Maij 1660.[7]

Other Anglicans also celebrated the restoration. At Tredunnock, whose Puritan minister Walter Prosser went off to serve a Baptist congregation at Hay on Wye, the churchwardens William Morgan and Philip Vane installed a new font in 1662. Penallt and Llandenny acquired new fonts, marked with the auspicious

Great Castle House, Monmouth. (© National Monuments Record for Wales, Royal Commission on the Ancient and Historical Monuments of Wales)

date, in 1660 and Skenfrith in the following year. At Llangibby the finely decorated font of 1662 was marked with the Prince of Wales's feathers and the names of the church-wardens, in honour of the new king. It is probably by the same hand as the Llandenny font and the Trellech sundial of 1689.[8]

Not all Puritan ministers disap-peared as rapidly as Edmund Rosser. In July 1660 Henry Walter, vicar of Newport, was preaching in Llantarnam church. Llantarnam was a catholic stronghold and before the end of the sermon, Walter was attacked by a company of soldiers, who, having disrupted the godly sermon, spent the rest of the day carousing and fighting. Walter, nevertheless, remained in post until 1662.[9]

Those Anglican clergy still alive rapidly reclaimed their livings. Where the expelled clergyman had remained in his parish, or even continued to exercise some of his functions, as at Bedwellty, this prob-ably took place quickly and with little formality. At Trellech the new vicar, Richard Meredith, was insti-tuted on Christmas Day 1660 — a significant date in view of puritan attempts to abolish the feast. In Usk Hundred, four of the ten ejected clergy lived to be restored, and a fifth, Henry Vaughan of Panteg, died during 1661, still headmaster of Abergavenny Grammar School. Where the incumbent had died or moved to another parish, the process of selecting and instituting the new priest naturally took longer, but three

Lady Magdalene Probert's sundial of 1689, Trellech, depicting the main antiquities of the village. She was the sister of Sir Trevor Williams and widow of another former Royalist, Sir George Probert. The sundial is by the same hand as the fonts from Llandenny (1661) and Llangibby (1662)

of the five vacant livings were filled in the early months of 1661, and Panteg towards the end of the year. In Caldicot Hundred, where only two clergy lived to be restored, of about a dozen excluded, five parishes were filled in February 1661, including three belonging to Eton College, and two others, later in the year following the death of the expelled vicar. This suggests a co-ordinated campaign and Green has shown the role of Anglican gentry in expelling puritan clergy and re-instating ejected Anglicans. No doubt lay patrons like Sir Charles Kemeys at Caldicot played a vigorous role in this congenial task. Gentry supporters of moderate puritan reform had been alarmed by the radical zeal of the Cromwellian reformers. The removal of many parish clergy; the icono-clastic fervour unleashed against fonts and stained glass windows (which often bore the arms of local families), but above all the threat to the gentry's patronage and tithes were a Reformation too far. At the Restoration, the gentry hastened to restore a Church properly respectful both of the social order and of their property rights over advowsons and tithes.[10]

Most replacements of parish clergy had thus taken place before the Act of Uniformity of May 1662, which required all clergy and schoolmasters to sign two declarations with 'unfeigned consent' and read Morning and Evening Prayer from the new revised prayerbook by St Bartholomew's Day (August 24). Among the 'Bartholomew ejections' were Thomas Barnes at Magor, Richard Blindman at Chepstow, Nicholas Cary at Monmouth and Henry Walter at Newport. Blindman had replaced Abraham Drew, vicar of Chepstow for nearly 40 years, who had died in 1646. Instituted in regular fashion to a vacant living, there had been no need for Blindman to resign earlier, but he now moved to Bristol as a minister, later emigrating to New England with other Welsh Independents. Cary resumed his secular avocation as a London doctor specializing in diseases of the eye and ear.[11] It was not only ministers who suffered. One group of dissenters met in Edward Webley's house in Caldicot. Five or six large cows belonging to Webley were seized and sold at the next market as distraint for his fine for religious nonconformity. His friends and neighbours refused to bid, whereupon they were snapped up at half their value by a lawyer who acted as Worcester's agent. Henry Baker of Abergavenny was also active distraining on the cattle of dissenters in the north of the county.[12]

Conformists and Papists—The Compton Census

The alleged strength of Catholicism in Monmouthshire was shortly to become an obsessive factor in national politics, as the nascent Whigs sought to control the king, and to exclude his brother, the catholic Duke of York (and future James II) from the throne. The fall from power of Clarendon and Sheldon in 1667 marked a relaxation of the persecution of dissenters. The main threat to the Restoration settlement was now seen as coming from influential catholics rather than from puritans. In the same year, Henry Herbert became Marquis of

Worcester. His aggressive hostility to anyone who stood in his way drew many moderate Royalists in Monmouthshire and Glamorgan into an anti-Worcester opposition. By a fortunate chance for historians, a religious census on the eve of the so called 'Popish plot' listed the numbers of 'conformists', 'papists' and 'nonconformists' in each county in England and Wales parish by parish. Though the returns present problems, their analysis of the religious allegiances of individual Gwent parishes is invaluable.[13]

The Compton census of 1676 was initiated by the king's first minister, the Earl of Danby, and by Archbishop Sheldon. It was primarily concerned not with the numbers of catholics, but with the numbers of nonconformists, and the feasibility of suppressing their conventicles. The intention was to list all adults, both men and women, of a legal age to take communion (*i.e.* over 16), but the instructions as transmitted to incumbents and churchwardens via the bishops and archdeacons of each diocese were not always clear. In most cases, they seem to have been carried out correctly, but sometimes only men were listed and sometimes the number of households. The returns do not indicate which of these alternatives were followed in particular cases, and it is necessary to deduce this from comparison with later population statistics.

Returns were presented as three figures for each parish: of 'conformists', 'papists' and 'nonconformists'. These categories are not without ambiguities. Though there was a legal requirement on all adults to take Anglican communion, in practice only a minority did so regularly. Was the figure for conformists, therefore, the number of communicants or of those who attended services in the parish church? In addition there were 'church papists' — catholics who occasionally conformed — whilst many Presbyterians and Independents saw no difficulty in conforming to the Anglican church when necessary, unlike separatist bodies such as Baptists and Quakers. Indeed, the question of 'occasional conformity' became a political issue when under the Corporation Act the Tories sought to exclude nonconformists from municipal bodies.

Thus, whilst the census gives an overview of religious allegiance, converting its statistics into population figures presents difficulties. Later surveys record, with varying degrees of disapproval, substantial numbers of people outside the ambit of organized religion. Philip Jenkins has estimated that the total population recorded in the Welsh dioceses was half that which can be calculated from the hearth tax returns, and that therefore considerable elements of the population were omitted. This was almost certainly the case at Caerleon. Overall, however, the picture is like that from the recusant rolls earlier in the century. The Deanery of Newport shows the same low numbers of catholics as neighbouring parts of Glamorgan, whilst virtually every parish had a respectable number of nonconformists. Conventicles had been reported in 1669 in Marshfield, Bedwas, Newport, Bedwellty and Mynyddislwyn. At

Marshfield, Baptists, including former Roundhead soldiers from Monmouthshire and Glamorgan, met at the house of Jane Reynolds, widow of a Parliamentary officer. Whatever the situation elsewhere in the county, Arnold would have had little cause for concern here. Similarly, catholic recusants were rare in Gwent Is Coed. Thirty-seven parishes contained only nine Catholics in total. The two exceptions were Christchurch, adjacent to the Catholic stronghold of Caerleon, with eight and Shirenewton, with 20. The latter figure is almost certainly a clerical error. Shirenewton already had both Baptist and Quaker meetings and the figures for papists and nonconformists have evidently been transposed.[14]

The situation in Usk Hundred is broadly similar. Frustratingly, returns for central and eastern Monmouthshire are incomplete and the gaps include Usk, Raglan and Trellech. The census returns for the diocese of Llandaff survive only in a single fair copy (Stafford, Salt Ms 33) and blocks of returns were evidently accidentaly omitted. Usk Hundred has figures for 14 of its 24 parishes, though possibly some small parishes were included with larger neighbours. Even so, the distribution of catholic recusants is clear. Four adjacent parishes —Caerleon; Llantarnam; Llanfrechfa and Llandewi Fach—have 45 recorded 'papists'. The remaining 11 have only nine, scattered over five parishes.

Catholicism in Monmouthshire was thus only numerous at this date north of the Wentwood ridge and east of the Usk, in the hundreds of Raglan, Abergavenny and Skenfrith. Entries for Raglan Hundred are incomplete. The catholic strongholds around Clytha and Dingestow stand out clearly, but in some cases the figures seem to represent the number of adults, in others the number of households.[15] To the east, in Trellech Hundred, there are no entries for its southern half, a large block of country comprising eight parishes. The remainder records few catholics, save in Mitchel Troy, adjacent to Monmouth.

Skenfrith Hundred was catholic heartland. The same cluster of parishes between Monmouth and Skenfrith that stand out in the recusant rolls appear here again. Monmouth itself has a respectably sized Catholic community (37), although numerically they were swamped by the 620 reported 'conformists'. There were also significant numbers of nonconformists in the immediate area of Monmouth.

Wentwood and the 'Popish Plot'

War had not ended the disputes between the Marquis of Worcester and local people with rights to graze cattle or take timber for building or fuel ('housebote and heybote') in Wentwood. Worcester's actions affected not only landless cottagers and squatters, but substantial local gentlemen with valuable rights in the Forest deriving from medieval manorial custom. In equivalent enclosures elsewhere the rights of such men had been protected, usually by agreement, but Worcester disregarded such niceties. For Worcester, the Civil War had been a financial disaster, and he was determined to recoup some of his losses. Tintern ironworks alone, to say nothing of the furnaces and forges around Usk and Pontypool in central Monmouthshire, consumed 2,000 tons of charcoal a year, representing 8,000 to 10,000 loads of wood worth about £2,500 a year, compared with the miniscule amounts raised in fines at the Speech Court. Others also had an interest in the Forest. In November 1661 Charles II appointed a commission to enquire into the king's rights in the woods and commons of Caldicot and Shirenewton and to compound with the tenants and commoners 'for setting forth a portion thereof for the king's use'.[16]

Extended conflict between major landowners and tenants claiming rights of common was not unusual in central Monmouthshire. The Earls of Pembroke around Usk, the Williamses of Llangibby and the Neville Lords of Abergavenny had all been involved in prolonged quarrels and litigation with tenants ranging from minor gentry to cottagers and squatters. Yet these disputes had not interfered with the normal patterns of patronage and lordship. At times, the breaking down of newly erected fences had the almost ritual quality of much popular protest, nor did they engender the intense bitterness of the Wentwood dispute. For this, other ingredients were necessary. One was the

Llanvihangel Court, the house of the priest hunter and anti-Papist John Arnold, one of the leading figures behind the 'Popish Plot'. (© National Monuments Record for Wales, Royal Commission on the Ancient and Historical Monuments of Wales)

bitterness and itch to settle old scores that follows a civil war. Worcester's wife was a daughter of Lord Capel, executed by Parliament at the end of the second Civil War, and his own family had suffered by its support for the king. In Glamorgan, Royalists like Sir Edward Stradling and the Bassetts of Beaupre had saddled themselves with massive wartime debts. Worcester on the other hand had every intention of repairing his financial fortunes and restoring his political status within the county.[17]

Any opposition to his plans was dealt with uncompromisingly. In November 1677, Henry Probert, who had gone into opposition after being passed over in the bye-election for his father's Parliamentary seat of Monmouth Boroughs (his mother Magdalene Herbert was the sister of Sir Trevor Williams), and John Arnold of Llanvihangel Court were removed from the Commission of the Peace at Worcester's instigation 'For affronts to the Duke [of York] and misdemeanors in office'. Arnold was also removed as Commander of the Horse in the county militia—an appointment in the gift of Worcester as Lord Lieutenant. The following March the king wrote to Worcester that Sir Edward Mansell of Margam and William Morgan of Tredegar had complained to him that 'gentlemen of good note and condition' had been expelled from the Commission of the Peace in Glamorgan and Monmouthshire at Worcester's instance, including the lawyer and former Cromwellian Evan Seys of Boverton, Glamorgan, whose Monmouthshire kinsmen were allies of Arnold. The Monmouthshire victims included Arnold and Probert, Charles Van of Llanwern, two of the Morgans and (an ominous name) Roger Oates of Cefn Tilla. The purging of puritans and former Parliamentarians from the Bench, or from municipal corporations, was commonplace after the Restoration, and Worcester used this weapon freely. Arnold was to prove a dangerous enemy however. He lived within sight of the medieval pilgrimage chapel of St Michael on the summit of the Skirrid, where large numbers of catholics assembled for Mass and which was the subject of a papal indulgence as late as 1676. At one time he had been sympathetic to catholics, a friend of the future martyr David Lewis, and was even said to have given a room in the Skirrid Mountain Inn, which he owned, for use as a catholic chapel. Whether his later fanatical anti-popery originated as opportunistic opposition to Worcester, or had other causes, is unclear.[18]

The following month Worcester entered Wentwood at the head of 100 men, who proceeded to fell trees and enclose the Chase. Some local gentlemen sought Counsel's opinion. Worcester retaliated by expelling five more from the Commission of the Peace, including Thomas Lewis of St Pierre and three of the Kemeys family and replacing them with the Deputy Governor of Chepstow, William Wolseley 'that had not a foot of land in the county' and by Worcester's steward, John Gwyn. Worcester then held a Forest Court and proceeded against tenants who had carried off wood. Edward Kemeys of Bertholey and Nathan

Rogers, who defended them, were arrested and taken to prison in Monmouth, though later released.[19]

Such activities were often countered by enclosure riots. Three generations of the Williams family of Llangibby tried to enclose common land and waste at Paynswood for almost 60 years, but were defeated by a mixture of legal action and riot, and when Lord Abergavenny enclosed common pasture at Drinos and leased it to a Bristol merchant, the inhabitants destroyed the merchant's fences. Such activities had a long history in the forest-edge areas of Monmouthshire. As late as 1861, attempts to enclose Glascoed Common resulted in 24 people being acquitted of riotous assembly and fence breaking at the Assizes and returning to Usk in triumph, with bands playing and church bells ringing.[20] In June, local people entered Chepstow Park Wood to test their legal right to carry away timber. Worcester reacted by guarding his enclosures with armed men headed by Wolseley, and proceeded against Nathan Rogers and six others in the House of Lords for breach of his privilege by inciting locals to resist his actions. Rogers and three others were imprisoned in London during July and August.[21]

John Arnold of Llanfihangel and John Scudamore of Kentchurch, just over the Herefordshire border, enemies of Worcester, were both to become notorious priest hunters.[22] Arnold was an ally of Sir Trevor Williams, whose kinsman Sir John Trevor of Brynkynallt was chairman of the Parliamentary enquiry into 'the growth and increase of Popery'. Williams had been active on anti-popery committees since his election to the House in 1667. In 1671 he told Parliament that half the county of Monmouth were papists and that more Catholic priests were seen there than Anglican clergymen. He served on other anti-popery committees in 1673 and 1675. On 27 March 1678 he told the Commons that 'Mass is publicly said in several places within the county of Monmouth, and there is one Mr Arnold at the door ready to make the same out'. Sitting in the Speaker's Chamber, the committee heard from Arnold, Scudamore and their informants—the vicars of Abergavenny, Llantilio Crossenny and Llanarth, parish constables and two embittered former catholics, William and Dorothy James of Lodge Farm, Caerleon—who were all too eager to give evidence against the Jesuit David Lewis. On 12 April a shocked House of Commons heard allegations of the numbers of catholic priests active in Monmouthshire, of houses where priests were kept and mass said, sometimes to congregations larger than those at the parish church. The evidence was presented in the format of a criminal trial, with Arnold making a brief statement for the 'prosecution' in the case of each priest, followed by witnesses supporting his allegations. He then moved on to various catholic gentry and local officials alleged to harbour priests and obstruct the prosecution of recusants.[23]

In reply, Worcester issued a pamphlet, ostensibly a letter from a Gloucestershire gentleman, a client of his, to a friend in London. It replied in detail to Arnold's charges with a series of documents and affidavits, some of which had been formally presented to the king in council. They included an autobiographical letter from Henry Milborne, testimonies from clergy to the Anglican conformity of some of those accused by Arnold and answers, at times a little evasive, to charges that they harboured catholic priests. A catalogue of Monmouthshire catholic families now extinct or turned protestant, beginning with the Marquis himself and his brother Sir Charles Somerset, was meant to show that, far from increasing, catholic families in the county were dying out, or converting to Anglicanism.[24]

Arnold's anti-papist propaganda campaign had been underway for several months when in mid August 1678 a religious zealot and pamphleteer named Israel Tongue confronted the king with details of an alleged Jesuit plot to murder the king and Ormonde, burn down London and invade with an army of French and Irish catholics. Charles was rightly sceptical, but in late September, shortly after Nathan Rogers and his colleagues had returned from their imprisonment in London, he referred it to the Privy Council. Tonge appeared before them with the informer and confidence trickster Titus Oates, who had infiltrated the English Jesuit colleges at Valladolid and St Omer, but whose sexual proclivities had caused his expulsion both from the seminaries and as a naval chaplain. On 17 October the body of the London magistrate investigating the plot was found on Primrose Hill. The death of Sir Edmund Berry Godfrey is one of the great murder mysteries of British history (if murder it was), but his funeral initiated a wave of national paranoia which was cleverly exploited by the Whig enemies of the king.

There is no need to discuss the so called 'Popish Plot' here, since it has already been treated in definitive detail elsewhere. Until the Chepstow born 'professional criminal, robber, highwayman and confidence trickster' (and one might add perjurer) William Bedloe wrote from Bristol in October offering information on the murder, Oates's allegations had lacked the second witness needed in cases of capital treason. Bedloe had links with several Whig Monmouthshire gentry, being the cousin of William Kemeys of Kemeys Inferior, the current sheriff, and a nephew by marriage of Charles Price of Llanfoist. Initially his claims merely confirmed some of Oates's allegations. No doubt after some prompting, they became more specific, aimed at Worcester's allies in Monmouthshire, and the enemies of the Arnold / Williams / Croft (the Bishop of Hereford) clique, including the Marquis's steward Charles Price; his cousin Milborne Vaughan of Monmouth; the Vaughans of Courtfield and Captain Francis Spaulding, Governor of Chepstow Castle.[25]

Pressure on the king built up. On 20 November he issued a proclamation for the immediate arrest of all priests and Jesuits who were to be imprisoned 'in order to their trial'. On 7 December Bishop Croft of Hereford, on the orders of the House of Lords, raided the Jesuit College at the Cwm, over the

Herefordshire border in Llanrothal. The priests, including the Jesuit Rector of the College, David Lewis (alias Charles Baker Lewis) had fled, but Lewis had been arrested at Llantarnam three days before the king's proclamation. Like several of the priest-hunters, Croft was an ex-catholic, and had been educated at Douai where his father had been a religious exile. His account of the raid tried hard to create an atmosphere of intrigue and plotting: 'There are one and twenty chimneys in both Houses, and a great many doors to go in and out at; and likewise many private passages from one room to the other'. A study (in 17th-century parlance a room or recess partitioned off) was found 'the door thereof was hardly to be discovered; being placed behind a bed and plastered over like the wall adjoining'. This contained 'a great store of Divinity Books and others in Folio and Quarto and many other lesser books'. A stone altar, vestments and liturgical items were also found. Croft finished his propaganda leaflet by retailing the story of Lewis, 'pretended bishop of Llandaff' cozening money from Dorothy James to free her father's soul from purgatory. Most of the books seized by Croft and his agent Captain Scudamore survive in Hereford Cathedral Library.[26]

Arnold, Trevor Williams and Bedloe kept up their offensive against Beaufort on other fronts. Two targets were Beaufort's steward, Henry Milborne of Wonastow, and the garrison of Chepstow Castle. Williams proposed in the Commons that 'the garrison of Chepstow should be disbanded, and the arms removed and the castle demolished, it having always been in ill hands'. On 5 December, Beaufort wrote to his wife 'not a day has passed this week, that I have not been forced to defend the garrison of Chepstow ... which Lord Shaftesbury will have to be all papists'. His pamphlet dealt with the allegations against the garrison in detail. All officers and soldiers had taken the oaths of allegiance and supremacy, received the sacraments and signed the declaration required by Parliament. Only one, John Rosser, had refused, some years ago, and he had duly been cashiered. The soldiers were fined if they skipped church, the proceeds being used 'towards making a walk in the castle for the ornament thereof' and for amenities for the soldiers. Every 5 November they had a church parade, marching to the Priory church for a service. The vicar of Chepstow and three J.P.s attested the truth of this.[27]

In his deposition to Parliament, Arnold claimed

> That he had seen a Publick chappel near the house of Mr Thomas Gunter, a papist convict, in Abergavenny, adorned with the mark of the Jesuits on the outside, and is informed that Mass is said there by Captain Evans, a reputed Jesuit, and by the aforesaid David Lewis in that very great numbers resort to the said chappel and very often at Church time, and he hath credibly heard that hundreds have gone out of the said chappel when not forty have gone out of the said church, that the said chappel is situate in a publick street of the said town, and doth front the street.[28]

The Catholic Martyrs: Philip Evans and David Lewis

Both priests mentioned by Arnold are now canonized saints. Philip Evans, a 33-year-old Jesuit from northern Monmouthshire, the son of William Evans of Llangattock Vibion Avel and Winifred Morgan of Llanvihangel Crucorney, served as a priest in Gunter's House and at Wernddu. In December, after the raid on the Cwm, he fled to the house of the Glamorgan recusant Christopher Turberville at Sker. Here he was arrested by Richard Bassett of Beaupre, son of the Civil War Royalist, and the former catholic Edward Turberville, after Arnold had offered a £200 reward for his capture. He was tried at Cardiff Assizes the following May with John Lloyd, a secular priest from Trivor at St Maughans near Monmouth. Both were sentenced to death. The witnesses against Evans included Arnold's creatures the dwarf Mayne Trott and Dorothy James of Caerleon, both of whom were to play a prominent role in the trial of David Lewis. Evans was playing tennis on the court near St John's church in

Engraving of St Philip Evans by Alex Vost, from Brevis Relatio Felicis Agonis quam pro Religione Subierunt *(Prague 1683).*
(National Portrait Gallery)

Cardiff, whose site is marked by the former Tennis Court public house, when news was brought that he was to be executed the next day. His reply was 'what haste is there, let me first play my game'. By coincidence, the Tennis Court (currently the Owain Glyndwr) is only yards from the spot where the Protestant martyr Rawlins White was burnt under Mary. A skilled musician and harpist, Evans was playing his harp when the sheriff's officers came for him the next morning. The two priests were executed at Cardiff on 22 July 1679. Whilst he was under sentence of death in Cardiff, his sister, unaware of this, was professed as a Blue Nun in Paris as Sister Barbara Catherine. His letter to her, gently breaking the news, has survived. When word of his execution was brought to David Lewis, in prison in Monmouth, he wrote to a friend 'I hope my turn comes next'.[29]

David Lewis, the 63-year-old Jesuit superior had been arrested shortly before Philip Evans in a dawn raid by a party of dragoons led by Roger Seys of Penrhos, petty constable of Arnold's parish of Llantilio Crossenny and kinsman of the Cromwellian Evan Seys, then M.P. for Gloucester. In his own words:

> After my full thirty years poor missionary labours in South Wales, on Sunday morning, a little before day, being the 17 November 1678 I was taken by six Armed men sent by Mr John Arnold and Mr Charles Price, until then my two very good Friends and Acquaintances. I was taken in a little house in the parish of St Michael-Lantarnam in the County of Monmouth. From thence by the souldiers, together with such church-stuff of mine they there found, carried I was to the House of Mr Charles Price in Llanffoyst.

The site of the smithy where St David Lewis was arrested is marked by a circular setting in the pavement opposite Llantarnam church, put there when the smithy was demolished for road widening. (Photograph by Jeremy Knight)

Waiting at Llanfoist were Thomas Lewis of St Pierre, John Arnold and Charles Price, the uncle by marriage of William Bedloe.

About 2 p.m. Lewis was escorted by a dozen armed horse to the Golden Lion in Frogmore Street, Abergavenny. They mounted to the Sheriff's Chamber ('together we went up to a chamber') and William Jones, Recorder of Abergavenny, was sent for. Lewis's former servant William James of Caerleon then gave evidence. His wife Dorothy had sued Lewis over a house and land at Llantarnam originally granted to her sister by Sir James Morgan of Llantarnam. Lewis had been chaplain to Lady Morgan at Llantarnam and Thomas Gunter of Abergavenny may have been involved as an attorney. Dorothy James lost her case after incurring considerable legal expenses, and had been heard threatening to wash her hands in Lewis's blood.

Site of the Golden Lion Inn, Frogmore Street, Abergavenny, where David
Lewis was taken after his arrest. The existing building is modern.
(Photograph by Jeremy Knight)

After James gave evidence that he and his wife had received mass from Lewis, he
was remanded in custody.[30]

What followed was curious. Arnold and Price were friends of Lewis and
throughout the three magistrates treated him with an oddly jocular courtesy,
though Arnold was not above making coarse jokes calling Lewis 'the pretended
bishop of Llandaff' or offering to show him 'his doll'—a grotesque effigy of the
pope. The contrast between the travelled and intellectual Lewis and the coarse
grained country squires comes over in Lewis's account not without a certain
humour. The party now adjourned to the dining room, a large room with a long
shuffle board table and a smaller square table, in which the four had supper
together. Afterwards, Thomas Lewis asked him if he would prefer to stay in
town at the inn, or at Arnold's house, Llanvihangel Court. Arnold assured
David Lewis that he would be 'most civilly entertained'. Thomas Lewis then
said 'why then, by consent, Mr Arnold, let my namesake be your guest this
night'. 'Content' said all.[31]

It was now 10 p.m. on a moonlit November night. Word had spread through
the town that Lewis was a prisoner and a large crowd had gathered outside.
Lewis spent the night at Llanvihangel Court and the next day was transferred

to Monmouth prison, where sympathisers procured for him a good lower room, at 14 shillings a week for the chamber, bed, linen, fire and candles and attendance. On 13 January Lewis was taken to Usk to the new gaol. There was deep snow. When the party stopped at an inn in Raglan, Lewis was sought out by a messenger from his fellow Jesuit, Walter Price of Clytha, who had been forced to flee in the winter weather, 'searched after ... by his own kinsman', Charles Price of Llanfoist. Price was now dying of exposure in a nearby barn, and entreated Lewis to visit him, but this was obviously impossible. Three days later, Lewis received news of Price's death and of his burial at Raglan. Later, his grave was opened by Charles Price to confirm his identity and because of rumours that he had been buried with a heavy gold cross.[32]

Price was not the only priest to die of his hardships. Father Andrews of Hardwick 'weakly ... and much stricken in years' fled to his brother Thomas Andrews in Skenfrith, who hid him in a wood for three months. He was then taken to the house of a widow, Jane Harris. She went to a butchers to get him fresh meat, but the butcher was suspicious 'for she was not in a condition to buy it for herself' and informed Arnold. Price fled yet again, but Jane Harris was committed to the Common Jail at Usk, where she still was some months later. No more was heard of Andrews until the end of June, when a farmer found his shallow grave in a barn at Werngochen in Llantilio Pertholey, a former monastic chapel. Another Monmouthshire Jesuit, Charles Pritchard, died in the house of a friend with whom he had taken refuge on 14 March 1680, and was secretly buried in a adjacent garden.[33]

Engraving of St David Lewis by Alex Vost from Brevis Relatio Felicis Agonis quam pro Religione Subierunt *(Prague 1683).* *(National Portrait Gallery)*

On 28 March, Lewis was back in Monmouth for trial before a single judge, Sir Robert Atkins. It was normal practice until recent times for gentry to sit on the bench alongside the Assize judges. Arnold, who may have been a kinsman of Atkins, seated himself on the judge's right hand and proceeded to challenge potential jurors of Lewis's 'neighbourhood or acquaintance' (of whom, says Lewis, there were many) until a jury satisfactory to Arnold had been chosen. There was no mention of any 'Plot' and the only charge was that of being a priest under the Treason Act of 1585.[34]

The witnesses against Lewis were an odd assortment of former catholics. They included Dorothy and William James, John James and a former Court dwarf, Mayne Trott, who had left Court under a cloud and was now a henchman of Arnold's. Trott's late wife had been a kinsman of David Lewis. They gave evidence that he had celebrated Mass, performed baptisms and weddings, including the marriage of Thomas Gunter's daughter, and preached in Welsh and English. Dorothy James was rebuked by the judge for laughing maliciously in court after giving her evidence, but others testified very unwillingly, despite pressure from Arnold. John James gave evidence under obvious agony of mind and Katherine Thomas refused to say more than that she had seen Lewis at Mass 'do what you please with me'. One Londoner at the trial was sure that he had often seen Lewis in his 'Great periwig' in Ferris's Coffee House, inferring that Lewis mixed with London society. The only allegations that Lewis denied were the claim by Dorothy James that he had received £8 in silver and a gold piece to free her father's soul from purgatory, and the pamphlets claiming that he had been arrested in a subterranean hiding place under a clay floor. The former fitted well into the propaganda stereotype of a greedy and corrupt priesthood and received wide publicity from the spin doctors and tabloid journalists of the day, even appearing as a topical joke in a stage play. The outcome of the trial was inevitable, and Lewis was sentenced to the terrible death of hanging, drawing and quartering reserved for treason. A secular priest, Walter Jones, and the Benedictine, William Pugh, were tried at the same assizes, but acquitted for lack of the second witness needed in cases of treason. In addition 14 catholics were bound over for refusing the oath of allegiance, and nine others sent to prison.[35]

By now, the alleged 'Popish Plot' was running out of steam. The executions of Lewis and the other priests was respited until further orders, on the king's instructions. In the month after Lewis's trial, the House of Lords ordered that priests under sentence of death should be brought to London in the hope of obtaining fresh evidence. Lewis, the aged John Kemble from Welsh Newton, just over the border in Herefordshire, and two others were brought up to London and lodged in a single cell at Newgate, where they were interrogated by Oates, Bedloe and others. Shaftesbury and Oates were now desperate to shore up the credibility of the plot. There were rumours that Shaftesbury himself had interviewed the convicted priests and offered them a pardon if they would confess and Lewis confirmed on the scaffold that he had been that to save his life and increase his fortunes he must 'make some discovery of the plot' or conform to the protestant religion. This mixture of threats and concealed promises did not work.[36] The four priests were taken back to their 'home prisons' in a coach, through hostile crowds in some towns. At Usk though, the sympathetic townspeople 'stared and pittied me' wrote Lewis 'thinking I came there to dye, and my executioner with me.' But there were still hopes that the sentences would not be carried out. On 12 June Lewis wrote 'hear I am, and well yet', although shortly after his return from London there was a muster of the county militia in Usk during which four drunken junior officers tried to break into the prison to murder him.[37]

The king delayed signing the death warrants in the hope that the 'Plot' would blow over. However, the political crisis following the fall of Charles's minister Danby in April resulted in the virulently anti-catholic Shaftesbury becoming Lord President of the Privy Council. A Bill to exclude the king's catholic brother James from the succession was going through a hostile House of Commons and the king was forced into a corner. Eventually on 11 July 1679 Parliament issued an order to the Assize Judges that they were to confirm the death sentences and see that they were carried out. Early on the morning of Wednesday 16 July word was brought to Lewis's bedside that Atkins was to return to Monmouthshire to confirm the death sentences, although official notice of this had not yet arrived. 'The next approaching Assizes will clear the matter' wrote Lewis, noting that Monmouth assizes were due to open on the Feast of St Augustine of Hippo (28 August) 'My God patron'. In the event, the Assizes were brought forward and the feast of St David Lewis (27 August) now stands next to that of St Augustine in the calendar of saints days.[38]

With Atkins on the Oxford circuit was Lord Chief Justice Scroggs, a foul mouthed and lecherous drunk ('like so many able men of that day' remarks Trevelyan), but who had, earlier that month, taken the first step in discrediting Oates when he was exposed as a liar and three Benedictine monks and the Queen's physician were acquitted of conspiring to poison the king.[39] On 31 July at Monmouth he confirmed the sentence on Lewis and Atkins signed the warrant before proceeding to Hereford, where they confirmed those on John Kemble and William Lloyd, brother of the Cardiff martyr, John Lloyd, though the latter died before execution. Cardiff lay in a different legal circuit, but Arnold had been involved in the arrest of Philip Evans. The strategy may have been intended to humiliate Worcester by the executions of priests in the three county towns where his influence was strongest. Lewis's execution may have been transferred from Monmouth, in view of the town's catholic tradition, to the more puritan inclined Usk, where it was hoped that sympathy for the victim would be less strong. The whole episode was marked, as Kenyon has observed, with a 'vicious obstinacy unique even at that time'. It is not hard to see the hand of Arnold behind this.[40] The High Sheriff, James Herbert of Coldbrook, found pretexts to delay Lewis's execution and Arnold, fearful that the volatile political climate would change and Lewis be reprieved, sent after Atkins, still on his Assize circuit, at Shrewsbury and Worcester, complaining of the delay. 'There now it lies' wrote Lewis, concluding his prison diary.

On 27 August 1679 Lewis was taken from the gaol near Usk bridge to the place of execution at a spot known as the Island, close to the site of the present Catholic church of St Francis Xavier and St David Lewis in Porth Y Carn Street. The transfer of the execution from the normal venue at Monmouth meant that the scaffold was an improvised affair (there were rumours that no local carpenter was prepared to carry out the work) and Lewis had to stand on a stool in a trench dug under a scaffold beam supported on a pair of forked posts. The 63-year-old Jesuit, who in 1642 had preached before Pope Urban VIII in Rome, now preached his last and most remarkable sermon. He took his

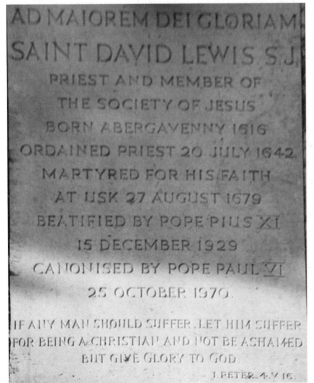

text from I Peter 4, vv.15-16: 'let none of you suffer as a murderer or thief, but if as a Christian, let him not be ashamed'. At the conclusion of the sermon, Lewis was hanged, but the crowd would not allow him to be cut down until he was dead.[41]

In the event Lewis's body was not quartered, but the spectators, led by the Under-Sheriff, escorted his body in a solemn procession to its burial place near the west end of St Mary's church. His tomb inscription 'Here Lies the body of Edward Lewis, who was condemned for a priest and a Jesuit, and executed the 27 August 1679 *Beati mortui qui in Domino Moriuntur*' (Blessed be the dead that die in the

Modern memorial to St David Lewis,
on the probable site of his burial, Usk Priory.
The biblical quotation was the text of his scaffold
sermon, 27 August 1679.
(Photograph by Jeremy Knight)

The attic chapel served by St John Lloyd survives in the roof space of Trivor, St Maughans. A niche in its east wall probably marks the position of an altar or cross. Drawing by Fred Hando in Journeys in Gwent *1951 (by courtesy of Chris Barber)*

Lord) was seen by a friend of the antiquary Thomas Hearne in 1734, but has since disappeared.[42] Between 20 June and 27 August, 13 priests had been executed in London and elsewhere, including seven Jesuits, though thankfully David Lewis was the last. Of the priests active in Monmouthshire before the Oates Plot, Philip Evans, John Lloyd and Lewis had been executed, Thomas Andrews, Charles Pritchard and Walter Price had died as fugitives in the bitter winter weather and William Lloyd had died in prison. Of the six Jesuits, only two or three remained. Under James II, the Franciscans opened missions in Monmouth and Abergavenny, the latter financed by Thomas Gunter's daughter, but by 1773 there were only nine catholic priests in Wales, few of them native or Welsh speaking.[43]

The chapel in Thomas Gunter's house at Abergavenny was rediscovered in 1908 when a new owner inserted stairs to a long disused attic in an Inn in Cross Street, once the Parrot, later the Cardiff Arms. Originally, the attic had only an external first floor door, and a lath and plaster partition had to be removed for access. The removal of lime wash revealed a painted altar piece representing the Nativity. on the sloping eastern ceiling of the attic. There were also painted graffiti and initials, including 'T[homas] G[unter] His Mark' and a crude drawing of a man in long black clothes adoring the matchstick figure of a woman. Above a little window looking out into Cross Street was the monogram IHS (the 'mark of the Jesuits' complained of by Arnold) on a red heart within a green oval, surrounded by golden rays, with a cross above.[44] Papers

Gunter House, Abergavenny. (Photograph by Jeremy Knight)

belonging to Thomas Gunter were found under the floorboards, including household bills, letters, a document relating to Thomas Gunter senior's sequestration, legal documents, a piece of music for the viol, and a valentine.[45]

The Mystery of Jackanapes Lane
Whilst Lewis was in prison in March 1679, the first Parliamentary election since 1661 took place. Worcester hoped to replace Sir Trevor Williams with his son, Charles Herbert, in one of the county seats. Williams in fact defeated Worcester's son, who was then left to fight Arnold for the Monmouth Boroughs seat. Arnold lost, but challenged the result and had it overturned by the Commons. The three members for Monmouthshire were thus Arnold, Williams and Sir

Gunter house, Abergavenny c.1907, and graffiti (© Abergavenny Museum)

*The rediscovered altar painting of the nativity from the catholic chapel in the
Gunter House, now in Abergavenny Museum. Drawing by Fred Hando in*
Out and About in Monmouthsire *1958 (by courtesy of Chris Barber)*

William Morgan. Nationally, a Whig government was returned, though the king
refused to allow it to sit. Later that year, there was a pope-burning in
Abergavenny, with the dwarf Mayne Trott, armed with a blunderbuss, as master
of ceremonies. 'Two lusty sow gelders with very large and shrill flagallets' led
the procession with a figure of the pope 'richly adorned with relics, pictures,
beads, bells and other superstitious emblems'—no doubt the 'doll' which
Arnold had offered to show to David Lewis. There were placards of the
Gunpowder Plot and the murder of Sir Edmund Berry Godfrey, but the carnival
proved unpopular with the townspeople, since it interfered with the annual fair.
Pope burnings were rare outside London, and usually celebrated Guy Fawkes
day or the accession of Elizabeth I on 17 November. Arnold's Abergavenny
pope-burning emphasises the relationship between political agitation in
London and events in Monmouthshire.[46]

The 'Plot' had by now imploded, but the search for fresh evidence
continued. When a suspected coiner and money clipper with links to
Abergavenny was arrested at the end of December, he was questioned about his
knowledge of the plot. In the February after the execution, Arnold and Bedloe
accused Thomas Herbert of Usk of seditious libel and alleged that Thomas
Gunter had used dangerous or seditious words against the king.

The allegations against Herbert were referred to the Privy Council, but the hearing was postponed repeatedly when Arnold failed to show up.[47] On 16 April the Privy Council issued an ultimatum, calling on Arnold to substantiate his allegations. The night before the deadline, Arnold claimed to have been beaten up in Jackanapes Lane in Little Lincoln's Inn Fields off Fleet Street. Three men in grey cloaks, one of whom he recognised as John Giles, Chief Constable of Usk and a friend of Herbert, had thrown a cloak over his head, dragged him into the lane and stabbed him with a rapier, wounding him several times, though he was saved, he claimed, by his whalebone corset. One of them then pulled out a knife and tried to cut his throat. Arnold claimed that one assailant 'bid him pray for the soul of Evans, a priest, whom Mr Arnold had prosecuted and … was executed in Monmouthshire'. Most historians have considered Arnold's wounds self-inflicted, but John Giles was arrested. A catholic, he had been 'very active at the Execution, dipping cloaths in Lewis his blood' and this and the fact that he gone around Usk denying that any plot existed may have brought the paranoid anger of Arnold upon him. The affair led to a flurry of pamphlets, with Arnold trying to restore his rapidly diminishing credit by setting himself up as a popular martyr in place of Sir Edmund Berry Godfrey. The unfortunate Giles was tried at the Old Bailey before Judge Jeffreys. It was alleged that he had taken a broken sword to an Usk sword cutler for repair and a series of witnesses who gave him an alibi were dismissed as 'for the most part Welsh people'. Giles was sentenced to stand in the pillories at Lincoln's Inn Fields, Grays Inn and the Maypole in the Strand for one hour each, pay a fine of £500 and be bound over to be of good behaviour. The fine was well beyond his means, and he was still in prison in May 1683, yearning to be home with his wife and children who were in 'a very sad condition', she having had her goods seized by the sheriff for catholicism.[48]

In November 1680, 34 catholics who had been remanded the previous Michaelmas appeared before the Quarter Sessions. The five magistrates included John Arnold; Sir James Herbert of Coldbrook (who had delayed the execution of Lewis); Charles Herbert; Trevor Morgan, son of Sir Thomas Morgan of Tredegar; and Captain Wolseley, Lieutenant-Governor of Chepstow Castle. Three were allies or clients of Worcester. The catholics were asked why judgement should not be given against them, whereupon they 'put on their hats and went laughing out of court'. The Sheriff, Thomas Morgan of Penrhos near Caerleon, who's daughter was a catholic and married to the Marquis of Worcester's agent, John Curre, did nothing to stop them and was alleged to have joined in the laughter. Arnold vented his anger on Francis Jenkins, the Under Sheriff, who was committed as a prisoner to the Sergeant at Arms.[49]

The king was still refusing to allow the Whig Parliament to sit and Arnold was feeling the strain. There were rumours that he was involved in a conspiracy to establish a Presbyterian republic. In May 1680 he wrote to Hugh Speke that he was tired and confined to his chamber 'being very weak and my cough very bad'. Returning home from Gloucester he had been met at Ross and Monmouth by 'hundreds of my friends' and 'almost hugged to death'. He anticipated another election, 'and I am confident that we are 20 to 1 against the great lord'. By the following year his mental state was unstable. He was assaulting strangers in the street and accusing them of popery. There were also allegations that he was inciting his followers to 'stab and kill' supporters of the Duke of York and the Marquis of Worcester and had supported Thomas Bassett, a seditious headmaster of Monmouth School. Sir Trevor Williams was accused of fomenting trouble in Monmouthshire among the youth of the county and nonconformists 'over barrels of ale', with Arnold as his chief of staff.

By the summer of 1681, the king had regained political control, and Shaftesbury was in prison charged with treason. The tide had turned. In 1684 Beaufort sued Arnold and Williams for *scandalum magnatum*, libel against a peer. Williams was fined £20,000, Arnold £10,000 and both were in prison for a considerable time.[50] At the election on the accession of James II in 1685, they lost their Parliamentary seats to Worcester and Sir James Herbert. In the same year, Nathan Rogers was imprisoned in Chepstow Castle for six weeks during the Monmouth Rebellion, and remained 'harrass'd and oppressed by the Tory High-Flying Party, till the Happy and Prosperous descent of our great Deliverer the late King William of Glorious Memory' in 1688.[51]

Arnold, Williams and his son John Williams sat in the new Convention Parliament of 1688, but lost their seats two years later. Their anti-catholic crusade continued, however. In 1690 Arnold and Matthew Powell, son of Walter Powell, summoned suspected catholics in the Hundred of Skenfrith to Grosmont to take the Oaths of Allegiance and Supremacy. In the same year the garrison of Chepstow Castle marched out for the last time and its guns were shipped to Chester for the Williamite war in Ireland.[52] On William III's return from his victory over James II at the Battle of the Boyne, he stayed with the Duke of Beaufort at Badminton. Beaufort's chaplain offered the usual prayers for the king, but onlookers noted that he omitted William's Christian name, so that it was uncertain which king he was praying for.[53]

Monmouthshire had undergone much change since 1640, and the period of actual fighting was only part of this. The catholic Worcesters were gone from Raglan. Although the protestant Tory Beauforts were still a power in the land, they were a distant presence. In the next century they shared power in the county with their Whig rivals, the Morgans of Tredegar. The once vigorous catholic community survived, and was still influential in some of its old strongholds, particularly Monmouth itself and a few places in central Monmouthshire. Elsewhere it was a spent force. It could no longer look to Raglan for support. Its priests had undergone the holocaust of the so-called Popish Plot and the catholic gentry who had supported and protected them were now politically powerless non-jurors, who in any case shared the demographic crisis of early 18th-century gentry. The psychological damage to the community was equally great. Many catholic girls from gentry families now went abroad as nuns rather than marry, reducing still further the pool of eligible marriage partners (and of dowries). A number of Monmouthshire catholic families ended in 18th-century French or Belgian nunneries. The established church had changed relatively little. It still had many poorly paid livings, leading to problems of pluralism and non-residence. However, the puritan expulsions of its clergy and the prohibition (however ineffective) of the Book of Common Prayer had given it a firmer sense of identity.

Though the short lived puritan regime failed at national level because of its inability to achieve a stable political settlement, in Wales it left a permanent legacy of religious nonconformity and political radicalism. In Gwent there were now Baptist, Independent or Quaker causes in most towns, and many villages, sometimes in former catholic strongholds. The county was to undergo another social revolution, this time industrial, at the end of the following century. The iron and coal industries which were to create it already existed on a small scale, awaiting the changes in ironmaking and transport technology, and the capital accumulation of the coming century. When the conflicts of that second revolution came, people from both sides of the political divide were keenly aware of their Civil War legacy, and anxious to promote their own versions of it. The Chartists took the six points of the People's Charter from radical Cromwellian thinkers. Samuel Etheridge, the radical Newport printer and antiquarian, produced a new edition of Nathan

In the 18th century, much of Monmouthsire was still Welsh speaking. This inn sign of 1719 on the Green house, Llantarnam, yards from the spot where St David Lewis was arrested, offers 'Cwrw da A seidir i chwi. Dewch y mewn Chwi gewch y brofi' — Good Beer and Cider for you. Come in, you shall taste it. (Photograph by Jeremy Knight)

Rogers's *Memoirs of Monmouthshire* in 1826, an election year, when the power of the Beauforts, attacked so bitterly by Rogers, was again being challenged. Thomas Wakeman, writing to his fellow antiquary, Ocatvius Morgan, in 1862 about the 1271 Wentwood Survey, compared Rogers with the Chartist, John Frost. Rogers was a 'violent puritan, and no doubt a troublesome meddling fellow, very much after the fashion of a noisy personage in your own neighbourhood in the present day.'[54] To some extent indeed, the Civil War is still a live issue in the county, reflecting the divide between radical, nonconformist industrial Gwent and rural agricultural Monmouthshire.

Chronology

1625		Accession of Charles I
1629–1640		Period of personal rule
1640	13 April–5 May	Short Parliament
	3 November	Long Parliament meet
1642	29 March	Parliament orders that county armoury be moved to Newport
	April	Dispute re county armoury
	23 April	King refused entry to Hull
	17 May	Monmouthshire Parliamentary petition
	12 July	Parliament votes to raise an army under the Earl of Essex
	22 August	King raises his standard at Nottingham
	17 September	Sir Edward Stradling's Regiment at Newport
	30 September	Stamford captures Hereford for Parliament
	3 October	Hertford flees to Cardiff, raises troops there
	do.	Royalists seize Cardiff, Newport and Caerleon castles
	23 October	Battle of Edgehill
	4 November	Hertford and Herbert advance on Hereford
	13 November	Skirmish at Pontrilas
	14 December	Stamford abandons Hereford, Royalists re-occupy
1643	9 January	Hertford leaves for Oxford. Edward Herbert Commander in Chief, south Wales and Marches
	5 February	Edward Herbert holds Council of War at Hereford
	6 February	Local gentry meet at Rockfield, pay 'Benevolence'
	7 February	Herbert advances into Forest of Dean. Skirmish at Coleford
	25 March	Waller crosses Severn at Framilode passage
	27 March	Herbert's army surrounded and captured at Highnam
	4 April	Waller takes Monmouth
	5 April	Waller takes Usk
	6 April	Waller takes Chepstow
	10 April	Waller retreats from Chepstow
	11 April	Cave reoccupies Monmouth for Royalists
	15 April	Royalist muster at Hereford
	22 April	Prince Maurice recalls Cave. Waller advances. Herbert to Oxford to seek help
	23 April	Waller captures Monmouth
	25 April	Waller captures Hereford
	28 April	Chepstow taken by amphibious attack, but re-taken by Royalists
	June	Vavasour made Colonel-General under Herbert
	26 July	Prince Rupert takes Bristol
	10 August	King besieges Gloucester
	5 September	King abandons siege of Gloucester
	20 September	First Battle of Newbury
		Sir John Wintour fortifies Lydney for the King

1644	6 January	Prince Rupert made commander of western regional army
	20 January	Massey makes amphibious raid on Chepstow
	2 July	Royalist defeat at the Battle of Marston Moor
	26 September	Monmouth taken by Massey
	28 September	Royalist attack on Wonastow House repulsed
1645	22 February	Royalists fortify Lancaut, driven out by Massey's brother
	March	Edward Herbert leaves for Ireland
	1 July	King at Abergavenny
	3 July	King at Raglan
	10 July	Battle of Langport (Somerset), Royalist defeat
	16 July	King to Cardiff
	17 July	King meets Glamorgan Commissioners
	19 July	King at Tredegar House
	20 July	King at Raglan
	22 July	Council of War at Crick
	24 July	Council of War at Crick
	25 July	King meets Monmouthshire Commissioners at Usk
	26–30 July	King at Ruperra
	29 July	King meets Glamorgan levies at Cefn Onn
	1 August	Glamorgan levies adopt name 'Peaceable Army'
	8 August	Astley calls meeting of gentry at Abergavenny for relief of Hereford. Sir Trevor Williams and others refuse to co-operate
	1 September	Meeting of Monmouthshire gentry at Penperllini
	2 September	King relieves Hereford
	7 September	King at Raglan
	10 September	Rupert surrenders Bristol to Parliament
	11 September	King summons Trevor Williams and others before him at Abergavenny. News arrives of fall of Bristol. Sir Trevor Williams changes sides. Peaceable army declare for Parliament
	2 October	Chepstow town taken by Sir Trevor Williams
	11 October	Chepstow Castle taken by Colonel Thomas Morgan
	24 October	Monmouth Castle taken by Morgan and Williams
	23 November	People of Brecon demolish own fortifications, declare for Parliament
	5 December	Royalists attack Parliamentary garrison of Abergavenny
	18 December	Hereford taken by Colonels Birch and Morgan
1646	22 January	Raglan horse rout parliamentary recruits at Caerleon
	24 January	Raglan horse attack Abergavenny
		Raglan horse attack Monmouth
		Charles Hughes of Trostrey submits to Parliament
	6 February	Royalists attack Cardiff
		Battle of the Heath, Cardiff
		General Thomas Morgan garrisons Llanarth

	14 March	Royalists surrender in Cornwall
	22 March	Last Royalist field army surrenders at Stow in the Wold
	13 April	Trevor Williams skirmishes with Raglan garrison near Monmouth
		Charles Prodger submits to Parliament
		Trevor Williams skirmishes with Raglan garrison at Usk
	20 May	Parliamentarians raid Raglan, seize horses
	24 May	Parliamentarians skirmish with garrison in Raglan village. Raglan garrison set fire to village, retreat into castle
	25 May	Siege of Raglan begins, Walter Powell imprisoned at Raglan
	6 June	Walter Powell freed
	28 June	General Thomas Morgan summons garrison
	5 August	Fairfax arrives at Raglan
	15 August	Marquis of Worcester opens negotiations for surrender
	19 August	Surrender of Raglan Castle
	25 August	Parliament orders demolition of Raglan Castle
	October	Marquis of Worcester taken to London
	18 December	Death of Marquis of Worcester
	25 December	Marquis buried at Windsor
1647	30 March	Kyrle orders demolition of Monmouth defences
	12 June	Glamorgan rising
	22 December	Keep of Monmouth Castle collapses
	27 December	Monmouth de-garrisoned
1648	23 March	Laugharne, Poyer and Powell seize Pembroke Castle
	1 May	Cromwell leaves London for South Wales
	8 May	Battle of St Fagans
	10 May	Royalists seize Chepstow Castle. Cromwell at Monmouth
	25 May	Ewer captures Chepstow Castle
	17 June	Cromwell orders arrest of Trevor Williams
	11 July	Surrender of Pembroke Castle
	6 December	Pride's Purge, moderates expelled from Commons.
1649	30 January	Execution of Charles I
1649–1653		The Commonwealth
1650	February	Act for Propagation of the Gospel in Wales
1652	August	Separated Baptist cause first meets in Abergavenny
1653	20 April	Cromwell dissolves the Rump
	4 July–12 Dec.	Cromwell's First Parliament ('Barebone's Parliament')
	16 December	Cromwell installed as Lord Protector
1654	August	Ordinance for ejecting scandalous ministers
	September	First Protectorate Parliament
1656–8		Second Protectorate Parliament
1656–7		Rule of the Major-Generals
1658	3 September	Death of Oliver Cromwell
1659	27 Jan.–22 April	Richard Cromwell's Parliament

	6 May	Rump Parliament restored
1660	1 January	Monck's army enters England from Scotland
	9 February	Monck enters London
	25 April	Convention Parliament meets
	1 May	Charles II's Declaration of Breda read to Parliament
	29 May	Charles II enters London (Oak apple day)

References

Abbreviations

Acts Ord. Interr.	Acts and Ordinances of the Interregnum
Add. Mss	Additional Manuscripts (British Library)
Arch. Camb	Archaeologia Cambrensis
B.L.	British Library
Bod.L.	Bodleian Library
Bradney J.A.	Bradney *History of Monmouthshire*
Cal. Cttee Adv.Mon.	Calendar of the Committee for the Advance of Money
Cal. Cttee. Comp.	Calendar of the Committee for Compounding
C.C.L.	Cardiff Central Library
C.S.P.D.	Calendar of State Papers, Domestic
C.S.P.V.	Calendar of State Papers, Venetian
D.N.B.	*Dictionary of National Biography*
D.W.B.	*Dictionary of Welsh Biography*
E.H.R.	*English Historical Review*
H.M.C.	Historical Manuscripts Commission
M.C.A.A.	Monmouthshire and Caerleon Antiquarian Association
Mon. Ant.	Monmouthshire Antiquary
N.A.: P.R.O.	The National Archives: Public Record Office
N.L.W.	National Library of Wales
N.R.L.	Newport Reference Library
S.A.L.	Society of Antiquaries Library, London.
T.T.	British Library, Thomason Tracts
W.H.R.	*Welsh History Review*

Introduction

1. Joshua Sprigge *Anglia Rediviva*, 300. Bayly *Apophthegm* no. 38. Some sources associate this passage with the existing Oriel window of the Great Hall. It could though refer to the window of the Great Chamber above and to one side, which would have commanded a view of Fairfax and his staff entering the Outer Ward in front of the main facade of the castle.
2. Clarendon *History of the Rebellion* V, 288-9.
3. See Clive Holmes 'County Community in Stuart Historiography' and *Seventeenth Century Lincolnshire* 1-5 and Ronald Hutton *Royalist War Effort* (2nd ed). xvi- xvii, xxxv.
4. Arthur Clark *Raglan Castle and the Civil War in Monmouthshire* (Chepstow 1953). Clark was senior history master at Jones's West Monmouth Grammar School, Pontypool, and the writer is glad to acknowledge his debt to his first mentor in historical studies. Warmington *Civil War, Interregnum and Restoration in Gloucestershire 1640–1672*; Underdown *Somerset in the Civil War and Interregnum*. Gaunt has argued that the war should be seen not as 'one civil war, but numerous regional conflicts, often with little ... communication between the various theatres' *The Cromwellian Gazetteer* (1987), p.x.
5. P.R.O. S.P. 23, Vol. 253, 96. *Cal Cttee Comp* 364 (29 November 1650). Aylmer notes the similar dearth in Herefordshire, with no Quarter Sessions or Commission of the Peace records before the Restoration.' Who was ruling in Herefordshire' 373.
6. Bradney *Diary of Walter Powell*.
7. *Letter from a Gentleman in Gloucestershire* 13-21; Foley *Records of the English Province* vol.6, 432.
8. Philip Jenkins 'Anti-popery on the Welsh Marches' 281.
9. Quoted W.S.K. Thomas *Stuart Wales* (Llandysul 1988), 204.

Chapter 1 Religious Change & Conflict in Stuart Monmouthshire

1. Pugh 'Monmouthshire recusants', 110. Mathias *Whitsun Riot* The Gunpowder plot led to stricter legislation on Catholic baptisms, marriages and burials. Thereafter, clandestine nightime burials became common, e.g. Powell *Diary* 20 January, 4 February 1640 (1641). Smith 'Herefordshire Catholics'. Foley (*Records* IV, 369) gave an incorrect reference (P.R.O. S.P. 14/14/52) for the Caerleon episode and McCoog was unable to trace it. ('Soc of Jesus' 5).
2. Mark Redknap 'The medieval wooden crucifix figure from Kemeys Inferior and its church' *Mon.Ant.* 16 (2000), 11-43. Edward Morgan- P.R.O. Star Chamber 8 James I 207/28, Owen *Wales in the Reign of James I* 83-5. Eure- *C.S.P.D. 1603-10*, 553.
3. Thomas *Welsh Catholic Martyrs* 9-17; Haigh *Reformation and Resistance* 249; Coffey *Persecution and Toleration* 85-93.
4. *H.M.C. Manuscripts of the Dean and Chapter of Wells* II (1914), 346-7. Pugh 'Monmouthshire recusants', 108. George Morris *clericus* 1588, Walter Powell *clericus* 1601–1608. *Alumni Oxoniensis* lists two George Morriss at about the right date, but neither seems to be our man.
5. J.H. Canning 'A Monmouthshire martyr'. Ellis *Catholic Martyrs* 36-9.

6. Augustine Baker *Memorials*, 81. Mathias *Whitsun Riot* 121-6. Meredith is not easy to identify. Abergavenny recusants in 1607- 8 included Jane Meredith, a widow and Isabel, wife of John Meredith, yeoman. Watson also referred to a Meredith whose seat was west of Abergavenny (Mathias 123).

7. *C.S.P.D. 1603-10* 253. P.R.O. *State Papers Domestic* S P 14/216 pt 1 (Gunpowder Treason Book) f. 128, Owen 76. Possibly William Vaughan of Tretower, the only Justice of that name active at the time (albeit on the Brecon bench.). Phillips *Justices of the Peace* 261-2. Mathias (p.125) suggests Henry Vaughan of Moccas and Rowland Vaughan of Whitehouse.

8. *H.M.C. Salisbury Mss XVIII* (1940), 35-6. Mathias *Whitsun Riot* 126-7.

9. B.L. *Harleian Ms 280*, fol. 157-164, Owen *Catalogue of Welsh Manuscripts* 1, 124. Bod. L. *Tanner Ms 146*. 1603- 145 Popish recusants in St Davids diocese, 381 in Llandaff diocese in Monmouthshire and Glamorgan. 1605- 21 men, 24 women Glamorgan; 336 (140 men, 196 women) Monmouthshire.

10. Haigh *Reformation and Resistance* 1-19.

11. M. Gray 'Change and continuity' 12-13. Wilcrick- *Cal. Comm.Comp* 3195, 3221.

12. *D.W.B.* 547-8, 645 (A.H. Dodd).

13. *C.S.P.D. 1581–1590*, 374. Do. 297, (1585) complaining of 'divers seminary priests and their receivers' in Monmouthshire.

14. *C.S.P.D. 1603–1610*, 553, Eure to Earl of Salisbury, 23 October 1609.

15. Pugh 'Monmouthshire recusants', Bradney 3.2 *Hundred of Usk* 250-52, 263-5. 'Anglican' (as an adjective) is first attested in 1635, but as a noun, describing an individual, only in 1797. The Compton census of 1676 uses the term 'conformist', as opposed to a nonconformist or a papist.

16. *Memorials of Father Augustine Baker* A.H. Dodd *D.W.B.* 22-23. Augustine Baker, Leander Jones and Clement Rayner *Apostolatus Benedictinorum in Anglia* (1626). M.D. Knowles 'The value of 16th and 17th century scholarship' in Levi Fox (ed.) *English Historical Scholarship in the Sixteenth and Seventeenth Centuries* (London 1956). Graham Parry *The Trophies of Time: English Antiquarians of the Seventeenth Century* (Oxford 1995), 70-71 and n.2.

17. Foley *Records* V, 912. Ellis *Catholic Martyrs* 178.

18. Nathaniel Pritchard- P.R.O. S.P. 23, Vol 17, 643. *Acts Ord. Interr* ii, 629, 637. *Cal. Cttee. Comp.* 3077. Originally sequestrated as a delinquent (royalist) and recusant, he appealed against the former charge and won his appeal. He was one of the ten capital burgesses of Abergavenny under the charter of 1638- Bradney 1.2 *Hundred of Abergavenny* 153.

19. Foley *Records of the English Province* V (series XII), 912-13. Canning 'Titus Oates plot', 160. Foley (p. 633) was unable to trace a Jesuit named John Pritchard. Charles Pritchard (1634–1680), though also a Monmouthshire man and a Jesuit, was a separate person.

20. Bradney 1.2a *Hundred of Abergavenny* 160. Symonds *Diary of the Marches of the Royal Army* 233. M. Gray 'Change and continuity' 13-16. Gunter 'Family of Gunter'. Walter Powell *Diary* 12 Jan 1648. 'Tho' Gunter dismissed because he had no good lease' *Cal. Comm. Comp.* V, 3233 (3 April 1655). Abergavenny Museum- Gunter Mss.

21. Thomas Gunter- *Commons Journal* ix, 467a. On the chapel see pp.171-2.

22. Bradney 1.2a *Hundred of Abergavenny* 199. Newman *Royalist Officers* nos.1181-2, p.307. *Alumni Oxoniensis* 1215. Only two officers of Prodger's Regiment are known- Captain Poyntz (on whom see n. below) and Lt William Jones of Monmouth. Reid *Royalist Army* III, 146.

23. Bradney 1.1a *Hundred of Abergavenny* 183-5.

24. *Monmouthshire Wills* no.84, pp.42-3. He appears both as 'John William, tanner' and as 'John William Tanner'.

25. *C.S.P.D. 1619–32*, 232. H.M.C. *Salisbury (Cecil) Mss XXIV, Addenda 1605–1668* 262. Notestein, Relf and Simpson *Commons Debates 1621* Vol 2, 544-5.

26. P.R.O. *Star Chamber* 8 James 1 207/30. D. Owen 108-9. David Morgan, Gentleman, was fined as a recusant four times between July 1607 and March 1624. Pugh 'Monmouthshire recusants' 85-105.

27. Thomas Churchyard *Worthines of Wales* (1587- edition of 1776), 21.

28. P.R.O. *Star Chamber* 8 James 1st (1609–10), 308/12, *Star Chamber Proceedings Relating to Wales* Complaints against George Langley of Caerleon, recusant convict, for purchase of meal in Christchurch whilst in dispute, forcible entry, cutting grass, assault and smuggling.

29. Pugh *Monmouthshire Recusants* 109. *Monmouthshire Wills* A5, p.219.

30. Rea *Popular Culture* 108-11.

31. *Calendar of the Bristol Apprentices Book, 1532–1565* Parts 1-3 (Bristol Record Society Publications XIV (1949), XXXI (1980), XLIII (1992) Philip Langley- Bristol Apprentices Book I, 159. Jones *Monmouthshire Wills* no.107, 166-7. Roberts *Letter Book of John Byrd*.

32. Whiteman *Compton Census*. Thomas *Religion and the Decline of Magic* 159-173. Jenkins 'Anti-popery' 276.

33. William Herbert- A.H. Dodd in *D.W.B.* 355. Despite his puritan sympathies, he was married to a daughter of William Morgan of Llantarnam.

34. *C.S.P.D. 1603–1610*, 553. Eure to Salisbury, 23 October 1609. M. Gray 'Change and continuity 23-6; 'Clergy as Rememberencers' 114; and 'Church in Gwent', with an edition of B.L. *Harleian Ms 595*, giving a full list of impropriations in the county, with their values. A source of *c.*1600 suggested that a stipend of £30–£50 per annum was barely adequate. Holmes *Seventeenth Century Lincolnshire* 56.

35. Bradney 3.2 *Hundred of Usk* 257.

36. Glanmor Williams in *Glamorgan County History IV* (ed. G. Williams), 239-42.

37. Between 1603 and the 1640s the percentage of Lincolnshire clergy with University degrees rose from 37% to 95%. Holmes *Seventeenth Century Lincolnshire* 54.

38. Bradney 1.1. *Hundred of Skenfrith* 47, 52; 4, 1 *Hundred of Caldicot* 122. Collington matriculated at Queen's College, Oxford in 1638. Reinstated at the Restoration, he resigned his living in 1664.

39. Bradney 3.2 *Hundred of Usk* 267. *Alumni Oxoniensis* II, 448. J. Gwynfor Jones 'Gentry of Gwent' 75-6.
40. Anthony Wood *Athenae Oxoniensis* (ed. Bliss, London 1817), 531; Foster *Alumni Oxoniensis* 111. Vaughan was the son of John Vaughan of Caethley in Merioneth. He lived to see the Restoration, but died the following year, still headmaster of Abergavenny Grammar School.
41. Robert Frampton (1604–1685) Bradney 2.1 *Hundred of Raglan* 106-7. Siddons *Visitations of the Heralds* 181. See below, Chapter 6, n 7.
42. E.g. *Monmouthshire Wills* no.28, pp.89-90 no. 87, p.146 no. 114, pp.173 Bradney 2.2 *Hundred of Trellech* 175. do 3.2 *Hundred of Usk* 135-6.
43. Madeleine Gray 'Lewis James'. Edmund Jones 141-2.
44. Monmouthshire Wills no.58, pp.117-18. Bradney 4.2 *Hundred of Caldicot* 28. The family claimed descent from a lieutenant of Edward Neville, steward of Chepstow in 1456. It was extinct by the Civil War.
45. *Monmouthshire Wills* nos.66, p 127 and 142, pp.202-3.
46. *Monmouthshire Wills* no.84, pp.142-3. M. Zell 'The use of religious preambles as a measure of belief in the sixteenth century' *Bull. Institute Hist Research* 50 (1997), 246-9; J.D. Alsop 'Religious preambles in early modern English wills as formulae' *J. Ecclesiastical Hist.* 40 (1989), 19-27. Books gave standard models for wills and the testator may have been more concerned with content than with formulae. However, it is hard to believe that they would have used formulae in conflict with their religious views and those of their family.

Chapter 2 The Anatomy of Stuart Monmouthshire

1. For 'deference', 'neutralist', 'class' and 'localist' models see Underdown *Revel, Riot and Rebellion* 1-8; 'The Chalk and the Cheese' and 'Reply to John Morrill' and J. Morrill 'Ecology of allegiance'. Mark Stoyle *Loyalty and Locality*. According to Richard Baxter 'a very great part of the Knights and Gentry of England and also most of the poorest of the people ... did follow the gentry and were for the King. On the Parliaments side were the smaller part of the gentry in most of the counties, and the greatest part of the tradespeople and freeholders and the middle sort of men, especially in those Corporations and counties which depend on clothing and such manufactures'. M. Sylvester (ed.) *Reliquae Baxterianae* (1696), 30.
2. John Aubrey *Monumenta Britannica* ed. John Fowles (1980), 414-15.
3. Lucy Toulmin Smith *Leland's Itinerary in England and Wales* (London 1906), Vol 3, 43.
4. Lucy Toulmin Smith Vol 3, 43.
5. J.K. Knight 'Newport Castle' *Mon.Ant.* 7 (1991), 17-42.
6. *Monmouthshire Wills* pp.14, 43. William Baker, father of the Benedictine priest Augustine Baker, was a major figure in the Abergavenny wool trade. A.H. Dodd *D.W.B.* 22-3.
7. William Coxe *Historical Tour,* 167-9. Glanmor Williams *Welsh Church*, 353
8. Clarendon *History of the Rebellion* IX, 67. P. Courtney *Medieval and Later Usk Report on the Excavations at Usk 1965–1976* (Cardiff 1994), 139. *Monmouthshire Wills* pp.5, 14, 43. In 1300 Abergavenny was in fifth place, judging by the number of burgesses, behind Chepstow, Usk, Trellech and Newport. (Griffiths 'Very wealthy by merchandise', 230-32.) It evidently escaped the late medieval depopulation that afflicted Trellech and Usk. By 1550 it seems to have been second only to Monmouth. However, as Griffiths has pointed out, these figures depend on a 'limited range of somewhat intractable sources'.
9. *Monmouthshire Wills*, 5. M. Gray 'The last days of the chantries and shrines in Monmouthshire' *J. Welsh Eccles. Hist. Soc* 8 (1991), 21-40. G.C. Boon *Welsh Tokens of the Seventeenth Century* (Cardiff 1973). The number of recorded specimens gives a similar order- Chepstow 24, Abergavenny 18, Caerleon 10, although Monmouth, with 42, outranks the rest, due to one or two particularly prolific issuers, or perhaps an unrecorded hoard.
10. *C.S.P.D 1631–3*, 43; *1634-5*, 145; *1636-7*, 177, 183. P. Slack 'Books of Orders: the making of English social policy 1577–1631.' *Trans. Roy. Hist. Soc.* 5th ser. 30, 1981. Holmes *Seventeenth Century Lincolnshire* 109-112. Robinson *Early Tudor Gwent* 51-2.
11. Stephen Rippon *The Gwent Levels: The Evolution of a Wetland Landscape* (C.B.A. Research Report 105, 1996).
12. *C.S.P.D. 1625–49*, 617.
13. Lhwyd *Parochialia* III 20.
14. Nathan Rogers 87. Lhwyd *Parochialia* III, 21. At the weekly Saturday market at Caerwent, much corn was bought for Bristol.
15. *Monmouthshire Wills* no.94. p.152.
16. P.R.O. Star Chamber, 8 James 1st 308/12, quoted Dyfnallt Owen, 84.
17. There were periodic attempts to make the sale of Welsh butter overseas illegal, but it was possible to circumvent this by the payment of fines. King James tried to establish a monopoly, but in 1621 the Commons passed a bill for the free export of Welsh butter and James agreed a compromise, though he tried to impose a customs duty of 2s. a barrel, equivalent to what he had hoped to raise from the patentees. Dyffnallt Owen 133, quoting P.R.O. E 148 no 3, pt 22. *State Papers Domestic James Ist, 1611–18* vol 94, f 180 'The state of the case concerning the transportation of Welsh butter out of Glamorgan and Monmouthshire'. Larkin and Hughes *Royal Proclamations I*, 518; Larkin *Royal Proclamations II* nos 198, pp.459- 62; 287, pp.678-9; 289, p.687.
18. Dodd *Studies in Stuart Wales* 24.
19. Bradney 4.1 *Hundred of Caldicot* 39. Ivor Waters *The Unfortunate Valentine Morris* (Chepstow 1964), 1.
20. Stoyle *Loyalty and Locality* 244. Edward Herbert to Rupert 25 July 1643. B.L. *Add Mss 18980*. I, f. 94. Warburton I, 501.
21. *C.S.P.D. 1625–49*, 247. Wintour was associated with the Jesuits around Henrietta Maria. The Papal envoy George Con secured his appointment as her secretary in the spring of 1638. Woolrych *Britain in Revolution* 127.

22. Bradney 4.1 *Hundred of Caldicot* 56. *C.S.P.D. 1625–49 Addenda*, 247. Harry was probably a client of Nicholas Kemeys. A lease of 1640–41 of a house and farm at Llanvair Discoed names a David Harry as his tenant. Gwent C.R.O. M.423.4 5626 (Kemeys Mss).

23. Rogers *Memoirs of Monmouthshire* 69-71.

24. Thomas Roberts *D.W.B.* 1093. Julian Mitchell 'Nathan Rogers' 24.

25. Edmund Jones *Geographical Account of the Parish of Aberystruth* 52, 141-2.

26. Lhwyd *Parochialia* III, 38-40.

27. W.G. Hoskins *Devon* (1954), quoted Andriette (1971), 22. D. Defoe *A Tour through the whole Island of Great Britain* (Everyman's library 1928), II 52. Fox and Raglan *Monmouthshire Houses* II, 14-15.

28. Edward Llwyd's correspondent noted *c.*1690 'The land in Trelech is generally barren, woods, heathy, abounding with wood and millstone quarries ... [but] ... very healthy for sheep'. *Parochialia* III, 20.

29. Catchmay- Bradney 2.2 *Hundred of Trellech* 214-15. Siddons *Visitations by the Heralds* 184. He spent the war in Gloucester and was on the County Committees both there (Warmington 63, 92), and in South Wales. Proberts- Bradney 2.2 *Hundred of Trellech* 141-2. Siddons *Visitations* 179. Newman *Monmouthshire* 577. He was descended from Thomas ap Robert of Pant Glas, receiver of the lordships of Usk, Caerleon and Trellech under Henry VIII. Robinson *Early Tudor Gwent* 21.

30. Richards *Puritan Movement* 127. Bradney 2.2 *Hundred of Trellech* 238. Walter Harris may have been a kinsman of George Harris, post-Reformation Ranger of Wentwood Forest and henchman of the Duke of Beaufort in his dis- afforestation schemes. John Clegge of Llantrisant (Usk Hundred), also vicar of Llansoy, was expelled from both livings.

31. William Llewellyn 'The iron and wireworks of Tintern' *Arch. Camb* 1863, 291-318. William Rees *Industry* 584-647. H.W. Paar and D.G. Tucker 'The old wireworks and ironworks of the Angidy Valley at Tintern, Gwent' *J. Hist. Metallurgy Soc.* 9.1 (1975). Lease of 1565 to William Humfray, assay master of the Royal Mint and Christopher Schutz, a German from Saxony and royal charter of 1568 to the Mineral and Battery Company. Foreign workers were brought in to make Osmund Iron for wireworking, but technical problems and embezellment by the company clerk made it unprofitable. By the early 1590s the lessees were paying no rent.

32. R.F. Tylecote 'Blast furnace at Coed Ithel, Llandogo' *Mon. Ant.* 2, part 3 (1967) 149-60. N.L.W. *Badminton Mss* 1631, p.12 (1651).

33. *V.C.H. Gloucestershire* 5, 340-41. Warmington. 51.

34. William Rees *Industry* 275. *Cal. Cttee. Adv. Mon.* 216, 1022. Kyrle at Monmouth- More Pye *Diary* (Warlow 96-7).

35. Edwards *Star Chamber Proceedings* P66/518; P38/ 29, pp.106-7. In 1575 William Morgan of Llantarnam sold Kemeys Commander woods to the partners of Tintern wireworks. Mathias *Whitsun Riot* 89, n.17.

36. Llangattock Vibion Avel had 115 convicted recusants, 29% 'papistae' in 1676. Comparable figures for Skenfrith were 63 and 20%; for Wonastow 11 and 22%; St Maughans 28 and 44% and Rockfield 13 and 29%, if, as seems likely, the figures for Catholics and Nonconformists have been transposed. In 1690 John Arnold listed 28 individuals, from 16 families, in Rockfield as alleged Papists. Bradney *List of Papists* 10. This agrees with the Compton census figure of 18 (? families). Grosmont had 23 convicted recusants (5% in 1676).

37. Lhwyd *Parochialia* III, 19. D. Defoe *A Tour through the whole Island of Great Britain* II, 52.

38. Bradney 1.1 *Hundred of Skenfrith* 58. *Cal. Cttee. Comp.* 2774-5, 2778-9. Arnold *Abstract of Several Examinations* 7- 8. St Noye's Chapel collapsed *c.*1680–1730. D. Williams *Mon. Ant.* 16 (2000), 112.

39. Lloyd lived at Trifor, said mass there and in the houses of Turberville Morgan at Llanfair Cilgoed and Mrs Scudamore at Penrhos. In 1690 Thomas Croft of Llanfair Cilgoed, son of Herbert Croft of Blackbrook, was fined for refusing the Oath of Allegiance and for 'notoriously abusing and affronting' the priest hunter John Arnold in open court. Bradney *List of Papists*. Archenfield- Mathias *Whitsun Riot* 77- 8. Philip Jenkins 'Anti-popery' 277.

40. Bradney 1.1 *Hundred of Skenfrith*29-31, 46-7, 59-60. N.L.W. *Milborne papers*.

41. *Cal. Cttee. Comp.* I, 311 'sequestrated by the late committee, also returned to us as a Papist in Arms for being in Raglan during the siege'. Thomas Richards *Puritan Movement* 128. N.R.L. M. 000 5461. Bradney 2.1 *Hundred of Raglan* 54.

42. *Letter from a Gentleman in Gloucestershire* 13-21. Bradney 1.1 *Hundred of Skenfrith* 37, 2.1 *Hundred of Raglan* 123- 6. N.L.W. *Milborne Papers*. In 1678 Milborne faced allegations from Bedloe that he and others were to join Lords Powis and Petre and march to join an invading Spanish army at Milford Haven. He was ordered to be brought to the bar of the House of Lords and questioned. *H.M.C. House of Lords Papers 1678–88*, 83. The Compton census records 10 Catholic households in Dingestow and 7 in Wonastow, suggesting a Catholic population of around 72 in the two parishes.

43. Seys family- Roberts *Letterbook of John Byrd* xiii-xvi and endpiece. Descended from Roger Seys, steward of the Earl of Pembroke from 1579, the family were prominent in opposition to the Worcester interest. Alexander Seys, John Byrd's father in law, and Byrd were customary tenants of Pembroke in Caerleon.

44. Murphy 'Jesuit College'. Priests at the Cwm in 1678 were Charles Pritchard, John Archer, Thomas Harris, David Lewis, Walter Price, Humphries and Dracot. *Short Narrative* 9. Dracot was of the recusant Dracot family of Paynsley, Shropshire Mathias *Whitsun Riot* 21. In 1655 the priests were Humphrey Brown, Charles and Thomas Harris, John Throgmorton, John Lloyd, Ignatius (Walter) Price, Charles Baker (David Lewis) and John Hughes. Foley vol 6, 439.

45. Morgans of Tredegar; Machen; The Friars, Newport; Crindau, Newport; Gwern Y Cleppa.; Coed Y Goras; Pencarn; Penllwyn Sarph and Llanrhymney. On the first see J. Gwynfor Jones *The Morgan Family*.

46. Henry Morgan *D.W.B* 645.

47. Pretty submitted to Parliament 24 March 1646. With property worth £84 10s. a year he was fined £126 15s. Newman *Royalist Officers* no.1167, p.305. *Cal. Cttee. Comp.* 1693.

48. Myles Morgan- Bradney 5 *Hundred of Newport* 73. Lewis Thomas compounded April 1649 in respect of both wars. (Newman *Royalist Officers* no.1413, p.369. *Cal Comm. Comp.* 2176.). Another (Glamorgan) Lewis Thomas, involved in the 1647 Glamorgan rising, was sentenced to death by court martial after the Battle of St Fagans the following year.Ashton *Counter Revolution* 345 and 22. Lewis Morgan- *A Loving and Loyal Speech*. At Raglan 1644 (Warburton II, 522), Indigent Officer, Glamorgan. David Morgan - R.H. Owen 'Jacobitism and the Church in Wales' *J. Hist. Soc. Church in Wales* Vol 3, no 8. (1953), 111-119.

49. *C.S.P.D. 1645–7* 96-7. *A Full Relation* (1647), 13.

50. N.L.W. 13072B. (*Llanover B* 12) '*Llyfyr Jenkin Richard*'.

51. Stoyle *Loyalty and Locality* 151-2. Holmes *Seventeenth Century Lincolnshire* 14-17.

52. F.J. Mitchell 'History of Monmouthshire' *Arch. Camb*. 1886, 1-12.

53. Julian Mitchell 'Nathan Rogers and the Wentwood case'.

54. Clarendon *History of the Rebellion* VI, 270.

55. J. Thirsk 'Seventeenth century agriculture and social change' in P.S. Seaver (ed.) *Seventeenth Century England* (1976), 71. Underdown *Revel Riot and Rebellion* and 'The Chalk and the cheese' John Aubrey quoted *Brief Lives* ed. Oliver Lawson Dick (Penguin Classics 1987), 25.

56. Underdown 'A reply to John Morrill'. For a judicious summing up see Woolrych *Britain in Revolution* 255-6. It would be interesting, and perhaps relevant to questions of popular allegiance in the British Civil War, to study the Spanish Civil War (an intensely regional conflict) on similar lines. In forested areas of western Europe like the Vendée the same radical opposition to central government is apparent, save that for historical reasons the radicalism is of the right, not the left.

57. *C.S.P.D. 1581–90* 108 (1583); Edwards *Star Chamber Proceedings* 106-7 (see n.35 above) Earl of Pembroke versus his tenants re. woods of Wyeswood, Glascoed and Gwehelog. Do. 49/19 and 120/9 (p.188) Lord Abergavenny re. destruction of enclosures at Goytre and Llandewi Rhydderch. *Exchequer Proceedings Concerning Wales* 107/ 72, p.258 (1613–14), Lord Abergavenny re. Parc Llingoed in Llanfihangel Crucorney and Llangattock Lingoed, where 'great numbers of freeholders pretend rights of common'.

Chapter 3 The Great Pyramid: Grandees, Gentry & Others

1. Edward Fisher *The Marrow of Modern Divinity, touching both the Covenant of works and the Covenant of Grace* (1645). John Edwards *Madruddyn y Difynyddiaeth Diweddaraf* (1651). J. Gwynfor Jones 'The Gentry of Gwent and the Welsh language' *Mon. Ant.* 18 (2002), 75-6.

2. Bradney 3.1 *Hundred of Usk* 97-8.

3. Leland *Itinerary in Wales* 14.

4. Symonds *Diary of the Marches of the Royal Army* 233-5.

5. Robinson *Early Tudor Gwent*. Coldbrook was demolished in 1954. Peter Smith *Arch. Camb.* 106 (1957), 64-72.

6. Bradney 3.2 *Hundred of Usk* 227- 8. *Monmouthshire Wills* 54, 113-14.

7. *P.R.O. Star Chamber* 8 James 1st, 207/32. Edwards *Star Chamber Procceedings* 193. Two north Walian Jesuits, John Salisbury and Thomas Pennant, were resident at Raglan Castle and at Llantarnam respectively. Salisbury was the Superior of the Welsh mission (missio Walliae). In 1622 this became the College of St Francis Xavier at the Cwm, of which the Earl of Worcester was regarded as founder. Foley *Records* IV, 335; Mc Coog 'Society of Jesus' 12-15.

8. E.g. Langstone, bought by his father, but sold to Sir Thomas Gore. Bradney 4.2 *Hundred of Caldicot* 203.Settlement with king- B.L. *Lansdowne Mss 153*, f. 78 Owen 103-4. *P.R.O. State Papers Domestic* James 1st 1611–18 vol 70, 6 July 1612.

9. Bradney 3.2 *Hundred of Usk* 231. Mathias *Whitsun Riot* 79-85 and 89 n.10.

10. Bradney 3.2 *Hundred of Usk* 230-31. *Cal. Cttee. Adv. Mon.* 1416, 1430. He was taken prisoner at Hereford in 1645.

11. Arnold *Abstract of Several Examinations* 12.

12. Eure to Lord Salisbury, 23 October 1609. *P.R.O. State Papers Domestic* James Ist 1603–10, vol 48, f. 163. Roberts 'Office holding and alleigance' 17.

13. Glanmor Williams *Wales and the Reformation* 331. Philip Jenkins 'Anti-popery in the Welsh March' 279-282. Austin Woolrych sums up the 'neutralist' group, particularly in south Wales:- (those) 'who bowed to the prevailing wind were not necesserily acting out of cynical opportunism, but rather out of a desire to preserve what they could of local autonomy and save the people under their charge from the worst depredations of war. In south Wales, where such gentry were in the majority, they were called 'ambidexters'and thought it no shame to transfer their nominal alleigance'. *Britain in Revolution* 248.

14. *C.S.P.D. 1648–9*, 272. Admits participation in Commission of Array, signing warrants for raising soldiers, was in Raglan in the siege and in the second war. Arnold *Abstract of Examinations* 12 and 17 (there is an hiatus in pagina-tion at this point). Lady Jones was named as a leading Monmouthshire Catholic under the *Papists (Removing and Disarming) Bill* of 1680 (*H.M.C. House of Lords Papers 1678–88*, 229-30.). Portraits of Sir Philip Jones, in armour, and of Lady Elizabeth Jones were formerly at Llanarth Court before the contents were dispersed in 1948. Steegman *Portraits in Welsh Houses II* 137-8.

15. Nicholas Kemeys was Royalist 'collector' (treasurer) in Glamorgan (Raymond *Glamorgan Arraymen* 16) David Kemeys- Ellis *Catholic Martyrs of Wales* 163-4; Kenyon *Popish Plot* 192-3. The Court House at Llanvair Discoed has a date stone of 1635, with a Welsh inscription, re-set in a house of *c.*1690. The earlier house was presumably built by Nicholas Kemeys soon after he acquired Llanvair.

16. Sir William Morgan was said in 1648 to have been Governor of Newport. In view of this age, the post was presum-ably nominal. The only other accusation was of having been a Commissioner of Array. *Cal. Cttee. Adv. Mon.* 977.

17. Newman *Royalist Officers* no.1579, p 414. The pulpit has been wrongly re-assembled at some date, but there is no doubt that it originally belonged to Caerwent, for it bears a carving of Llandaff Cathedral, and the then vicar of

Caerwent was John Dowle, Treasurer of Llandaff. Dowle may have been involved in the Wentwood feuds, for in 1630 his churchwardens accused him of neglect of his clerical duties and 'acts of immorality with many of his female parishoners' *C.S.P.D. 1629–1631*, 364.

18. Bradney 1.2a *Hundred of Abergavenny* 177.

19. Newman *Royalist Officers* nos.719 and 1575, pp.188, 719. Reid *Officers and Regiments of the Royalist Army* 2, 94; 4, 151-2. Richard Herbert's Regiment was mainly from mid Wales, but he was a Commissioner of Array for Monmouthshire and other Monmouthshire men served in it. Warburton II, 237. *Gallant Siege of Parliament's Forces* 2. Siddons *Visitations by the Heralds* 178-9 confirms that Trevor Williams had no other brother. Bradney (3.1 *Hundred of Usk* 101) notes that Edward Williams was present at the siege, and was wounded, but assumed that he was among the defenders.

20. A.H. Dodd *D.W.B.* 353. Henry Herbert sat in the High Court of Justice and the Council of State in 1651. He died in 1656.

21. Thomas Hughes (d.1667)- Parliamentary County Committee for Monmouthshire 1646, Governor of Chepstow 1647, Commissioner for county militia 1648, M.P. for Monmouth 1654–5, for Carmarthen 1659. Monument in Mathern church- Bradney 4.1 *Hundred of Caldicot* 70. A letter of Cromwell to Hughes, preserved at Moynes Court in the eighteenth century is Abbott *Letters and Speeches* I, 617. Charles Hughes of Trostrey (d.1676)- Bradney 2.1 *Hundred of Usk* 92; Reid *Royalist Army* I, 32.

22. Clarendon *History of the Rebellion* VI, 283. Bradney 2.2 *Hundred of Trellech* 215. Siddons *Visitations by the Heralds* 184.

23. Jenkins 'Anti-popery' 278-282. Woolrych *Britain in Revolution* 248. Andriette *Devon and Exeter in the Civil War* 38.

24. *Commons Journal* 27 September 1642.

25. Symonds *Diary of the Marches of the Royal Army* 233, 238.

26. *C.S.P.D. 1636–7*, 177, 183. H.M.C. *12th Report, Appendix. Mss of Earl Cowper Part II* (1888), 101. The term 'fifth column' derives from an episode in the Spanish Civil War, when a Nationalist general told a journalist that he had four columns of troops outside a city 'and a fifth column inside it'.

27. *C.S.P.D. 1640*, 483. Gardiner *History of England 1602–1642* IX, 289. Eales *Puritans and Roundheads* 97-8, 118-20. *Great Discovery of a Damnable Plot at Ragland Castle.*

28. Northamptonshire Record Office *Finch-Hatton Ms 133* f. 45. They were Sir Robert Cooke of Highnam outside Gloucester; Sir William Morgan of Tredegar; Thomas Morgan of Machen; William Herbert of Coldbrook; William Baker of Abergavenny; Sir Charles Williams of Llangibby and James Kyrle of Ross on Wye. This may have been the context for the anecdote of 'rustics' arriving to search Raglan Castle for arms, only to be frightened off by the noise of Edward Herbert's steam engine, which they took for escaped lions.

29. B.L. *Harleian MS 6988*, f.66. Webb and Webb *Civil War in Herefordshire* 98.

Chapter 4 Community in Conflict: 1642–3 'That Mushrump Army'

1. Ian Roy 'England turned Germany' 130.

2. Gwent C.R.O. *Misc Mss 648* (Letterbook of Richard Herbert) 10. P.R.O. S. P.16 381/66 quoted Malcolm *Caesar's Due* 234-5.

3. Gwent C.R.O. *Misc. Mss. 648*, 10-11. There are two lists. The first 'Arms in Monmouth Proper' merely gives totals e.g. 'All sorts of Coursllets- 163'. The second, on the verso of the same sheet 'A Note of such Arms as are in the Magazine of the town of Monmouth' breaks these down into 'White Corslets with Pauldrons and Taces' (shoulder pieces and articulated thigh pieces); Black Corslets with Pauldrons and Taces and the same types without Pauldrons and Tassets. Similarly pikes are classified as 'New pikes with heads', 'Ould pikes without heads' and 'Ould pikes with heads'.

4. P.R.O. *Star Chamber* 8 James I st, 207/28. D. Owen 67. B.L. *Harleian Ms* 6988, 66, 11 December 1641.

5. Bod. L. *Tanner Ms 66* f. 244 Jan 23 1642. *H.M.C 13th Report, Portland Manuscripts* I, 62-3; *Lords Journal* May 10 1642; *Commons Journal* March 29, April 14 and 28, Webb I, 104. For a similar quarrel elsewhere see Lucy Hutchinson *Memoirs* 81-7. Mason- N.L.W. *Milborne Ms* 1380 .

6. *A True Copie of the Petition ... of the County of Monmouth. Commons Journal* II, 575; *H.M.C. 13th Report Appendix 1 Portland Mss 1*, 39 17 May 1642 'A brief information of the present state of our County of Monmouth'. Woolrych *Britain in Revolution* 217-18.

7. *Letter from Mercurius Civicus to Mercurius Rusticus* (August 1643) 11, *SomersTracts* IV, 580-98. Nathaniel Stephens-Warmington, p.30.

8. *Portland Mss 1*, 30 Warrant 13 Jan 1642 to Mayor of Monmouth and Chief Constables of Hundred to raise 20 men to secure magazine at Monmouth and those of three other Hundreds to raise nine men to secure the powder at Caerleon.

9. Webb I, 105.

10. Stradling to Morgan 17 September 1642. N.L.W. *Tredegar MSS* 911. Reid *Royalist Army* 4, 166-7

11. Peter Young *Edgehill* 223-4. Stradling was released in May 1644 by exchange, but died of fever in Oxford the following month.

12. Northampton County Record Office *Finch-Hatton Ms 133* ff 44-5. B.L. *Harleian Ms 6804*, f. 17 lists members of a 'Commission of Impress' charged with raising '100 men a Peece'. Four of the 15 are not in the Finch-Hatton list. Two (Sir Edward Morgan of Llantarnam and Sir Charles Somerset) were Catholics, excluded from the Commission of Array. The other two, Thomas Morgan of Llanrhymney and Edmund Morgan of Penllwyn Sarph, were from the western fringes of the county, under represented in the original Commission, but likely to be a fruitful source of recruits.

13. The full list of Commissioners, in alphabetical order, was Thomas Berrington (Tintern Parva); William Blethin (Dinham); John Gainsford (Upper Dyffryn, Grosmont); Sir Richard Herbert (St Julians); Edmund Jones (Llansoy);

Philip Jones (Treowen); Sir Charles and Sir Nicholas Kemeys (Llanvair Discoed); William Kemeys (Kemeys Inferior); David Lewis (Llandewi Rhydderch); John Milborne (Wonastow); George Moore (Crick); Nicholas Moore (Crick); Sir Edmund Morgan (Pen-worlod, Penhow); Philip Morgan (Penllwyn Sarph); Thomas Morgan (Machen); Thomas Morgan (Llansor); Sir William Morgan (Tredegar); Sir George Probert and Henry Probert (Pant Glas, Trellech); Sir Trevor Williams (Llangibby). Blethin, Edmund Jones and Thomas Morgan (Machen) appear on both lists. The six only on the 'omitted' list are William Baker (Abergavenny); William Herbert (Coldbrook); Edward Morgan (Pencoed); William Morgan (Pencrug, Llanhennock); John Parry and (Llantilio Pertholey)Roger Williams (Cefn Ila, Llandadoc). For discussion see Knight 'Taking Sides : Royalist Commissioners of Array for Monmouthshire in the Civil War *Mon. Antiq.* (forthcoming)

14. *True News out of Herefordshire; A Most Blessed Victory Obtained Against the Marquess of Hertford. True and Happy News from Wales.* Hutton *Royalist War Effort* 34. Webb I, 176. *H.M.C. 7th Report* (1879), 689.

15. Webb I, 197-8. Walter Powell *Diary* 13 Nov 'The men slayne at Pontrilas'.

16. Edward Herbert to Stamford at Hereford, 6 November 1642. *Lords Journal* 21 November 1642. Webb I, 192-5.

17. Clarendon *History of the Rebellion* V, 287.

18. Gwynne was from Llanbrayne, Carmarthenshire. Reid *Royalist Army* 4, 166-7. P. Young *Edgehill* 223-4. Newman *Royalist Officers* no.656, 170.

19. Hutton *Royalist War Effort* 53. Clarendon *History of the Rebellion* V, 288-9. Walter Powell *Diary* 6 Feb. 1643 'Benevolence p(ro) Rege at Rockfield £1'.

20. Herbert to Rupert, 7 March 1643. B.L. *Add Mss 18980* f. 94 Warburton II, 501.

21. Stoyle *Loyalty and Locality* 244. Corbet *True and Impartial History* 27. Webb I, 229. Monmouth Parish Register (N.L.W. Pa 32, Vol 1)- 12 Feb (1642/3). Mr Richard Lawdey, Baronett, Serjeant Major General for his M[ajest]y in south Wales and Colonel of a Regiment of Dragoons. Randall Wallinger, Lieut to a troop of horse under the command of Capt Henry. Capt Burke yt commanded Colonell Lawdey his company These three slayne at ye taking of Colford in ye forest and were buried in Mon[mou]th Church.
16 [Feb] Richard Smith, a soldier
29 [Feb] John Stradling, a troop[er], hurt at Colford.
Lawdey- Newman *Royalist Officers* no.857, p.224-5; *Cal. Cttee. Adv. Mon.* 973.

22. Clarendon *History of the Rebellion* V, 290-91. Hutton 1982a, 73 and *Royalist War Effort* 54.

23. Clarendon V, 292. *Victorious and Fortunate Proceedings; Copy of a Letter sent from Bristol;* Corbet *Military Government;* John Putley *The Battle of Highnam House.* A memorial at Barber's Bridge on the Leadon three miles north-west of Highnam records the finding of a mass grave of 86 skeletons, said to be Royalists fleeing from Highnam, in 1868. There is nothing to confirm this antiquarian guess and the date of the skeletons is unknown. 'Welch Thomas'- Bod.L. Archdeacon Furney Mss (Washbourne 272-3). John ap John- Edmund Jones *Geographical, Historical and Religious Account* 112-114.

24. *Mercurius Aulicus* 28 March, 1642-3. Webb I, 238-9.

25. Clarendon V, 293.

26. *H.M.C 13th Report Portland MSS* 1, (1891) 703-4. L.W. Dillwyn *Contributions Towards a History of Swansea* (1840), 27; M. Price *Account Book for the Borough of Swansea* p.96, f.49. 'Aprill last 1643 for my lord Marquesse of Worcester his servants dyet, and housement £10.9.4d. and 19s 2d more … for one nights enterteynment to Sir Marmaduke Loyd, all being £11.8.6d. whereof we had receavd out of the contribution moneys for making up our Magazine: and the other £8.8.6d. wee payd out of the Towne money'.

27. Edward Herbert, 19 March 1643- 'God forgive those of the king's party who were the occasion that 1,500 gentlemen were surprised, and I not despatched from Oxford until the day after'. Rushworth, quoted Dircks *Life … of the Second Marquis of Worcester* 57. Hutton (*Royalist War Effort* 56) notes that 'what [Herbert] had been doing for the past month [before 15 April] is a complete mystery'. However, a cryptic undated letter to Sir Nicholas Kemeys from his 'unanimous kinsmen' refers to Herbert's expected return from 'a hazardous journey' and his 'favourable encounter' with the King. Herbert, excluded from command at the outbreak of war because of his catholicism, was now being sent a commission via Lord Hertford. From the reference to Hertford, the letter seems to slightly pre-date Highnam, but business connected with the commission (and perhaps opposition to it) could explain his stay in Oxford at the time of the disaster (N.L.W. *Kemeys Tynte Mss* C.1).

28. J.E. Lee *Isca Silurum* (London 1862), 121 and plate 50, 1, now Gwent C.R.O. *Misc. Mss 1357.* Thomas Morgan- *Cal. Ctte. Comp.* 1710, 1882, 2816.

29. Roy 'England Turned Germany' 131.

30. Gwent C.R.O. *Misc Mss 648*, 10. P.R.O. State Papers 16/381/ 66

31. Webb II, 249-51. 'One of the sons of Sir William Morgan of Tredegar, Sir William Herbert of Coldbrook and others had sent [to Waller] to invite him hither'. Corbet *Military Government.*

32. *Victoriovs and Fortunate Proceedings.* Walter Powell *Diary* 11 April 1643 'Sir Richard Lane [? Cave] and soldiers at lantilio'. Johns *Historical Traditions* Part V, 90.

33. *Mercurius Britannicus* 9-15 April 1643. Muster- Duncumb 245-58; Bod. L. *Tanner Ms 303* ff.113 -20 Webb I, 254 and 275.

34. King to Sheriff of Monmouthshire, 26 April 1643- N.R.L. M000 946.Walter Powell *Diary* 23 April 1643 and 28 April 1643 'Chepstow taken by Bristow men and re-taken'. Cave's lengthy defence was printed (Webb I, 274-84).

35. Dircks *Life … of the Marquis of Worcester* 60.

36. Warmington *Civil War, Interregnum and Restoration* 48 (Clarendon VII, 201). Hutton *Royalist War Effort* 114. King on Vavasour- Malcolm *Caesar's Due* 94, Raymond 'Glamorgan Armaymen'. Miners- Warburton II, 501.

37. Bassett- N.L.W. L1/MB/ 17. ff 25, 29.Raymond 'Glamorgan Armaymen'. Bennet 'Dampnified villagers', Symonds *Diary of the Marches of the Royal Army* 204. Walter Powell *Diary* 28 August 1643. *A True Relation of a Plot Against*

the City of Gloucester T.T. E.45 (12) 7 May 1644.Lingen and Williams's commissions- B.L. *Harleian Ms 6852*, 9 June 1643.

38. *C.S.P.V 1643–7*, 51-2.

39. Hutton *Royalist War Effort* 118-19, Bod.L. *Firth Ms* C8, f. 337, B.L. *Harleian Ms 6802* f. 60. H.M.C. *Stuart Papers* I (1902), 1-2. Sir Richard Herbert, Governor of Aberystwyth, was replaced by Roger Whitley under the same policy and given the consolation prize of Newport, close to his house at St Julians. Hutton *Royalist War Effort* 140. Tucker 'Colonel Roger Whitley'.

40. C.S.P.D. 1644, 8. *Chepstow Parish Register* (Gwent C.R.0. D/Pa 86.1.) 20 Jan 'Bur(ied) Captain Carvine, who was killed in his chamber at the George by certain souldiers that came from Gloucester'. Do. Feb 1644 'A souldier dyinge at the George, his name unknown' and 'Reece Williams, who dyed at the George'.

41. B.L. *Add Mss 18981* f. 36. Warburton II, 511, 507. Newman *Royalist Officers* no.1070, p.278; Daniel F. Cregan 'An Irish cavalier: Daniel O'Neill in the Civil Wars 1642–165' *Studia Hibernica* 4 (1964), 104-33. Elements of Sir William Russell's Regiment from Worcester garrison may have been active locally at this time. One of the regiment, a Suffolk man, killed in action, was buried at Chepstow 15 March 1644.

42. *Mercurius Aulicus* 22 May 1644. Webb II, 33-4. Warburton II, 507.

43. Arthur Trevor to Ormonde, 13 September 1644. Carte 61-2. Ernley to Rupert 19 September 1644 B.L. *Add Mss 18981* f. 259 (Warburton I, 519). Mynne- Newman *Royalist Officers* no.1031, p.270. Earlier in the summer, the Northern Horse, of two brigades under Sir William Blackiston, totalled 1,500 horse. They had been much reduced by defeats at Naseby and Montgomery (where the 'Lancashire horse' broke) and by their long retreat. Symonds *Diary of the Marches of the Royal Army* 182.

44. Corbett *Diary of the Campaigns of Massey* 117, 356-7. *Commons Journal* 28 September 1644. *C.S.P.D. 1644*, 512-13 Major Robert Harley to Colonel Edward Harley 21 September 1644. The cavalry troops were those of Robert and Edward Harley and two of Colonel Stephens's. *H.M.C. 14th Report, Duke of Portland Mss* 128-9, Bod. L. *Firth Mss* C7 ff 178-9, 183, 215. B.L. *Add. Mss 18981*, ff. 268, 294. Warmington *Civil War, Interregnum and Restoration* 64.

45. Rushworth 743; Luke *Letter Books* 63; J.L. Malcolm *Caesar's Due* 74.

46. Tuke to Rupert 19 Sept.-1 Oct. 1644. B.L. *Add Mss 18981* II, ff. 255, 257, 268, 274, 285. Tuke became a Roman Catholic, one of the courtiers around Henrietta Maria. Miller *Popery and Politics* 97-98. A 'playwright, courtier and occasional diplomat', Pepys attended one of his plays- *Diary* Vol 4, 8, 16 ; Vol 9, 429, 450. Tax revenue- Thomas Price to Rupert B.L. *Add. Mss 18981* II, f. 251.

47. Lewis Morgan to Rupert, 17 October 1644. B.L. *Add Mss 18981* f. 293b (Warburton II, 522). Possibly kinsman of Sir Lewis Morgan, Pencarn, Bassaleg (d.1636). Bradney 5 *Hundred of Newport* 74. Lewis Morgan (probably the same) brought a piece of plate with his arms 'massy and of great value' to Prince Charles at Raglan in 1642 (*A Loving and Loyal Speech*). List of Indigent officers (Glamorgan).

48. Warmington 70. Holtby- Newman *Royalist Officers* no.750, 194-5. Walter Powell *Diary* 23 September 1644 'Monmouth taken p[er] Massy'. Monmouth Parish Register (N.L.W. Pa 32, Vol 1)- Burials of John Hannes 'a soldier slayne by Coll. Massie's entering the toune'. (Sept 24); 'A trayned [train band] soldier slayne the 24th in entering the toune by Collo Massey' (25th) and 'Richard W[i]ll[iams] a soldier slayne ye same time' (Sept 26th). Kyrle- Newman *Royalist Officers* no.750, 194-5. He published a lengthy justification for his first change of side- *A Copy of a Letter*, printed Webb II, 349-353. Memorial of James Kyrle (d.1645) in St Mary de Crypt church, Gloucester.

49. Powell *Diary* 28 September 1644 'Ffire [? ffite] at Wonastow'. *Mercurius Aulicus* Oct 7, 1644. The more colourful version occurs in the *Country Messanger*. Webb II, 100.

50. Rushworth II, iii. 742. Phillips II, 210-11. Blackiston- Newman *Royalist Officers* no.130, p.31. Dore *Letter Book of Sir William Brereton* 1, 229. County Committee to Rupert, 30 Sept. 1644. B.L. *Add Mss 18981*, f. 237. Webb II, 100 n.7.

51. *H.M.C. 14 th Report, (Portland Mss 3)* 128-9. Robert Harley to Edward Harley October 1644; Throckmorton to Edward Harley 7 October 1644.

52. *C.S.P.D. 1644–5*, 42; (14 Oct 1644). *H.M.C. 14 th Report (Portland Mss 3)* 127. *Moderate Intelligencer* 19 October 1644.

53. *C.S.P.D. 1644–5*, 42. Thomas Lewis v Duke of Beaufort, April 1723. Bradney 4.1 *Hundred of Caldicot* 107. S.A.L. Mss 790 (Wakeman papers). William Coxe *Historical Tour in Monmouthshire* 366n; Ormerod *Archaeologia* 1841, 13-17.

54. *H.M.C. 14th Report part 3* (1894), 130. Robert Harley to Edward Harley 15 November 1644; 131 28 November. *Mercurius Aulicus* 23 November 1644. Webb II, 101.and 113-14. Walter Powell *Diary* 18 November 1644 'Monmouth retaken p(ro) Rege by Raglan men' *Perfect Diurnall* Corbet 'True and Impartial account' 361-2; Camden Miscellany 2, 9-10 Rushworth III, ii, 743. The garrison of Monmouth comprised the foot companies of the Governor and Captains Rodiford, Elsing, Mallory and Mercer, and Edward and Robert Harley's troops of horse, 80 combined. After the disaster, Edward Harley had 36 troopers, but 20 were without horses. Some foot companies were down to 20 or 25 men.

55. Two of the Committee, Colonel Stephens and William Jones of Usk, were exchanged for the Earl of Cleveland, captured at Second Newbury. *Commons Journal* 26 March 1645, Webb 114 n.2. By December 1644 Wintour was blocked in at Lydney by three Parliamentarian outposts, one commanded by a Captain Gainsford. Webb II, 123-4. As Webb realised, this was not the Royalist, whose daughter claimed that he died in prison for his loyalty.

56. Hutton *Royalist War Effort* 167-8. Hereford Ref Lib. Webb Ms 1, ff. 129 -91 (Accounts of Receiver of Tax, Skenfrith Hundred), Lunsford- B.L. *Sloane Ms 1519*, f. 60, *Harleian Misc* 7, 557.

57. *Harleian Misc* 7, 557, Hutton *Royalist War Effort* 173. Lunsford's statement tht he had 200 men at work on fortifications has sometimes been applied to Monmouth, but his letter to Rupert (B.L. *Sloane Ms 1519* f. 60, 9 March 1645)

is dated from Bristol, and probably refers to work there. In contrast to Abergavenny, Monmouth, despite extensive excavations, has produced no trace of Civil War fortifications.

58. Raymond 'Glamorgan Arraymen'; Bennet 'Damnified villagers'; Symonds *Diary of the Marches of the Royal Army* 204. Gwent C.R.O. *Letterbook of Richard Herbert.*

Chapter 5 The Royalist Ebb, 1644–45 Civilians and the War

1. N.L.W. *Ms 17091* C44 and 46 (Walter Powell Diary); C 85-6 (Bradney Contributions). On 'contributions' Roy 'England turned Germany'136. Lawes- Webb II, 167.

2. Walter Powell *Diary* 11 April 1643 'Sir Richard Lane and soldiers at Llantilio'. 14 April 1643 'souldiers from Monmouth at Llantilio.' do. November 1644 'Bergevenny troops every night at my house' 11 Jan. 1645 'Sir William Blackstone and [Sir James] Proger at my house'. Bennet 'Dampnified villagers' 36-7. Abergavenny Museum Gunter Papers A/44-61. Looting by Rupert and others- Roy 'England turned Germany' 137.

3. N.L.W. 13072B. 'Llyfyr Jenkin Richard' p.159 (1646); 161-3 (1643–4). He may have been a son of Richard ap Jenkin of Llanover. Bradney 5 *Hundred of Newport* 69; Huws 'Llengarwch Reciwsantiaid' 6-7.

4. B.L. *Harleian Ms 6804* f. 107. *Moderate Intelligencer* 16 April 1645, Webb II, 171-2.

5. *Letter Book of John Byrd* nos.283-4, pp.135-7; 295, 141-2. Whitley later replaced Sir Richard Herbert as Governor of Aberystwyth. Hutton *Royalist War Effort* 140. Roberts 'Office holding and allegiance' 17; Morrill *Cheshire 1630–1660* 304-6; N. Tucker 'Colonel Roger Whitley'.

6. Wintour to Rupert 26 October and 20 November 1644. B.L. *Add Mss 18981* II, ff. 36b, 308, 324 (Warburton II, 525.)

7. Gwent C.R.O. D/Pa 86.1. James *Registers of Chepstow Parish Church* ,Waters *Chepstow Parish Records*. Deaths in Gloucester doubled in 1645-6 and in 1644–5 a quarter of the population of Bristol perished, mostly by plague. By 1646-7 however, things were back to normal. Ian Roy 'England turned Germany' 142.

8. Symonds *Diary of the Marches of the Royal Army* 231 and Webb II, 102. Rushworth III, 743. Hoard- H.E. Shepperd 'Monmouth Castle and Priory' *Papers on Monmouth Castle and Priory* ... M.A.A. Gloucester 1896.

9 F. Radcliffe and J.K. Knight 'Excavations at Abergavenny, 1962–1963 Part 2' *Mon. Ant.* 3, part 2 (1972–3), 73-7. K. Blockley 'Excavations at the Roman fort at Abergavenny, Orchard Site 1972–3' *Archaeological J.* 150 (1993), 193-6 and personal information from Fiona and Patrick Ashmore. Symonds *Diary of the Marches of the Royal Army* 206, 212.

10. *Chepstow Parish Register* (Gwent C.R.O. D/Pa 86.1) 25 Feb. 1645. 'Captain Poore was killed in a Battell at Lancaute, being Governor of Berkeley Castle, and was buried in the church of Chepstow'. 27 Feb Conrad Gamme a soldier dying at Pearsfield was buried. 15 March- 'William Morgan, a soldier of Sir John Winter drowned at Longkate in the battell fought there was buried' 16 March- 'A souldier drowned at Longhute in the battell there was buried'. Colonel Veale was a kinsman of the Veales of Chapel Hill, Tintern, tenants of the Earl of Worcester. *Monmouthshire Wills* no.146, pp.205-6. Corbet *Diary of Massey's Campaigns* 137.

11. Corbet *Diary* 329. *Mercurius Aulicus* 13-20 April 1645 Corbet 'True and Impartial Account' 365-7, Bod. L. *Clarendon MS 28*, f. 129.

12. *Letter Book of John Byrd* no.8, p.3 Two Captain John Morgans, Senior and Junior were in Raglan Castle in 1646. The episode may have been a straightforward requisition, though it has some odd features.

13 Dabridgecourt to Rupert, 11 March 1645. B.L. *Add Mss 18981* f. 83. Warburton II, 385. Phillips Civil War 139 (both displaced among papers of 1644). Dabridgecourt was taken prisoner at Rowton Heath the following September. Phillips *Civil War* II, 272. Osborne 'The war, the people and the absence of the Clubmen'. Gaunt *English Civil War* 246.

14. Phillips *Civil War* II, 155. *C.S..P.D. 1644–5*,356. *Cal. Cttee. Comp.* 3, 2123. (6 Oct 1652). The land had been sequestrated, and Morgan was trying to recover it. Elizabeth Mansfield, presumably a widow, held only a life interest. Fox and Raglan *Monmouthshire Houses* II, 89 and 126. Bradney 5 *Hundred of Newport* 69-70. Hutton *Royalist War Effort* 189. Anthony Morgan of Cilfegan should not be confused with the Catholic Anthony Morgan of Llandewi Skirydd, uncle of St Philip Evans.

15. Bod. L. *Tanner Ms 60* f. 440. Astley to Digby, 30 August 1645 from Abergavenny- *C.S.P.D. 1645–47*, 96-7. Thomas Morgan *H.M.C. 13th Report, Portland Mss Part 1,* 286-7.

16. John Aubrey *Brief Lives* ed. Oliver Lawson Dick (Penguin Classics 1987), 284. Warmington 74, *C.S.P.D. 1644–5*, 599, 602. *H.M.C. 7th Report Part 1 Appendix (House of Lords Papers 1648–65)*, 68-9.

17. Clarendon *History of the Rebellion* IX, 67. Larkin *Stuart Royal Proclamations II* no.516, pp.1065-6 'A proclamation for the Raising of Auxiliaries in the Co. of Hereford'.

18. B.L. *Plutarch Ms 64 F* quoted Raglan Somerset *Guide to Raglan Castle* (1923), Malcolm *Caesar's Due* 96-8. Morrill 'Ecology of allegiance' 455. Symonds *Diary* 181-2.

19. Clarendon *History of the Rebellion* IX, 67. B.L. *Harleian 6852* ff. 285,292. Symonds *Diary* 233, 238. Hutton *Royalist War Effort* 183.

20. Bayly *Certamen Religiosum* (1649) and *Apophthegms* no 4. Heath *Raglan Castle* 83.

21. Clarendon *History of the Rebellion* IX, 67-68. Symonds *Diary* 210 (22 July 1645) 'about the 8 of July the two trooples were going to Black Rock, and the king intended to goe over, had not Goring's news stopt [him]'- presumably misdated. Gilbert- Coxe *Historical Tour* Vol 1, p.2. S.A.L. Ms 790 Wakeman Collection. Later folklore- W.N. Johns *Historical Traditions and Facts* V, 115- *Moderate Intelligencer* 5 August 1645 claims that the captives were carrying £1,600.

22. B.L. *Harleian 6852*, f. 302. Hutton *Royalist War Effort* 183.

23. C.J. Spurgeon and Howard J. Thomas 'Caerphilly Castle; The Civil War redoubt' *Arch. Camb.* 147 (1998), 181-93. Symonds *Marches of the Royal Army* 210.

24. Clarendon *History of the Rebellion* IX, 71. B.L. *Harleian 6852*, ff. 305, 308, Symonds *Marches of the Royal Army* 212. Astley to Rupert from Newport, 30 July 1645. Warburton II, 526. Leaders of the Peace Army- Roberts *Parliamentary Politics* 659

25. Astley to Rupert 11th, 15th August 1645. Warburton II, 526. Lunsford to Rupert 25 July 1645 Warburton II, 529.

26. *H.M.C. 13th Report, Appendix 1 Portland Mss 1*, 362-3, examination of William Barry of Tregate, Herefordshire Chepstow 16 May 1646. For his family see Bradney 2.1 *Hundred of Raglan* 64.

27. Symonds *Diary of the Marches of the Royal Army* 27 July, 238-9. Astley to Digby, 30 August 1645- *C.S.P.D. 1645–47*, 96-7. Walter Powell Diary 1 September 1645. *Cal. Cttee. Comp.* 1537.

28. Symonds *Marches of the Royal Army* Sept 11, 233, 238. Bayly *Apothegums* Roberts 'Office holding and allegiance', 18. do 'Parliamentary politics' 659. *Moderate Intelligencer* 10 October 1645. *City Scout* 28 October 1645.

29. Clarendon *History of the Rebellion* IX, 89-128. Clarendon thought Digby 'the sole cause of revoking ... {Rupert's} commission and of the order ... to leave the kingdom without being heard'. *Ibid* IX, 121. Charles to Rupert and Maurice October 27 and 30 1645. Warburton II, 527, Clarendon IX, 70. Symonds records an angry exchange between the King, Rupert and Charles Gerard at Newark in which the latter two blamed Digby for all these distractions' and their own dismissals. *Diary of the Marches of the Royal Army* 268-9.

30. Williams- Bod. L. *Tanner Ms 60* f. 440-41. Morgan *H.M.C. 13th Report Portland Mss Part 1*, 286-7. (October 10 1645). Walter Powell 'Chepstow taken by Parliament' 2 October 1645. This may record Williams's capture of the town, though he claims that the castle held out 'above a fortnight.'Symonds *Diary of the Marches of the Royal Army* 239. According to the Webbs (p.238) Fitzmorris was an Irish Catholic.

31. Bod. L. *Tanner Ms 60* f. 440-4. *C.S.P.D. 1645–47*, 200, 204. *The True Informer* 22 October 1645 (S.A.L. 790/5).

32. Walter Powell *Diary* 13-14 October 1645 'Washington at Bergavenny'. Moulton to Lenthall October 22, 1645. *H.M.C. Portland Mss 1*, 294 *A Full Relation of the Desparate Design*. *True Informer* 1 November 1645. Its claim that Sir Edward Morgan 'came in' to Parliament soon after 'rather for fear than favour'is mistaken. He was taken prisoner on the fall of Hereford in the following month.

33. *H.M.C. Portland Mss 1*, 294. Ashton *Counter Revolution*. Symonds *Diary of the Marches of the Royal Army* 263. *Gallant Siege of Parliaments Forces* 4.

34. *Letters from Colonel Morgan* Original account, in Morgan's hand, signed by Williams *H.M.C. Portland Mss 1*, 295. *Kingdom's Weekly Intelligencer* 28 October 1645; *Mercurius Veridicus* 18, 25 October. ('the country Clubmen' or 'The Monmouth and Glamorgan Clubmen'; Bod. L. *Tanner Ms 60* f. 440 K.R. *Two Letters from an Officer*. Dean miners had assisted Fairfax at the siege of Bristol (Warmington 75).

35. *A Full Relation of the Desperate Design* gives most of the credit to Kyrle, who may have had a hand in its writing. Captain Gainsford was the son of John Gainsford of Grosmont, Lt. Colonel of the Marquis of Worcester's Foot. See note 4.55 above.

36. Wintour- Warburton II, 511. Captain Wathen- Webb II, 252-3.

37. *C.S.P. Venetian 1643–6*, 223, Nov 9 1645.

38. Walter Powell *Diary* 27 November 1645 'The P'liament army at my house, Collonell Morgan coming from Gloucester towards Bergavenny'. Colonel Thomas Herbert to Speaker Lenthall, 6 December 1645- Col. Morgan occupies Abergavenny, Raglan troops attack, kill three and carry away 'divers well affected gentlemen'. Col. Morgan then planned to garrison a house three miles from Raglan (probably Clytha) but finding it unsuitable, returned to Gloucester. *H.M.C. Portland Mss 1*, 320.

39. *Severall Letters from Colonel Morgan* Dec. 18 1645, Phillips II, 286-7, 349. Walter Powell *Diary* 18 December. Symonds *Diary of the Marches of the Royal Army* 276.

40. *A Declaration of the Gentlemen and Inhabitants of the County of Brecknock* (London, Edward Husbands, Dec. 6, 1645). Phillips II, 284-5. *H.M.C. 13th Report, Appendix 1. Portland Mss 1*, 345. *Mercuricus Belgicus* March 25, 1646. Astley commented to Rupert (Warburton II, 526) that the gentry of Brecon were 'most of them inclined to be neutral, and to join with the strongest party'.

41. *Cal. Cttee. Comp.* II, 1589. Reid *Royalist Army* 2, 98.

42. *C.S.P.D. 1645–7*, 248, 259, 311.

43. Herbert to Lenthall Dec. 6 1645 *H.M.C. Portland Mss 1*, 320. Bod. L. *Tanner Ms 60* f. 440.

Chapter 6 End Game; Raglan and Chepstow 1646–48

1. *Great Overthrow Given to the King's forces in Wales* 5-6. Laugharne to Speaker, 2 January 1646 ' the Ragland and Ludlow horse prove very active' *H.M.C. 13th Report Appendix Portland Mss I*, 346. *Mercurius Belgicus* 25 March 1646. *Mercurius Britannicus* 2 March 1646. Williams- Bod.L. *Tanner Ms 60* ff. 440-41.

2. *A Great Overthrow* claims the Llanarth garrison was to prevent raids on Monmouth from Raglan, but it is in the wrong direction. Captain 'Wastman' was presumably Edward Wakeman.

3. Webb II, 339. Kissack *Monmouth* 41

4. *Great Overthrow Given to the King's Forces in Wales* ... Lord Charles Somerset to Commander in Chief and 'his Majesty's loyal subjects in Glamorgan' 13 February 1646. *H.M.C. Portland Mss 1*, 350. Roberts 'Parliamentary politics' 664-5. Joyce Lee Malcolm *Caesar's Due* 221.

5. Lowe 'Glamorgan mission to Ireland' 159. Woolrych *Britain in Revolution* 327-8, 345.

6. Lowe notes (p.157) Glamorgan's 'quixotic and steadfast fidelity' whilst his father, despite his unflinching loyalty, was more sceptical of the king's motives and honesty.

7. *C.S.P.D. 1645–47*, 312-13. Bradney 5 *Hundred of Newport* 69-70. For another Anthony Morgan (b.1627), a Catholic in the service of the Earl of Worcester see P.R.O. SP.23, Vol 163, 85-7, Lindley *Catholics* 83. Roberts 'Parliamentary politics' 656-7, 666-7.

8. Bod.L. *Carte Mss* 30 f. 307, r-v.- 'Boteler's account of his business at Oxford, 1646', Webb II, 418-20. Newman *Royalist Officers* no.217, p.51. By this time, Royalist communications were difficult and hazardous. Messages between Denbigh and Raglan were carried by an intrepid woman courier 'quilted up in a truss of linen tyed next to her body'. Boteler names Colonel Butler and Major Butler as quitting the castle.

9. Sprigge *Anglia Rediviva* 291.

10. *Cal. Cttee. Comp.* 1356, 1693. Walter Powell *Diary* 19 Dec. 1645; 17 Jan. 1646, 14, 23, 26 March, 25 May 1646. N.L.W. *Ms 17091*, C 85-6, printed Bradney *Contributions Towards the Royal Army*. The Nelsons of Penrhos were a recusant family, mentioned several times in Walter Powell's diary.

11. Walter Powell *Diary* July 9-10, November 27, 1646.

12. *A Great Overthrow Given to the King's Forces*. Prodger- *Cal. Ctte. Comp.* 1571

13. Heath *Raglan Castle* 82. N.L.W. *Ms 1307B (Llyfyr Jenkin Richard)* f. 159.

14. *Gallant Siege of Parliament's forces* 1-3. It was normal for a Colonel's brother to serve as Lieutenant-Colonel. Edward Williams disappears from royalist records after summer 1643 and Edward Williams had no other brother. Newman *Royalist Officers* no.1575, p.413, Siddons *Visitations by the Heralds* 178-9. *Moderate Intelligencer* 28 May 1646 blames the execution of the Corporal (whom it calls a Lieutenant) on 'the Irish part of the garrison'. Other details in this account are also unreliable.

15. *Gallant Siege of Parliament's Forces* 3-6. In the 20 May skirmish, the Parliamentarians admitted losing three men, but claimed five or six Royalist dead, plus 12 prisoners.

16. Lucy Hutchinson *Memoirs* 151. do 200- 'Mr Hooper the engineer, a man very faithful to the cause, and very honest, but rough withal ... the priests (i.e. Presbyterians) having a particular spite at him, as one they esteemed a leader of the separatists; yet he was very ingenious and industrious ... and most faithful ... To the public service'. Sprigge *Anglia Rediviva* 291. Rowland Laugharne from Abergavenny May 25 1646, *Perfect Occurances* Phillips II, 369.

17. *Letter to the Hon . William Lenthal...from Colonel Morgan* July 3 1646. Phillips II, 314-18.

18. Coxe *Historical Tour in Monmouthshire* 1, plate opp. p.137. J.R. Kenyon 'The Civil War earthworks around Raglan Castle'.

19. Heath *Raglan Castle* 25 (unpaginated, but pencil pagination in Haines Collection copy, Newport). Elizabeth Whittle 'The ... gardens at Raglan Castle' and 'The Renaissance Gardens of Raglan Castle'.

20. *Gallant Siege Before Raglan* (1646). Sprigge *Anglia Rediviva* 292.

21. *An Exact and True Relation* (19 August 1646); *A Letter from His Excellencies Quarters* by W.C. (probably Walter Cradock- 27 August 1646); *A Perfect Diurnall* no. 160, 35th week (28 August 1646). Sprigge *Anglia Rediviva* 293-6.

22. G. Ormerod *Tracts Relating to the Military proceedings in Lancashire during the Great Civil War* (Chetham Society 1844), 177. E.A. Halsall *Journal of the Siege of Lathom House in Lancashire* (1902). Sprigge *Anglia Rediviva* 297. Lucy Hutchinson *Memoirs of ... Colonel Hutchinson*.

23. *A Letter from His Excellencies Quarters*. *A Perfect Diurnall* 160, 28 August. *Anglia Rediviva* 298. The parliamentary commissioners were Colonels Thomas Morgan, Birch and Thomas Herbert of Usk; Quartermaster General Grosvenor; Lt Col. Ashfield and Major Tuliday. The following year, Tuliday lobbied parliament in support of a Leveller petition, only to be physically assaulted by the Presbyterian M.P. Philip Stapleton and imprisoned. Ashfield was also a leading army radical and a Baptist. Woolrych *Britain in Revolution* 355, 714-18.

24. *A Perfect Diurnall* 160, 24 August 1646. Articles of surrender- *Anglia Rediviva* 298-300.

25. W.C. *A Letter from His Excellencies Quarters*. Bayly *Apophtegm* no. 53. *Anglia Rediviva* 300.

26. *Perfect Occurances* 35th week (28 August 1646). Phillips II, 323-7. *Anglia Rediviva* 301. Passes- J.L. Malcolm *Caesar's Due* 117. The Colonels were Ratcliffe Gerard, Hubert Price, John Morgan and Ralph Neale.

27. *Anglia Rediviva* 301, *C.S.P.D. 1625–49, Addenda*, 699. Monmouthshire's share of the estate rental was £4,631 4s. 5d. Of this, £465 17s. was granted to Cromwell, plus the let of a farm worth £200; £765 for preachers; £866 11s. 8d. for the Marquis's two grandchildren; and two manors worth £161 16s. 8d. per annum were sold. Webb 285. Lewis-N.L.W. *Milborne Mss* 2644 31 August 1646.

28. Heath *Raglan Castle* 45-7 (no page numbers, but the Newport Reference Library copy is paginated in pencil). The document used by Heath can be dated on internal evidence to between *c*.1670 and 1760. Kenyon 'Cannon shot mould'. Members of Cadw works staff told me that the shot mould and other cannon shot fragments were found east of the Closet Tower, outside the inner walls of the castle. The measured positions of the shot in the east curtain were recorded in the site foreman's register book, now in the archives of Cadw. Shot of 18 and 20lb weight were found some time before 1879 and one of the Webbs had met an old man who salvaged enough lead piping from the well in the Great Tower to buy a pair of shoes (Webb 284).

29. *C.S.P.D. 1625–49, Addenda*, 700. *Lords Journal* VIII, 498.

30. *C.S.P.V 1643–7*, 223. Bayly *Apothegm* no.57.

31. Bod.L. *Tanner Ms 58* f. 218-218v. Ashton *Counter Revolution* 341-6. Bradney 5 *Hundred of Newport* 95. Roberts 'Parliamentary politics' 669-70.

32. Bod.L. *Tanner Ms 58* f. 218v lists ten clergy involved- Iorwerth Lloyd, Francis Davies, Thomas Bassett, Edward Davies, Jenkin Williams, John Butler, Thomas Morgan, Evan Price, Theodore Price and Nathaniel Gamage.

33. Bod.L. *Tanner Ms 58* f. 173. Warrant to Constables of Miskin Hundred- *Full Relation* (Phillips 336).

34. Summons to Garrison,signed by three Stradlings, Robert and Edward Thomas, Thomas Nott, Charles Kemeys and Richard Bassett, 16 June and Pritchard's reply- Bod.L. *Tanner Ms 58* f. 174-175.

35. Laugharne's report on the affair to Parliament- *A Full Relation of the Late Proceedings* . The Committee at Usk's is *A Declaration of the Proceedings of Divers Knights and other Gentlemen*. Phillips *Civil War* II, 335-343. That of the Cardiff parliamentarians- Bussey Mansell, Edward Pritchard, Edward Stradling and Thomas Herbert- Bod.L. *Tanner Ms 58* ff. 218-218v.

36. *Heads of the Present Grievances* has no date, or, significantly, name of a printer. Walter Powell Diary 14 June 1647 'Sturre in Glamorganshire'. John Pyne- Underdown *Somerset*, Ashton *Counter Revolution* 89-91; 95-105. Dodd *Studies In Stuart Wales* 110-76.

37. *A Full Relation of the … late Rising and Commotion in Wales* 13. Ashton *Counter Revolution* 343.

38. *Declaration of the Proceedings*. The Usk Committee thought that the plot was hatched by Judge Jenkins and other Royalists in the Tower of London.

39. Bod.L. *Tanner Ms 58* f. 218 v.

40. Heath *Historical Account of … Monmouth* 49 (unpaginated). *Monmouth Beacon* 1859. Warlow *History of the Charities of William Jones* 92- 99. Kissack *Monmouth* 313, n.53. M.W. Thompson *The Decline of the Castle* (Cambridge 1987), 179, quoting *Commons Journal* 1, 3 March, 19 July 1647.

41. Roy 'England turned Germany' 144. *A Declaration of the Proceedings* Chepstow bridge- T. T. E 435.7 (April 3 1648).

42. Walter Powell *Diary* 12 Jan 1647/8 'Uske Committee to app'r and s' (? apprehend and suppress). The Breconshire demonstration involved Hugh Games, father-in-law of Edmund Jones of Llansoy. Ashton *Counter Revolution* 347-8, 416-22, 459. Roberts 'Parliamentary politics' 670.

43. *C.S.P.D. 1648–9*, 40-41, 64-5. *Acts. Ord. Interr.* ii, 543-4. *Moderate Intelligencer* 18 May 1648- an eye witness ('next day we marched to Chepstow'). The story (Heath *Handbook to Monmouth* 10) that a Royalist named Evans attempted to shoot Cromwell through the parlour window of Mr Fortune's house at Monmouth is simply one of the many folk tales which Cromwell's name attracted. Contemporery sources are silent on this sensational event.

44. *Cal. Cttee. Comp.* 1276, (Vol 3, 104.7, May 1646); 2351. Underdown *Somerset in the Civil War* 148-9.

45. *Moderate Intelligencer* 18 May 1648; 'R.W.' Fight at Chepstow.

46. Newman *Royalist Officers* no.823, pp.213-14.

47. *A Full Relation of the Taking of Chepstow Castle*. Prisoners included Thomas Lewis and Major Francis Lewis of St Pierre; Major Thomas; Captains Morgan, Buckeswell, John Harris, late of the Marquess of Worcester's Foot, and Christopher Harris; Mancell; Pinner; Doule and Rosstree; Lieutenants Kemeys, Leach, and Codd; and Ensigns Watkin and Morgan. The Harriss may have been kinsmen of William Harris of Gwernesney, Ranger of Wentwood Forest, and so neighbours of Nicholas Kemeys.

48. *Kingdom's Weekly Intelligencer* 24 May 1648. *C.S.P.D. 1660–61*, 438. Miles and Florence Button and Poyer's widow were asking for a warrant to make a Baron (which could be sold).

49. Abbott *Letters and Speeches of Oliver Cromwell* Vol 1, 615-17. The original was in the possession of Hans Winthrop Mortimer in 1762.

50. Abbott *Letters and Speeches* Vol 1, 616. The Letter was found in the attics of St Julians shortly before September 1845, when it appeared in the *Monmouthshire Merlin*. This was Carlyle's (and Abbott's) source.

51. *C.S P.D. 1648–49*, 246. (August 18 1648). Walter Powell *Diary* 22 October, 4 November 1648, 9 February 1648/9.

52. Ashton *Counter Revolution* 51-2, *Acts. Ord. Interr.* ii, 13, *C.S.P.D. 1649–50*, 13 'An act concerning the sequestration of South Wales and the County of Monmouth' (Feb. 23 1649). Income tax- Morrill *Cheshire* 97.

Chapter 7 A Reformation too Far?

1. A. de Tocqueville *Souvenirs, 1848–1851*. In 1640, at the opening of the Long Parliament, the Earl of Northumberland wrote to the Earl of Leicester that parliament was 'fully resolved upon a reformation of all things'. Zagorin *Court and Country* 212.

2. *Perfect Diurnall* no.156 1646. Sir William Catchmay- *Cal. Cttee. Comp.* III, 1678. Jones- Bradney 3.1 *Hundred of Usk* 50-51, 56. The Earl of Pembroke sold Usk Priory to an ancestor of Sir Trevor Williams, who sold it to William ap John, ancestor of William Jones. Jones' tomb in Usk church was recorded in a Herald's visitation of 1683.

3. Dinham was bought by William Blethin, bishop of Llandaff, in 1589. His grandson,William Blethin III, (died unmarried 1676) was the Civil War activist. Dodd *Studies in Stuart Wales* 125. Bradney 4.2 *Hundred of Caldicot* 150-51. Other members included William Herbert; Rice Williams; Roger Williams and Edward Morgan. In November 1651, James Sydwell of Abergavenny replaced James Rumsey (*Cal. Cttee. Comp.* I, 507). There were three committees- for Sequestration; Assessment; (responsible for the monthly tax) and the Militia. The first was the most active and vexatious. Contemperories referred to 'the County Committee' or ' the Committee at Usk'. Herefordshire usage was 'the Committee at Hereford', Aylmer 'Who was ruling in Herefordshire?' 378-80.

4. These included Catchmay, Blethin, Roger Williams and Henry Baker of Abergavenny. William Jones, John Walter and Rice Williams were added soon after. Phillips *Justices of the Peace* 359.

5. Madeleine Gray 'clergy as rememberencers', 118. Warmington *Civil War, Interregnum and Restoration*, 113. Underdown *Somerset in the Civil War* 145 Hart *Country Clergy* 119-32. A.G. Matthews *Walker Revised* (Oxford 1947), updating John Walker *Attempt Toward Recovering an Account of the Numbers and Sufferings of the Clergy of the Church of England who were Sequestrated, Harrassed etc in the late … Great Rebellion* (London 1714) covers only English dioceses, and for Monmouthshire only Monmouth and Dixton, then in Hereford diocese. Commissioners for Monmouthshire under the 1654 Act- *Acts Ord. Interr.* II, 973. Quarrell- Richards *Penal Code* 93-4.

6. Green 'persecution' 510. Durston *Cromwell's Major Generals* 159-166.

7. Anthony Wood *Athenae Oxoniensis* (3rd ed. edited Bliss, London 1817), 531; Foster *Alumni Oxoniensis* 111. The son of John Vaughan of Caethley Merionethshire, evicted 'before the Act' (Richards *Puritan Movement* 229 and n), his appeal was refused- (Richards 55). He became headmaster of Abergavenny Grammar School. Parish register- Gwent Record Office D/ Pa 111.1. Petition- B.L. *Harleian Mss 163*, f. 740v., quoted Eales *Puritans and Roundheads* 106. Gray 'Clergy as Rememberencers' 118-19.

8. Green *Persecution* 510-12. Clegg- Walker *Sufferings of the Clergy* (1714) 222.

9. Gwent C.R.O. D/ Pa 30.1. 'The old Register Book of Bryngwyn deliver ... seige of Raglan by Wm. Jones of Usk Esq, Parliament Commissioner, to his Kinsman David Pritchard of Bryngwyn, was all torn in pieces and lost saving this one poor leaf, hereunto affixed. Teste Roberto Frampton, Rector.' Bradney 2.1 *Hundred of Raglan* 106. *Alumni Oxoniensis 1500–1714* II, 528. Siddons *Visitations by the Heralds* 181. His son, William Frampton, was senior proctor of the University of Oxford. Robert Frampton was a kinsman of Robert Frampton of Pimperne in Dorset (1622–1708), a former royalist officer, later chaplain to the Levant Company's factory at Aleppo and bishop of Gloucester, deprived of his see in 1690 as a non-juror. *Alumni Oxoniensis loc. cit.*

10. J. Foster *Alumni Oxoniensis*; J. and J.A. Venn *Alumni Cantabrigiensis Part 1* (Cambridge 1922-7).

11. T. Richards *Religious Developments in Wales* 46, 55-6; *Puritan Movement in Wales* 67, 129, 229. Stephen Roberts *Parliamentary politics* 655-6 and n.33. In 1670 he was resident at Woolton in Gloucestershire *Alumni Oxoniensis* II, Diary- W.H. Green *Monmouth Beacon* 1859 W.H. Warlow *History of the Charities of William Jones* 1899, 92-99.

12. Bedwas font- Walker Mss C.4, folio 16, Richards *Puritan Movement* 66.

13. Walker Mss C.4, folio 65, quoted Richards 345.

14. Henry Walter's maintenance was from the tithes of Machen and rectorial tithes of Bassaleg, Peterston Wentloog and Newport. Richards 88-9. Bradney 4.2 *Hundred of Caldicot* 189. Blindman- Nuttall *Welsh Saints* 9-10.

15. *C.S.P.D. 1651*, 339; *C.S.P.D. 1657–58*, 363. Nuttall 'The faith of Walter Cradock' *Welsh Saints* 18-36. Major Richard Creed had been secretary to Admirals Blake and Sandwich. His brother was a friend and colleague of Pepys and frequently appears in the Diaries. Richard Creed's memorial is in Llangwm church. Julian Mitchell 'Monmouthshire Politics'.

16. Walter Powell *Diary* 27 May, 30 June, 1 September 1650; 2 May 1651; 8 March 1654. Bradney 1.1 *Hundred of Skenfrith* 122.

17. Gwent C.R.O. D/ Pa.14. 104. Gray 'Clergy as Rememberencers'. James's note of 1660 in his parish register distinguishes between 'all the children w'ch Lewis James, cler' christened ... as if they had bin christened *in facie ecclesiae*' and 'all such persons w'ch were buried (and also all those persons w'ch were married) in Bedwelltie' in the Interregnum. Rosser would hardly have permitted his expelled predecessor to perform burials in the parish churchyard.

18. Claims in the Exchequer Court that these included Caldicot, Llanwern and Portskewett were clearly false, unless by the latter Sudbrook was meant. Playfair Field of Penhow officiated in Raglan church in 1660 'Reading of Common Prayer' and a new vicar was appointed in 1661. Richards *Puritan Movement* 229 and n; 242; 50; 431. For a description of the monuments before their destruction see Symonds *Diary* 207. *Gallant Siege of Parliament's Forces* postscript. *Montgomeryshire Collections* 20 (1886) 35-8.

19. Wright 'Church Bells of Monmouthshire' 5, 42-3.

20. Panteg, Christchurch and Llanwenarth acquired new bells in 1661, (Panteg and Christchurch two apiece), Llanelen and Penallt in 1662 and Bishton in 1663 Wright 'Church Bells' part 4, 89-90.

21. In 1645 wheat was 35s. a quarter; 1647–8 62s.; 1649–50 65s. 6d. By 1653–4 it had fallen to 25s. and by 1654–5 to 21s. Firth *Cromwell's Army* 184-5, quoting Rogers *History of Prices* V, 826.

22. Wright 'Church Bells' part 2, 62, 68; part 3, 226; part 4, 88; part 6, 230, 238-9.

23. Wright 'Church Bells' part 1, 307; part 2, 58; part 3 226; part 4, 81; part 5, 42-3.

24. J.A. Bradney *Registers of Llandewi Rhydderch 1670–1783* (London 1919); *Registers of Caerwent 1568–1812 and Llanfair Discoed 1680–1812* (London 1920); *Register of Grosmont 1589–1812* (London 1921).

25. Siddons *Visitations of the Heralds* 215.

26. Bradney 1.2b *Hundred of Abergavenny* 355.

27. Richards *Religious Developments* 156, 284. John Tombes *A Plea for Antipaedobaptists* (London 1654); John Cragge *The Arraignment and Conviction of Anabaptism* (London 1656).

28. Cragge was author of *The Light of God's Counterance*, preached at Llantilio Pertholey on June 5 1653 by 'John Cragge, Master of Arts and Dispenser of the Gospel there' (1654). N.L.W. *Civil War Tracts* 188, p.64.He also wrote *The Royal Prerogative Vindicated and the converted recusant convinced* (1661). This claimed to attack both 'Romish superstition and fanatic disorder', but apart from a brief reference to nonconformity, was a sustained anti-Catholic attack. Cragge was a client of Sir Trevor Williams and William Morgan of Tredegar. Jenkins *Anti-Popery* 282.

29. Walcott- *Cal. Ctte. Comp.* 1060. Nuttall *Welsh Saints* 12-16. Eales *Puritans and Roundheads* 10 and n.27. Ap Howell- *Cal. Ctte. Comp.* 3007.

30. *H.M.C. 14th Report, part 3* (1894), 130. Lucy Hutchinson *Memoirs* 259. *Cal. Ctte. Comp.* III, 1882, 1711. Walter Powell *Diary* 2 August 1651.

31. *Cal. Cttee. Adv. Mon.* 1399 (30 September 1651).

32. P.R.O. S.P. 23, Vol 8, 203, 209; Vol 10, 59, 160; Vol 11, 126. Vol 95, 232. *Cal. Cttee. Comp.* 364, 2406, 3193.

33. P.R.O. S.P. 23, Vol 24, 1125. *Cal. Cttee. Comp.* 2406. During the 'Popish plot' the family were accused of harbouring the priest Thomas Andrews. 'J.D.' *True Narrative of ... Father Andrews* (1679).

34. *Cal. Cttee. Comp.* V, 3233. Walter Powell *Diary* 12 Jan 1648. Abergavenny Museum Gunter Papers A /44-61. Pritchard- P.R.O. S.P. 23, Vol.17, 643. Lindley 'The part played by Catholics in the Civil War' 38.

35. *Cal. Cttee. Comp.* 1514 (Sir Philip Jones); 1967 (Roger Williams, Kinhiley); 2310-11 (Sir Edward Morgan;). Sequestration elsewhere- Morrill *Cheshire 1630–1660*, 203-15.

36. Ashton *Counter Revolution* 100. *Cal. Cttee. Comp.* 644, 722, 739.

37. *H.M.C. Manuscripts of the Earl of Egmont I*, part 2 (1905), 344, 350-1, 410-11, F. Fernandez-Armesto *The Spanish Armada: The Experience of War in 1588* (Oxford 1988), 1-5.

38. *Cal. Cttee. Comp.* 1130–31, 1537. Durston *Cromwell's Major Generals*. Basset claimed to have gone in search of the king at Abergavenny and Hereford to surrender his commission, but was captured before he could do so. The formal

gardens shown in a painting of Tre-Worgan *c*.1670 (Bradney 2.1 *Hundred of Raglan* 44), now at the Museum of Welsh Life, St Fagans, are a fantasy of Netherlandish inspiration, intended as interior decoration. Another version locates them at Carshalton, Surrey (home of the Grosmont Gainsfords) and others are known. John Harris *The Artist and the Country House* (1979), 58. I am grateful to Elizabeth Whittle and Julian Mitchell for these details. The absence of traces on the ground confirm that the garden never existed.

39. *Acts Ord. Interr.* I, 1136. The commissioners included Sir Trevor Williams; Thomas Morgan and William Morgan of Machen and William Baker of Abergavenny, all active Whigs in the next reign, and the Parliamentarians Thomas Herbert of Usk, Christopher Catchmay, Thomas Hughes, William Blethin and William Packer.

40. A.H. Dodd *D.W.B.* 917-18. *Cal. Cttee. Adv. Mon.* 1466.

41. *Cal. Comm. Comp.* 1705. Bradney 2.1 *Hundred of Raglan* 27.

42. Newman *Royalist Officers* no.1596, pp.419-20. *C.S.P.D. 1654*, 273- prisoners in Tower for high treason, including Wintour and Gilbert and Charles Gerard. Marriage portions- N.L.W. *Tredegar Mss 916* (Dec 29, 1653). On Wildman's other money making activities, including treasure hunting, see Keith Thomas *Religion and the Decline of Magic* 236-7.

43. *C.S.P.D. 1660–7 Addenda* 55.

44. Newman *Royalist Officers* no.1341, p.822. P.R.O. S.P. 23, Vol 206, 272, May *Cal. Comm. Comp.* 1276. do. Vol 12, 210, May 1651 (discharge of sequestration). Parliament used the fine to pay rewards. *Cal. Cttee. Comp.* 808-10.

45. *Cal. Cttee. Comp.* 623. A manuscript collection of documents on the trial and execution of Sir Walter Raleigh. belonging to Sir Charles Kemeys survives as B.L. *Add Mss 73086*.

46. *C.S.P.D. 1660–61*, 150-51. Newman *Royalist Officers* no.576, p.147.

47. *C.S.P.D. 1660–61*, 433, 444.

48. *Harleian Miscellany* (London 1745) III, 325-335.

49. P.R.O. S.P.23, Vol 109, 725-29. Reid *Royalist Army III* 146. *C.S.P.D. 1655*, 294. I am grateful to Conleth Manning for information on his later career in Ireland. Unfortunately, the evidence is complicated by the presence of several namesakes.

50. Huws 'Llengarwch Reciwsantaid' 14. Pugh, Philip Evans and Sullard are referred to by Arnold as Captains (*Abstract of Examinations* 5). With Evans (b.1645) this obviously cannot refer to wartime rank. Sylliard- Reid *Royalist Army* III, 192-3. His appearance in the Indigent Officers list shows that he had been a serving soldier. William Pugh-Raglan surrender list 1646 and Indigent officer, Herefordshire (Reid 164). There is confusion in the sources between the secular priest William Pugh of Skenfrith and the north Walian Jesuit Robert Pugh, alias Robert Phillips. According to Anthony à Wood *Athenae Oxoniensis* the latter was chaplain to English Catholic troops fighting for Spain in Flanders, and during the Civil War was dismissed by the Jesuits for accompanying the royal army without the consent of his superiors (Ellis *Catholic Martyrs* 162-3). This parallels William Pugh's possible role as military chaplain. Arnold's 'Doctor Pugh' and 'Captain Pugh' are probably simple duplication. Robert Pugh's documented post-war career until his death in Newgate in January 1680 shows that he was not in Monmouthshire.

51. Berry and Lee *Cromwellian Major General* Appendix E, 287- 90, from P.R.O. *State Papers Domestic* Interregnum 25/77. This was the normal establishment of a New Model Army cavalry troop. At the time of Penruddock's rising, Nicholas reported to Cromwell (16 March 1654) that he had posted troops, sent 100 horse and dragoons to reinforce Major Creed at Gloucester and kept others in Monmouth. He had also imprisoned those whom 'the honest people thought most dangerous' in Chepstow castle. (Webb II, 322-3).

52. Durston *Cromwell's Major Generals* 140-47. Bradney 4.2 *Hundred of Caldicot* 150-1.

53. Berry and Lee *Cromwellian Major General* 183-5, quoting P.R.O. *Order Book Council of State- State Papers* 25, 77 f.920 (10 July 1656) and *State Papers Domestic 1661* Vol 34, f.27. *C.S.P.D 1656–7*, 16-17.

54. Berry to Thurlow 19 February 1655 (old style), Bod. L. *Rawlinson Mss A 35* f.172. Berry and Lee *Cromwellian Major General* 158-9 and photograph of letter plate VI. Durston *Cromwell's Major Generals* 75, 90, 173,

55. Durston *Cromwell's Major Generals* 87-90. *C.S.P.D. 1656–7* 161, 233-4. Jenkins *Making of a Ruling Class* 111. Abergavenny lost its borough charter after 1688 when its burgesses refused to swear an oath of loyalty to the new regime. The folk tale that the windows of St Mary's church were buried to protect them in the Civil War is also told of the Jesse window at Llanrhaeadr in north Wales. Gaunt *Nation under Siege* 39.

56. *Letter Book of John Byrd* 230-31. *C.S.P.D. 1661–2*, 141.

57. Colonel Thomas Horton wrote from Bridgend with news of St Fagans:- 'Captain Nicholets (this bearer) with Col. Okey's own troop of dragoons, mounted with some horses on the right wing, disputed the first encounter very hotly, where he showed much resolution, and beat the enemy out of two closes and over a little brook and they maintained the ground under command of the enemy's shot until the forlorn hope of foot, commanded by Captain Lieutenant Fann, and horse came to the relief. Then they beat the enemy from hedge to hedge …' *Confirmation of a Great Victory in Wales, sent in a letter from Colonel Horton* (1648), printed Phillips M*emoirs of the Civil War* II, 365-9. Letter from Colonel Okey, 8 May 1648, printed Johns *Historical Traditions* V, 147-8. Siddons *Visitations by the Heralds* 178-9.

58. D. Underwood 'Settlement in the counties, 1653–1658' in Aylmer *Interregnum* 179-80.

59. *Cal. Cttee. Comp.* 2311. ('Bartholemew Morgan' is a clerical error for Sir Edward Morgan Bart). *C.S.P.D. 1649–50*, 176, 509. Repair of castle- *C.S.P.D. 1654*, 52.

60. *C.S.P.D. 1651*, 339 (18 August).

Chapter 8   Restoration and Reaction 1660–90. Plus ça Change

1. Cromwell- Abbott *Letters and Speeches* III, 318-19 June 1654. Warmington *Civil War, Interregnum and Restoration* 158-161, 168. Underwood *Royalist Conspiracy* 260-264.

2. Clarendon *History of the Rebellion* XVI, 35-43. *C.S.P.D. 1659–60*, 114, 205.

3. *Cal Cttee Comp.* 3248. Thomas Veale was in royalist plots from 1648 on and received a commission from Charles II to raise regiments of foot and horse. Underdown *Royalist Conspiracy* 204. Hutton *Restoration* 68- 84. Morgan and Fairfax- Woolrych *Britain in Revolution* 750-51.

4. *C.S.P.D. 1666–7*, 500. A.H. Dodd *D.W.B.* 918-19. Julian Mitchell 'Nathan Rogers' 37-8. Charles had promised Worcester the Dukedom of Somerset and the Garter. Warburton III, 18-20.

5. *C.S.P.D. 1663–4*, 103; *1664–5*, 446, 470; *1665–6*, 16 (supply of timber planks); *1664–5*, 22, 169; *1665–6*, 364, 384 (prisoners). In May 1656, 123 Dutch prisoners were transferred from Bristol to Chepstow Castle. Particularly unfortunate were people like Rowland Gilbert, an Englishman long resident in Holland, captured on a Dutch merchant ship and imprisoned in Chepstow *C.S.P.D. 1665–6*, 411. There is a muster roll of the Chepstow garrison of October 1662 in Society of Antiquaries Library, Wakeman Mss, 790/ 1.

6. Newman *Monmouthshire* 400-401

7. M. Gray 'clergy as rememberencers'. Gwent Record Office D/Pa. 14. 104.

8. Newman *Monmouthshire* 310.

9. Henry Jessey *The Lord's Loud Call* (T.T.E. 1038.8). Richards *Religious Developments* 396.

10. Green *Re-Establishment of the Church* 179-202. Do. 'Persecution of 'Scandalous' and 'Malignant' clergy' 531. An unusual case was that of John Boncle at Christchurch. Regularly instituted in April 1659, on the death of the unejected Lancelot Warneford, he nevertheless resigned his living in 1660.

11. Green *Re-Establishment* 143-54, Richards *Puritan Movement in Wales* 51, 488, quoting Calamy II, 473, 610. Nuttall *Welsh Saints* 9-10.

12. Nathan Rogers *Memoirs of Monmouthshire* 83-4. Bradney 4.1 *Hundred of Caldicot* 112, 148. A conventicle existed in Caldicot in 1669. Edmund Jones *Geographical … Account of the Parish of Aberystruth* 96. Coffey *Persecution and Toleration* 166-179.

13. Jenkins *Making of a Ruling Class* 124-8. Whiteman *Compton Census*. All figures are taken from her edition.

14. Jenkins 'Anti popery' 276. Michaelston Y Vedw had 72 conformists, 8 nonconformists and no papists. From the 1811 census, Whiteman deduces a population of 80 men and women over 16 (there were 176 inhabitants in 1801). Yet similar figures for nearby Bassaleg (89 conformists, 8 nonconfomists) may represent households. The parish is six times the size of Michaelston and the 1801 population was 986. Shirenewton and Marshfield- Richards *Wales under the Penal Code* 93-4.

15. Raglan, Llandenny and Bryngwyn are missing. Penrhos (35), Clytha (36) and Bettws Newydd (21) have high figures which Whiteman saw as the total of men and women over 16, though Arnold claimed there were 80 'reputed Popish recusants, besides women and children' in Clytha (*Abstract of Several Examinations* 5). However, the figures for Dingestow (10), Tregaer (9) and Llanfihangel Ystern Llewern (3) probably represent households. The livings of Dingestow and Tregaer were held together and the same incumbent was presumably responsible for both entries.

16. Dodd *D.W.B.* 652-3. *C.S.P.D. 1660*, 433, 444. *Letter Book of John Byrd* no.386, p.176. *C.S.P.D. 1661–2*, 138. Julian Mitchell 'Nathan Rogers' 26-7, do. 'Speech Court of Wentwood' 66.

17. Jenkins *Making of a Ruling Class* 68.

18. Phillips *Justices of the Peace* 364 (24 Nov 1677); *H.M.C. Finch Manuscripts Vol 2, 1670–90*, 44. King to Worcester, March 9, 1678. *C.S.P.D. 1678, Addenda 1674–9* . Probert and Arnold were restored to the Bench on 16 April 1679, with Edward and Edmund Morgan, Charles Van and Roger Oates. Phillips 365. Sir Edward Morgan of Llantarnam had been removed as a Papist in June 1676 at the instance of the Bishop of Llandaff. Philip Jenkins 'Glamorgan gentry' and 'Anti-Popery' 287-8.

19. Nathan Rogers *Memoirs of Monmouthshire* 84-85, Julian Mitchell 'Nathan Rogers and the Wentwood case'. William Wolseley J.P. appears thus in the heraldic visitation of 1683. Siddons *Visitations by the Heralds* 219. He was probably a kinsman of the Staffordshire royalist Colonel Devereux Wolseley (Newman *Royalist Officers* no.1600, p.420).

20. D. Owen *Wales in the Reign of James Ist* 123-4. A.G. Mein *Norman Usk: The Birth of a Town* (Usk 1986), 98, quoting *Free Press of Monmouthshire* 16 February 1861.

21. Phillips *Justices of the Peace* 364. Those imprisoned were Rogers; Nathaniel Field of Penhow; Philip Edwards of Llanvaches; Meredith Howell. The others were Edward and John Kemeys and Thomas Blethin.

22. Dodd *Studies in Stuart Wales* 83.

23. Mitchell 'Nathan Rogers' 37-38. Arnold *Abstract of Several Examinations*.

24. *Letter from a Gentleman in Gloucestershire*. A draft, in the Marquis's hand, survives at Badminton. Mc Clain *Beaufort* 145. Glamorgan gentry and the anti-Worcester 'Popish plot' agitatation- Jenkins *Making of a Ruling Class* 128-31.

25. Kenyon *Popish Plot* 93-6. Bradney 3.2 *Hundred of Usk* 177. Newport Public Library M.000 282.5 (Kemeys Mss)- copy of Bedloe's allegations, Nov 19 1678, of a Jesuit plot to assasinate the king at Newmarket, involving a group of Worcester's associates, including his steward Charles Price, two Vaughans of Courtfield and Charles Milborne. Chepstow Castle was to be surrendered to Charles Wintour of Lydney by the Governor.

26. Herbert Croft *Short Narrative* 3-7. There were Catholic Crofts at Blackbrook, Skenfrith and at Llanfair Cilgoed. The Crofts of Llanthony remained Catholic until Victorian times. Philip Jenkins 'Anti-popery' 287. The present house at the Cwm was built in 1830.

27. McClain *Beaufort* 140-45. *Letter from a Gentleman* 29-35. The King's Council ordered that Milborne be prosecuted for keeping a Jesuit and speaking dangerous words on the bench. Miller *Popery and Politics* 61.

28. Arnold *An Abstract of Several Examinations* 8-9.

29. *A Short Memorandum* (1679). After studies at Watten and Liege in Flanders, Evans joined the English Mission in 1675. Canning 'Cardiff Martyrs' 38-47. Foley *Records of the English Province* Vol 1, 232 and 5 (series XII), 882.

Lewis's letter is signed with a pseudonym, but is certainly by him. Greenhaugh *Abstract of Several Examinations* 8-9, 17- 'Mr Evans, a reputed Popish priest, entertained at the house of Charles Prodger Esq … a Justice of the Peace … great numbers of Men and Women resort thither to mass'. William James:- 'great numbers of Roman Catholics resort to the house of Mr Thomas Gunter at Abergavenny, … [who] … entertains one Captain Evans, a popish priest'. *Trial of John Giles* 18- When the under sheriff came to give him notice that he had a warrant for his speedy execution, the said Evans being in a game at Tennis said '… I will play out my set first'. Jenkins ' Glamorgan gentry'. Kenyon *Popish Plot* 214.

30. David Lewis *Narrative of the Imprisonment and Tryal of Mr David Lewis* … Canning 'Titus Oates Plot'. *C.S.P.D. 1678, Addenda 1674–9*, 592- report on arrest by Thomas Lewis and Charles Price. Lists the books, vestments and liturgical material in Lewis's possession at his arrest, but omits the silver plate (2 chalices and patens, pair of flower pots, thurible and cover, cruet, altar bell and pair of candlesticks). When they were found in Price's possession in the next reign, he had some explaining to do. Price was uncle to William Bedloe and the Abergavenny apothecary Christopher Price, former clerk of the Monmouthshire section of the Committee for the Propagation of the Gospel in Wales, who in 1695 gave land at Llanwenarth for the first Baptist chapel in Wales. The site of the smithy where Lewis was arrested is marked by a circular setting in the pavement opposite Llantarnam church.

31. The Golden Lion, a large and commodious inn, first recorded in 1592, stood at the corner of Frogmore Street and Lion Street (to which it gave its name). I am very grateful to Frank Olding and Alan Probert for information about the inn and its internal arrangements. Rebuilt on a smaller scale in Edwardian times, it was later demolished.

32. Ignatius (Walter) Price S.J.- Ellis *Catholic Martyrs* 112-13. Foley *Records of the English Province* Vol 1, 12. Kenyon *Popish Plot* 214. A Monmouthshire man, born 1610, he had served in the Jesuit Welsh mission since 1644.

33. *A True Narrative of that Grande Jesuit Father Andrews* (Andrews was not in fact a Jesuit). Pritchard was from Blaen-Lymman, Monmouthshire Foley *Records of the English Province* Vol 1, 633-4.

34. David Lewis *Narrative*. Lewis says that he 'had a strong influence on the judge, or being his kinsman' (Gwent C.R.O. D 3267.114)

35. *State Trials* (London 1810), 250-59. The same sentence was passed at Monmouth in January 1840 on the three leaders of the Chartist rising. William Pugh OSB 'Captain, doctor, monk, priest, and bard' - Daniel Huws 'Llengarwch Reciwsantiaid Gwent' 14 and Geraint Bowen 'Gwilym Pue "Bardd Mair" a thelu'r Penrhyn'. *Efrydiau Catholig* 2 (1947), 11-35. Oath of allegiance- Kenyon *Popish Plot* 227. There is no reference to Ferris's Coffee House in Bryant Lillywhite *London Coffee Houses: A Reference Book* (1963).

36. *Lords Journal* XIII, 517. H.M.C *11th Report, part 2*, 151. David Lewis *Narrative*. Kenyon *Popish Plot* 152-3.

37. Gwent C.R.O. D. 3267.114 (notebook of Henry Phillips), a copy, dated 1780, of Lewis's account of his arrest and trial. It is a transcript of a manuscript by Lewis, preserved at Llantarnam, where he was a priest for many years and where he was arrested. The account of his arrest and trial are almost identical to the printed versions, but the section dealing with events following the London visit seem to be unique to this version. Several episodes are dated by Lewis as in a diary. I am very grateful to David Rimmer for drawing my attention to this source.

38. Gwent C.R.O. Henry Phillips notebook.

39. G.M. Trevelyan *England Under the Stuarts* 330. Kenyon *Popish Plot* 178.

40. Kenyon *Popish Plot* 214.

41. N.L.W. *Baker-Gabb Mss 723, Tredegar Park Mss 105/64*. David Lewis *Narrative* and *Speech*. A contemporary copy, with what seems to be Lewis's signature, once belonging to his kinsmen the Baker-Gabbs of Abergavenny, survives in the National Library of Wales, together with another copy from the Tredegar House Mss. There are at least two printed versions, including Lewis's own account.

42. Thomas Hearne- P. Bliss (ed.) *Reliquiae Hearnianae* (1734).Vol 2, 838-9.

43. Holt 'Glamorgan Mission'. Miller *Popery and Politics* 242, 248.

44. Haines *Abergavenny Chronicle* 17 and 31 January 1908 and *Arch. Camb.* 1908, 291-2. There is a photograph of the mural before removal in the Haines Collection in Newport Public Library.

45. Abergavenny museum Box 22A

46. *Pope's Downfall at Abergavenny*. Miller *Popery and Politics* 182-8.

47. *C.S.P.D. 1678, addenda 1674–9*, 592. P.R.O. *Privy Council Office Register* no.68, p.406. quoted Canning 'Titus Oates Plot' 7, part 3, p.100.

48. *H.M.C. Finch Manuscripts Vol 2, 1670–1690*, 77, Daniel Finch to Sir John Finch. *Trial of John Giles*; *England's Second Warning Piece*; *Tryal and Condemnation of John Giles*. Sir John Pollock *The Popish Plot* (London 1903), 394-9. Kenyon *Popish Plot* 191. Mitchell 'Monmouthshire Politics' 8-9.

49. *H.M.C. House of Lords Mss 1678–88*, 207-9. Kenyon *Popish Plot* 227. Miller *Popery and Politics* 61, *Lords Journal* XIII, 621-2. The number of Catholics involved varies between sources. Francis Jenkins was married to the widow of Thomas Morgan's son Edmund Morgan, killed in a duel by Charles Williams, founder of the Williams Charity, Caerleon.

50. Kenyon *Popish Plot* 214-15. Arnold to Speke, May 17, 1680- *C.S.P.D. 1679–80*, 483. Worcester- *C.S.P.D. 1680–81*, 38; *1682*, 221-2, 275-6, 288-9, 538-9, 575-6. Jenkins *Making of a Ruling Class* 129. *H.M.C. 12 th Report*, Appendix 9, 88 (Marquis of Worcester's Papers). Mitchell 'Monmouthshire Politics' 10-11. Canning 'Titus Oates Plot' 7, part 3, 105.

51. Rogers *Memoirs of Monmouthshire* 90.

52. *C.S.P.D. 1690–91*, 11. Warrant to Sir Henry Goodrick, Lt Gen of the Ordnance, to dismantle Chepstow Castle and send ordnance to Chester, 13 May 13, 1690. Mitchell 'Monmouthshire politics' 11-12.

53. Horatia Durant *Henry, First Duke of Beaufort* 71.

54. Julian Mitchell 'Nathan Rogers and the Wentwoiod case'. N.L.W. Tredgar Mss 1461-3, Thomas Wakeman to Octavius Morgan 1863.

Bibliography

Unpublished Primary Sources

Abergavenny Museum
Box 22 A. Thomas Gunter Papers

Bodleian Library
Carte Ms 30 f.307 r-v. Ormonde's Papers.Alan Boteler's journey to Raglan 1646
Tanner Ms 58 Glamorgan Rising, 1647
Tanner Ms 60 ff.440- 41 Sir Trevor Williams's services to Parliament
Tanner Ms 66 Thomas Morgan and Nicholas Kemeys re county magazine 1642
Tanner Ms 303 Fitzwilliam Coningsby's papers.

British Library
Additional Mss 18980-18982. Prince Rupert's correspondence 1642- 1658.
Harleian 280, ff.157-164. List of Welsh recusants
Harleian 595, ff.1-8. Bp Godwin of Llandaff- impropriators, communicants and recusants, diocese of Llandaff 1603
Harleian 986, ff.77-143. Symonds Diary of the Marches of the Royal Army
Harleian 6804 f.107 (Papers of Royalist Council of War). List of Commissioners of Impress for Monmouthshire
Harleian 6852 (do.) King and Gerard in South Wales July 1645
Plutarch 64 F. Raglan cavalry garrison 1645
Sloane 1519 f 60 Thomas Lunsford to Prince Rupert. 9 March 1644

Cardiff City Library
Ms 4. 1224/1-3. Augusta Rayer-Jenkins. Biographical list of clergy, Llandaff diocese

Gwent County Record Office, Cwmbran
D./ Pa 14.104 Parish Register, Bedwellty
D./ Pa 30.1. Parish Register, Bryngwyn
D./ Pa 86. 1. Parish Register, Chepstow
D/ Pa 111.1 Parish Register, Panteg
Misc Mss 253-8. Letters Charles 1st to Sheriff, November 1642–August 1643.
Misc. Mss 648 Letterbook of Richard Herbert
Misc. Mss 1357 Edward Herbert to Thomas Morgan, 28 March 1643
D. 1059.26 The Tregaer manuscript
D. 3267.114. Llantarnam Estate Records. Notebook of Henry Phillips, 1780

National Library of Wales
Ms 11420 E (Pandy 65) Notes on Gunter papers by Rev.John Davies F.S.A.
Ms 13072 B. (Llanover B.12) Llyfyr Jenkin Richard
Ms 17088A Diary of Walter Powell
Ms 17091 Walter Powell Mss:-
    C.44 Letters and papers of Walter Powell relating to the Civil War
    C.45 Accounts of Llantilio mill, 1621–1637
    C. 85-86. Contributions of parish of Llantilio Crossenny towards support of royal army at Raglan, Feb-April 1646, printed Bradney *Contributions towards the Royal army in 1646* (Newport 1921)
    C. 261, 253. Assessment of taxes, Llantilio Crossenny, towards the maintainance of Sir Thomas Fairfax's army in Ireland 1648
    C. 625, 648. Will and probate of Walter Powell 1654–6
Tredegar Park Ms 93/52 List of Papists in Monmouthshire, 1690
Tredegar Park Ms 93/ 53- 58. Lists of Papists in Monmouthshire 1706
Tredegar Park Ms 911 Edward Stradling to William Morgan 17 September 1642
Tredegar Park Ms 916 Mary Wintour to Thomas Morgan 29 December 1653
Tredegar Park Ms 1461-3 Thomas Wakeman to Octavius Morgan 1862
Baker Gabb Ms 723 Dying speech of David Lewis- contemperory copy with signature
Kemeys-Tynte Mss
Milborne Mss 2644 Thomas Lewis to Sir Thomas Fairfax 31 August 1646
Pa. 32 Parish Register, Monmouth, Vol 1, 1598–1686

Newport Reference Library
M 000 282.5 Collection of documents, pamphlets etc relating to the 'Popish plot'
M 000 946 Collection of material relating to the Civil War in Monmouthshire

Individual items and pamphlets listed separately below.

M 000 946 Photocopies of six letters from Charles 1st to High Sheriff of Monmouthshire November 1642–August 1643 (originals at Llanarth Court 1958)

M 000 282.5 'Interesting discovery (of the Gunter chapel) at Abergavenny' (Haines Collection)

M 000 282.5 (Kemeys Mss) Copy of Bedloe's allegations before the House of Lords re involvement of various Monmouthshire gentlemen in a Jesuit plot to assasinate the king at Newmarket, 19 Nov 1678.
List of Priests and Jesuits in Monmouthshire 1678

M 000 5461 List of property in Monmouthshire belonging to Catholic non jurors (1720)

M 000 282.5 K.J. Lindley *The Part played by the Catholics in the Civil War in Lancashire and Monmouthshire* University of Manchester M.A. thesis 1965 photocopy)

Northamptonshire Record Office
Finch Hatton Mss 133 ff.44-45. List of Royalist Commissioners of Array

National Archives/ Public Record Office
S.P. 16 State Papers Domestic
S.P. 19 Papers of the Committee for the Advance of Money
S.P. 23 Papers of the Committee for Compounding with Delinquents

Society of Antiquaries Library, London
Ms 790. Thomas Wakeman Collection.
Ms 790 /1 Muster roll, Garrison in Chepstow Castle 4 October 1662
Ms 790/5 Transcripts of Civil War newsletters
Ms 790/ 21 Printed pamphlets relating to Popish Plot

William Salt Library, Stafford
Salt Ms 33. Fair copy of Compton census, diocese of Llandaff 1676

Official Publications

Acts and Ordinances of the Interregnum 1642–1660 ed. C.H. Firth and R.S. Rait (3 vols, 1911)

Calendar of the Proceedings of the Committee for Compounding with Delinquents1642–1660 ed. Mary A.E. Green (London 1889–92, 5 vols.)

Calendar of the Proceedings of the Committee for the Advance of Money ed. M.A.E.Green (London 1881), 3 vols.

Calendar of State Papers, Domestic ed. M.A.E. Green (London 1867-95, 40 volumes)

Calendar of State Papers relating to English Affairs....in the Archives and Collections
of Venice ed. H. F. Brown and A.B. Hinds (London 1864–1940, 38 vols.)

Historical Manuscripts Commission

Third Report Appendix 1, 420. Marquis of Worcester's Papers. Grant of Earl of Pembroke's lands in Monmouthshire

Seventh Report (1879) Appendix 1, 689 Papers relating to Herefordshire and Monmouthshire. Complaints re taxation assesments in Monmouthshire

Eleventh Report Appendix 2 Manuscripts of the House of Lords 1678–1688 (1887)

Twelfth Report Appendix 9 (1891) 12-14 Marquess of Worcester's Papers

Thirteenth Report Appendix 1 Portland Manuscripts Vol 1 (1891)

Clerk of the Parliament's Papers. Lord Edward Herbert and outbreak of war

Thirteenth Report Appendix 2 Portland Manuscripts Vol 2 (1893)

Fourteenth Report, Appendix 2 Portland Manusripts Vol 3 (1894)

Calendar of the Manuscripts of the Marquess of Bath (1904)

9. *Salisbury (Cecil) Manuscripts* XIV, Addenda (1923); XVIII (1940);

12. Manuscripts of the Dean and Chapter of Wells II (1914)

Journals of the House of Commons

Journals of the House of Lords

Newsletters- Civil War and Popish Plot

1641

A Great Discovery of a Damnable plot at Rugland Castle in Monmouthshire in Wales. Related to the High Court of Parliament by John Davis The Chief Actor being the Earle of Worcester
Bernard Alsop, Nov. 12 1641
T.T. E 176 (13) . N.R.L. M.447. 900. C.C.L. W3 3565

A Discovery of a horrible and bloody treason and conspiracie ... with a plot by the Earle of Worcester in Wales
John Thomas, Nov 15 1641
NLW 186

REFERENCES & BIBLIOGRAPHY

1642

A True Copie of the Petition of the Knights, Justices of the Peace and Other Gentlemen, Ministers and Freeholders (in numbers many thousands) of the County of Monmouth
William Larner, May 17 1642
T.T. E 669 f.6. (20) N.L.W. 199. N.R.L. M.000 282.5.

A Loving and Loyal Speech spoken unto the excellency of our Noble Prince Charles by Sir Hugh Vaughan, the 2 of October at Raglan Castle in Monmouthshire
John Johnson, October 2, 1642.
T.T. E 122. 14. N.L.W. 185. C.C.L.

True and Happy News from Wales, declaring the proceedings of the Marquis of Hertford in Glamorganshire
Phillips II, 23-4

A True and Joyful Relation of a Victory obtained by the Inhabitants of Glamorganshire against the Marquess of Hertford and the Caveleers
Fowler 5 October 1642
T.T. E 119 (31)

1643

The Copy of a Letter Sent from Bristol wherein is set down the Relation of the Great Victory obtained by Sir William Waller against the Welsh Forces under Lord Herbert
R.D. 30 March 1643 (2nd impression 4 April)
T.T. E 94 (30)

The Victorious and Fortunate Proceedings of Sir William Waller and his Forces in Wales and other places ... with the true manner of the taking of Highnam and 150 Commanders and Gentlemen and 1,444 common prisoners well armed ... as was sent in a letter from Sir William Waller and Sir Arthur Haselrig, and was read in both Houses of Parliament Aprill 15 1643
April 17, 1643, John Wright, Old Bailey
T.T. E 97 (2) N.L.W. 320

The Welchman's Lamentation and Complaint for the Losse of her great Towne and City of Hereford, which was taken from her by her Creat Enemy Sir William Waller
April (no printer)
T.T. E 101 (12) C.C.L. W3 10329. N.L.W.

1644

Three Severall Letters (including) the Late loss of Monmouth
G.B, Nov.10 1644
T.T. E 21 (6)

1645

Two Letters from Colonell Morgan, Governor of Gloucester, ... Relating the ... taking [of] the Towne and Castle of Monmouth ...
Thomas Bates, Holborn Conduit Oct 28 1645
T.T. E. 307. 14 ; N.L.W. 94. N.R.L. M 000 946. C.C.L.W3 16.

K. R. *Two Letters from an Officer in Monmouthshire to a Gentleman in London* October 1645
S.A.L. 790/5 (transcript)

C.W. *A Full Relation of the Desparate Design of the Malignants for the Betraying of Monmouth Towne and Castle. With the particular manner of the discovery thereof by Sir Trevor Williams and the meanes used to prevent it by Col. Morgan and Lieut. Col. Kerle And divers malignant families thereupon by Proclamation put out of the said town. Also how Lt. Col. Kerle fell at the enemies Quarters near Hereford and took divers prisoners*
Thomas Bates, 4 Nov 1645
T.T. E 308.19 ; N.L.W. 18; N.R.L. 140.900 C.C.L. W 6 189 reprint J Norris 1888

Severall Letters from Colonell Morgan, Governour of Gloucester, and Colonell Birch. Fully relating the manner of the taking of ... Hereford ... with a perfect list of the prisoners
John Wright 18 Dec 1645.
T.T. E 313 (17). N.L.W. 19.

Two letters ... concerning the taking of Hereford by Col. Morgan and Col. John Birch
Edward Husband, 18 Dec 1645
T.T. E 313 (11).

1646

Two letters to the Speaker of the House of Commons (on the) Victory at Cardiff
Edward Husband 21 Feb 1646
T.T. E 325 (17)

Letters Intercepted by Sir Thomas Fairfax from the Earl of Glamorgan to His Majesty
23 Feb 1646
T.T. E 329 (12)

A Great Overthrow Given to the King's Forces in Wales, Under the Command of Sir Charles Kemish and Kerne the
    Sheriffe : By Lieutenant Colonel Laugharne, Colonell Morgan and Sir Trevor Williams ...
Matthew Walbanke 26 February 1645.
T.T. E 325. 8., N.L.W. 216. N.R.L. M.000. 946. 35331.

The Earl of Glamorgan's Negotiations in Ireland demonstrated; or the Irish plot for bringing ten thousand men and arms
    into England discovered in letters taken in a packet boat by Sir Thomas Fairfax at Padstow, with other letters taken
    by Captain Moulton at sea near Milford Haven
Edward Husband March 7 1646
T.T. E 328 (9)

Three Victories in Wales, 100 Horse and foot of the Lord Summersets routed at Ragland ...
Matthew Walbanke April 14, 1646
T.T. E. 338 (8). N.L.W. 70

M.P. (probably Revd. More Pye) *The Gallant Siege of the Parliaments Forces before Ragland Castle, Maintained by*
    Colonel Morgan, Major-General Laughorn, Sir Trevor Williams Baronet and Colonel Robert Kirle, ... The desparate
    exploits of the besieged in Ragland, who have burned Ragland Town to the ground, and have levelled that stately
    Steeple with the earth ...
Elizabeth Purston May 30, 1646
N.L.W. 308. N.R.L. M. 000. 946

A Letter from the Marquesse of Worcester to the Committee of Parliament sitting in the County of Monmouth, Concerning
    his Sons landing with Irish forces ... : and the Committees Answer thereunto
Edward Husband, June 9 1646
T.T. E 340 (11) N. L. W. 207

A Letter ... from Col. Morgan Governor of Gloucester concerning the whole proceedings of the siege before Raglan
    Castle. Together with the several Summons of the said Colonel to the Earl of Worcester and the Earl's Obstinate
    Answer
Edward Husband June 29 1646
T.T. E 342.16., N.L.W. 208

An Exact and true Relation of the many severall Messages, That have passed between his Excellency Sir Tho. Fairfax, and
    the Marquesse of Worcester, Governour of Ragland Castle, touching the Surrender thereof ...
Fra Coles, Old Bailey,August 18, 1646
T.T. E 350. 18. N.L.W. 121

A Letter from his Excellencies Quarters ... with a Conference between his Excellency and the Marquess of Worcester, also
    a full relation of of all the Proceedings at Ragland Castle 21 and 22 August 1646
Bernard Alsop, 21 August 1646
T.T. E 351 (13)

A Letter from ... Sir Thomas Fairfax ...With a Conference between his Excellency and the Marquesse of Worcester .... at
    Ragland Castle And a perfect list of the Names of the Colonels, Majors ... And other officers therein ...
Bernard Alsop, August 27, 1646
N.L.W. 95

1647

A Declaration of the Proceedings of divers Knights and other Gentlemen In Glamorganshire who declared themselves for
    the King and Sir Thomas Fairfax
I. Coe and A Coe June 15 1647
T.T. E.394 (5). Phillips II, 341-3.

The Heads of the present Greevances of the County of Glamorgan (July 1 st)
No printer given
T.T. E.396 (3). C.C.L. W 3 527

REFERENCES & BIBLIOGRAPHY

A full Relation of the whole Proceedings of the late Rising and Commotion in Wales represented in letters to the Parliament and Sir Thomas Fairfax
Frances Leech, June 15 1647.
T.T. E 396 (9). Philips II, 335-40

1648
R.W. *A Great fight at Chepstow Castle betwixt the forces under Lt. Gen Cromwell and the Cavaliers commanded by Sir William Kelmish, Governor of the said Castle*
Williamson, May 13 1648
T.T. E 443 (14)

A full and particular relation of the manner of the late besieging and taking of Chepstow Castle in Wales ... expressed in a letter from Col. Ewer to the Honorable Wm. Lenthal, Speaker of the House of Commons
Matthew Simmons May 25 1648
T.T. E 445 (6). C.C.L. (Phillips II, 375-6).

1649
An Act Concerning the Sequestration of South Wales and Monmouth
S.A.L. 790/21 (7)

1678
A Letter from a Gentleman in Gloucestershire to a friend in London in vindication of an eminent, and some other persons (of approved loyalty to his Majesty and unquestionable affection to the religion of the Church of England) from certain aspertions cast on them
1678–9 (after 26 Dec 1678- no printer).
N.R.L. M.000 282.

1679
A Short Memorandum upon the deaths of Mr Philip Evans and Mr John Lloyd, both priests, who were executed at Cardiff in Glamorgan the 22 Day of July 1679
N.R.L. Pq. M000 282.5

David Lewis *A Narrative of the Imprisonment and Tryal of Mr David Lewis, Priest of the Society of Jesus : Written by Himself. At the assizes held at Monmouth March 28 1679: to which is annexed his last SPEECH at the place of Execution Aug 27 1679*
N.R.L. M.000. 282.5

David Lewis *The Speech of Mr Henry Lewis, a Jesuit, who was executed at Usk in Monmouthshire The 27 (August) 1679* (London 1679)
N.R.L. Pf. M.000 282.5.(Haines Collection)

Herbert Croft *A Short Narrative of the Discovery of a College of Jesuits, at a place called the Come in the Co. of Hereford, which was set up unto the ... Lords assembled in Parliament ... by ... Herbert, Lord Bishop of Hereford ... To which is added a True Relation of the Knavery of Father Lewis, the pretended Bishop of Llandaffe, now a prisoner in Monmouth Gaol* (London 1679).
N.R.L. M.000 282.5

D.J. (Skenfrith) *A True Narrative of that Grand Jesuite Father Andrews who lived at Hardwick in Monmouthshire*
2 July 1679
N.R.L. M000 282.5

The Pope's Downfall at Abergavenny
printed for T. C. and N. L.
N.L.W.

1680
An Abstract of several Examinations, and taken upon oath, in the Counties of Monmouth and Hereford, and delivered unto the Honourable House of Commons: reported by Sir John Trevor ... at a conference to prevent the growth of increase of Popery... with the account given to the House of Commons the 12 of April 1678 by John Arnold and John Scudamore Esqs of the encouragement given to Popery in the counties of Monmouth and Hereford
J.C. for John Gain
N.R.L. Pq M. 000 282.5 (Haines Collection)

The Tryal of John Giles at the Sessions House in the Old Bayly: held by adjournment from the 7th day of July 1680 ... for a barbarous and inhumane attempt to assasinate and murthur JOHN ARNOLD ESQ
Thomas Jones for Randal Taylor 1681.
N.R.L. Pf M 000 282.5

England's Second Warning Piece: or observations on the barbarous attempt to murther Justice Arnold April the 15th
   1680. Containing a true copy of the pretended speech of Evans, the Popish Priest, executed in Glamorgan ... in
   revenge of whose prosecution, the assassination is presumed to have been committed 1680
N.R.L. M 000 282.5. S.A.L. 790/21 (3)

The Tryal and Condemnation of John Giles that Notorious Ruffian for that he in the company of 2 more fell upon and
   grievously wounded John Arnold Esq of Monmouthshire
1680 (no printer given).
N.R.L. Pq M 000 282.5

An Account of an attempt made upon ... Mr Arnold
S.A.L. 790/21 (1).

Editions and Catalogues of Contemporary Books and Papers

Abbott, W.C. (1937-47), *Letters and Speeches of Oliver Cromwell* ed. W.C. Abbott, 4 vols (Harvard)

Baker, David *Memorials of Father Augustine Baker* (Catholic Record Soc. Pubs XXXIII)
   (1922) *The Confessions of the Venerable Father Augustine Baker O.S.B.* ed. Dom Justin Mc Cann (London).

Bayly, Dr Thomas (1650) *Apothegems of the Marquess of Worcester, or Witty Sayings of the Right Honourable Henry, late*
   Marquess and Earl of Worcester (London)
   (1649) *Certamen Religiosum or, a conference between His late Majestie Charles, King of England, and Henry, late*
   Marquess and Earl of Worcester concerning religion 1646 at Raglan Castle T.T. E 1355 (1)

Bradney, J.A. (1921) *Contributions Towards the Royal Army in 1646 and Lists of Papists in 1690* M.C.A.A. (Newport)

Carte, Thomas (ed.) (1739) *A Collection of Original letters and papers, concerning the affairs of England from the year*
   1641 to 1660

Clarendon, Edward Hyde, Earl of (1888) *The History of the Rebellion and Civil wars In England* ed. W.D. Macray
   (Oxford) (reprinted 1958, 6 vols)

Corbet, J. (1825) *Diary of the Campaigns of Massey west of Severn* (1645) ed. J. Washbourn

Corbet, J. 'A true and impartial account of the militarie government of the Citie of Gloucester' in *Somers Tracts* V, 296-
   374.

Cromwell, Oliver see W.C. Abbott

Dineley, Thomas 1888 *The Account of the Official Progress of ... the first Duke of Beaufort ... through Wales in 1684*

Dore, R.N. 1990 *The Letter Books of Sir William Brereton* (Record Soc of Lancashire and Cheshire, 2 vols)

Edwards, I ap.O. 1929 *A Catalogue of Star Chamber Proceedings Relating to Wales* (Cardiff)

Emanuel, Hywel D *A Preliminary Schedule of the Tredegar Park Muniments Deposited by the Rt Hon. Lord Tredegar*
   (N.L.W. typescript, no date)

Firth, C.H. and Rait, R.S. (1911) *Acts and Ordinances of the Interregnum 1642–1660*

Foley, Henry 1887–1883 *Records of the English Province of the Society of Jesus*

Fortescue G. (1908) *Catalogue of the Pamphlets, Books, Newspapers and Manuscripts relating to the Civil War,*
   Commonwealth and Restoration, collected by George Thomason (London, 2 vols). = Thomason Tracts

Gough, Richard (1981) *Human Nature Displayed in the History of Myddle* ed. David Hey

Hutchinson, Lucy (1908) *Memoirs of the Life of Colonel Hutchinson* ed. Revd Julius Hutchinson (Everyman's Library,
   1968) ed. James Sutherland (Oxford 1973)

James, W.H. (1913) *The Registers of Chepstow Parish Church*

Jones, Edmund (1779) *A Geographical, Historical and Religious Account of the Parish of Aberystruth in the County of*
   Monmouth : To Which Are added Memoirs of several Persons of Note who lived in the Same Parish (Trevecca).
   Reprint of 1988

Larkin, J.F. and Hughes, P.L. (ed.) (1973) *Stuart Royal Proclamations: Vol 1 Royal Proclamations of King James 1 st,*
   1603–1625 (Oxford)

Larkin, J.F. (1983) *Stuart Royal Proclamations: Vol II, Charles 1st, 1625–1646* (Oxford)

Leland, John (1906) *The Itinerary in Wales of John Leland in or about the years 1536–1539* ed. L. Toulmin Smith

Lhwyd, Edward (1909–11) *Parochialia: Being a Summary of Answers to Parochial Queries* ed. R.H. Morris, 3 parts.
   Cambrian Archaeological Association

Luke, Samuel (1963) *The Letter Books, 1644–45 of Sir Samuel Luke, Parliamentary Governor of Newport Pagnall* (Hist.
   Mss Commission)

National Library of Wales (1939) *Schedule of Manuscripts, Letters and Manorial records from the library of the late*
   Major Addams Williams, Llangibby Castle Vol 1 Mss, letters etc. Vol 2 Deeds and Documents (typescript)

Owen, Edward (1900) *Catalogue of Welsh Manuscripts in the British Museum*

Pepys, Samuel (1970–1983) *The Diary of Samuel Pepys* ed. R. Latham and W. Matthews 11 vols.

Phillips, J.R. (1874) *Memoirs of the Civil War In Wales and the Marches 1642–1649* Vol 1 narrative, Vol 2 printed sources

Powell, Walter (1907) *The Diary of Walter Powell of Llantilio Crossenny in the County of Monmouth, Gentleman,*
   1603–1654 ed. J.A. Bradney (Bristol)

Price, M. (1990) *The Account Book for the Borough of Swansea, Wales 1640–1660 : A Study in Local Administration*
   during the Civil War and Interregnum (Lampeter)

Roberts, S.K. (1999) T*he Letter Book of John Byrd, Customs Collector in South-East Wales 1648–80* (Cardiff, South
   Wales Record Soc.)

Rogers, Nathan (1983) *Memoirs of Monmouthshire* (1708) reprinted Chepstow

Roy, I. (ed.) (1964) *The Royalist Ordnance Papers* (Oxfordshire Hist. Record Soc. xliii)

Rushworth, J. (1680–1701) *Historical Collections of Private Passages of State* (8 vols)

Scott, Walter (ed.) (1810) *A Collection of scarce and valuable tracts … Selected from … libraries, particularly that of the late Lord Somers* (13 vols)

Siddons, M.P. (1996) *Visitations by the Heralds in Wales* (Harleian Society, new series 14).

Sprigge, Josuah (1647) *Anglia Rediviva: England's Recovery : Being the History of the motions, actions and successes of the Army under the immediate conduct of … Sir Thomas Fairfax* (1647, new ed. Oxford 1854).

Symonds, R. (1859) *Diary of the Marches of the Royal Army during the Great Civil War : Kept by Richard Symonds* ed. C.E. Long (Camden Soc LXXIV, 1859). Reprinted Camden Classic Reprints 3 (Cambridge 1997) with introduction by Ian Roy

Warburton, E. (1849) *Memoirs of Prince Rupert and the Cavaliers* (3 vols)

Washbourne, J. (1825) *Bibliotheca Gloucestrensis* (Gloucester)

Webb, Revds John and T.H. (1879) *Memorials of the Civil War between King Charles Ist and the Parliament of England As it affected Herefordshire and the adjacent Counties* (2 vols)

Whiteman, E.A.O. (1986) *The Compton Census of 1676: A critical edition*

Secondary Sources

Allen, R. (1999) 'Catholic records in the attic … found in the seventeenth century Catholic household of the Gunter family of Abergavenny' *Gwent Local History* 86 (Spring 1999), 17-30

Andriette, E.A. (1971) *Devon and Exeter in the Civil War* (Newton Abbot)

Apted, M.R. (1973) 'Social conditions at Tredegar House, Newport, in the 17th and 18th Centuries' *Mon. Ant.* III, part II, 125-154

Ashton, R. (1994) *Counter Revolution : The Second Civil War and its Origins, 1646–8*

Atkin, M and Laughton, M. (1992) *Gloucester and the Civil War* (Stroud)

Aylmer, G.E. (1972) 'Who was ruling in Herefordshire from 1645 to 1661?' *Trans. Woolhope Naturalists Field Club* 40, 373-387

(1972a) (ed.) *The Interregnum: The Quest for a Settlement 1646–1660*

(1986) *Rebellion or Revolution, England 1640–1660* (Oxford)

Bennett, M. (1998) 'Dampnified Villagers : Taxation in Wales during the first Civil War' *Welsh History Review* 19, 1 (June 1998), 29-43.

Berry, J. and Lee, S.G. (1938) *A Cromwellian Major General: The Career of Colonel James Berry* (Oxford)

Canning, J.H. (1923–4) 'The Titus Oates plot in south Wales and the Marches' *St Peter's Magazine* (Cardiff) 3-4; 38-47 The Cardiff martyrs; 74-101 John Kemble; 159-168, 189-197, 219-226 David Lewis

(1929) 'A Monmouthshire martyr, Venerable William Gunter' *St Peter's Magazine* 9.8 (August 1929), 234-6

Clark, Arthur (1953) *Raglan Castle and the Civil War in Monmouthshire* (Chepstow)

n.d. *Chepstow : The Castle and Lordship* (Newport)

Coffey, J. (2000) *Persecution and Toleration in Protestant England, 1558–1689*

Coxe, William (1801) *An Historical Tour in Monmouthshire* (reprinted 1995)

Davies, E.T. (1976) 'The Popish Plot in Monmouthshire' *J. Hist Soc Church in Wales* 25 (1976), 32-45

Davies, Linedd Mair (2000) 'The Tregaer Manuscript : An Elegy for Charles I' *Nat. Library of Wales Journal* 31.3, 243-270

Dircks, Henry (1865) *The Life, Times and Scientific Labours of the Second Marquess of Worcester*

Dodd, A.H. (1945–7) 'Wales in the Parliaments of Charles 1st' *Trans. Honorable Soc. of Cymroddorion* 1945, 16-49 and 1946-7, 59-96

(1948) 'The pattern of politics in Stuart Wales' *Trans. Honorable Soc. of Cymroddorion* 1948, 8-91

(1971) *Studies in Stuart Wales* (2nd ed., Cardiff)

Duncumb, J. (1804) *Collections Towards the History and Antiquities of the County of Hereford*

Dunn, Diana (ed.) (2000) *War and Society in Medieval and Early Modern Britain* (Liverpool)

Durant, H. (1973) *Henry, first Duke of Beaufort and his Duchess, Mary* (Pontypool)

Durston, C. (2001) *Cromwell's Major Generals: Godly Government during the English Revolution* (Manchester)

Eales, J. (1990) *Puritans and Roundheads: The Harleys of Brampton Bryan and the outbreak of the English Civil War* (Cambridge)

Ellis, T.P. (1932) *The Catholic Martyrs of Wales, 1535–1680* (Cardiff)

Emery, F. (1967) The farming regions of Wales J. Thirsk (ed.) *The Agrarian History of England and Wales IV* (Cambridge)

Firth C.H. (1902) *Cromwell's Army* (University paperback reprint 1967)

Foley, H. (1877–9) *Records of the English Province of the Society of Jesus* (8 vols)

Foster, J. (1891–2) *Alumni Oxoniensis: The Members of the University of Oxford 1500–1714* (Oxford, 3 vols).

Fox, C. and Lord Raglan (1951–4) *Monmouthshire Houses* Part 1 *Medieval* (1951); Part 2 *Sub-Medieval* (1953); Part 3 *Renaissance* (1954). Cardiff, National Museum of Wales

Gardiner, S.R. (1883–4) *History of England 1603–1642* (10 vols)

(1893) *History of the Great Civil War 1642–1649* (4 vols)

(1903) *A History of the Commonwealth and Protectorate 1649–1660* (4 vols)

Gaunt, P. (ed.) (2000) *The English Civil War*

(2000) 'One of the Goodliest and Strongest Places that I Ever Looked upon : Montgomery and the Civil War' Dunn (ed.) 180-203

Gray, M. (1985) 'The Church in Gwent in 1603' *J. Welsh Ecclesiastical Hist.* 2 (1985) 7-26.

(1989) 'Change and Continuity: The gentry and the property of the Church in south-east Wales and the Marches' J. Gwynfor Jones (ed.) *Class, Community and Culture* 1-38

(2000) 'The clergy as rememberencers of the community: Lewis James, curate of Bedwellty 1633–1667' *Mon. Ant.* 16, 113-120

Green, I.M. (1978) *The Re-Establishment of the Church of England 1660–1663* (Oxford)

(1979) 'The persecution of "scandalous" and "malignant" parish clergy during the English Civil War' *E.H.R* 94, 507-31

Griffiths, M. (1989) 'Very wealthy by merchandise? : Urban fortunes' J. Gwynfor Jones (ed.) *Class Community and Culture* 197- 235

Gunter, G.W. (1990) 'Pedigree of the Gunter family of Abergavenny and London' *Gwent Local History* 69 (Autumn 1990), 8-12

Haigh, C. (1975) *Reformation and Resistance in Tudor Lancashire*

Hart, A. Tindal (1958) *The Country Clergy in Elizabethan and Stuart Times, 1558–1660*

Heath, C. (1804) *Historical and Descriptive Accounts of the Ancient and Present State of the Town of Monmouth* (1825) *Raglan Castle* (10th edition)

Holmes, C. (1980) *Seventeenth Century Lincolnshire* (History of Lincolnshire Vol VII, Lincoln)

(1980a) 'The County Community in Stuart Historiography' *J. British Stud.* 19 (1980), 54-73.

Holt, T.G. (1984) 'The Glamorgan Mission after the Oates Plot' *J. Welsh Ecclesiastical Hist.* 1, 11-27.

Howell, B. (1995) *Law and Disorder in Tudor Monmouthshire* (Cardiff)

Hughes, Ann (1987) *Politics, Society and Civil War in Warwickshire 1620–1660* (Cambridge)

(1989) 'Local history and the origins of the Civil War' in *Conflict In Stuart England : Studies in Religion and Politics 1603–1642* ed. R Cust and A Hughes, 224-253

Hutton, R. (1982) 'Clarendon's History of the Rebellion' *E.H.R.* 97, 70-88

(1985) *The Restoration : A Political and Religious History of England and Wales 1658–1667* (Oxford)

(2003) *The Royalist War Effort* Second edition (first ed. 1982)

Huws, Daniel (2002) 'Llengarwch Reciwsantiaid Gwent' *Y Cylch Grawn Catholig* XIV, 2-15

Ingram, M. (1984) Ridings, rough music and 'the reform of popular culture' in early modern England *Past and Present* 105, 79-113

Jenkins, G.H. (1987) *The Formation of Modern Wales, 1642–1780* (Cardiff)

Jenkins, Philip (1980) 'The origins of anti-popery on the Welsh Marches in the seventeenth century' *Historical Journal* 23, 275-93

(1981) 'The Old Leaven: The Welsh Roundheads after 1660' *Historical Journal* 24, 807-823.

(1983) *The Making of a Ruling Class: The Glamorgan gentry 1640–1790* (Cambridge)

(1987–8) 'The Glamorgan gentry in 1677 *J. National Library of Wales* 25, 53-70

John, M. (ed.) (1976)*Welsh Baptist Studies* (Cardiff)

Johns, W.N. (1885) (Anon- 'By a Member of the Caerleon and Monmouthshire Antiquarian Society') *Historical Traditions and Facts Relating to Newport and Caerleon* (Newport)

Johnson A.M. (1976) 'Bussey Mansell' *Morgannwg* 20, 9-36.

(1978) 'Wales during the Commonwealth and Protectorate' in D.H. Pennington and K.V. Thomas (eds.) *Puritans and Revolutionaries*

Jones, J. Gwynfor (ed.) (1989) *Class, Community and Culture in Tudor Wales* (Cardiff)

(1995) *The Morgan Family of Tredegar c.1340-1674* (Newport).

(2002) 'The Gentry of Gwent and the Welsh language after the Acts of Union' *Mon. Ant.* 18, 65-84.

Kenyon, John (1972) *The Popish Plot*

Kenyon, J.R. (1982) 'The Civil War earthworks around Raglan Castle, Gwent: an aerial view' *Arch. Camb.* 131, 39-42

(1982a) 'A Cannon Shot Mould from Raglan Castle, Gwent' *Arch. Camb.* 131, 142-3.

(2003) *Raglan Castle* (Cadw, revised edition)

Kissack, K. (1975) *Monmouth: The Making of a County Town*

Knight J.K. (2004) 'A nonconformity of the gentry? Catholic recusants in seventeenth century Abergavenny' *Mon. Ant.* 20, 145-152

'"From the Welsh good lord deliver me"; soldiers, papists and civilians in Civil War Monmouthshire' *Archaeologia Cambrensis* 151 (for 2002) 1-18

Lovering, G.W.J. (2002) 'Dissenting communities in Monmouthshire 1639–1715' *Gwent Local History* 93, Autumn 2002, 3-23

Lowe, J. (1964) 'The Glamorgan mission to Ireland 1645-6' *Studia Hibernica* 4, 161-6

Malcolm, J.L. (1978) 'The king in search of soldiers : Charles I in 1642' *Historical Journal* 21, 2, 257-68

(1983) *Caesar's Due : Loyalty and King Charles, 1642–1646* (London, Royal Hist. Soc.)

Manning, B. (1996) *Aristocrats, Plebeians and Revolution in England 1640–1660*

Mathias, R. (1963) *Whitsun Riot: An account of a commotion amongst Catholics in Herefordshire and Monmouthshire in 1605*

Matthews, A.G. (1947) *Walker Revised* (Oxford)

McClain, Molly (2001) *Beaufort: The Duke and his Duchess, 1657–1715*

McCoog, T.M. (1997) 'The Society of Jesus in Wales and the Welsh in the Society of Jesus 1561–1625' *J. Welsh Eccl. Hist.* 5, 1-27

Miller, J. (1973) *Popery and Politics in England 1660–1688* (Cambridge)
Mitchell, Julian (1988) 'Nathan Rogers and the Wentwood Case' *W.H.R.*14, no.1 23-53
    (1990) 'The Speech Court of Wentwood' *Mon. Ant.* 6, 61-67
    forthcoming 'Monmouthshire Politics 1660–1702' in *Gwent County History vol III*
Morrill, J. (1974) *Cheshire 1630–1660 : County Government and Society During the English Revolution* (Oxford)
    (1976) *The Revolt of the Provinces*
    (1982) ed. *Reactions to the English Civil War 1642–1649*
    (1987) 'The ecology of allegiance in the English Revolution' *J. British Studies* 26, 453-67
    (1993) *The Nature of the English Revolution*
Murphy, Paul (1971) 'The Jesuit College of the Cwm, Llanrothal' *Severn and Wye Review* Vol 1, 6, 135-139
Newman, J. (2000) *The Buildings of Wales : Gwent/Monmouthshire*
Newman, P.R. (1981) *Royalist Officers in England and Wales 1642–1660* (Garland Press, New York and London)
    (1983) 'The Royalist officer corps 1642–1660' *Historical Journal* 26 945-58.
    (1987) 'The 1663 list of indigent royalist officers considered as a primary source for the study of the royalist army'
        Historical Journal 30, 885-904.
Nuttall, G.F. (1957) *The Welsh Saints 1640–1660* (Cardiff)
O'Keefe, M. (1970) *Four Martyrs of South Wales and the Marches*
Osborne, Susan (1994) 'The war, the people and the absence of the Clubmen in the Midlands 1642-46' *Midlands History*
    19, reprinted Gaunt *English Civil War* 226-48.
Owen, G. Dyfnallt (1988) *Wales in the Reign of James 1st* (Woodbridge)
Peacock, E. (1874) *The Army Lists of the Roundheads and Cavaliers*
Phillips, J.R.S. (1975) *The Justices of the Peace in Wales and Monmouthshire, 1541 to 1689* (Cardiff)
Porter, S. (1994) *Destruction in the English Civil Wars* (Stroud)
Price, M. (1990) *The Account Book for the Borough of Swansea, Wales 1640–1660 : A study in local administration*
    during the Civil War and Interregnum (Lampeter)
Pugh, Frank H. (1957) 'Monmouthshire recusants in the reigns of Elizabeth 1st and James 1st, from the returns in the
    Public Record Office' *South Wales and Monmouthshire Record Society* 4, 59-110
Putley, J. (2002) *The Battle of Highnam House, 1643* (Bristol, Stuart Press)
Raymond, S.A. (1980) 'The Glamorgan Arraymen 1642–1645' *Morgannwg* 24, 9-30
Rea, Barry (1988) *Popular Culture in Seventeenth Century England*
Rees, William (1968) *Industry Before the Industrial Revolution* (Cardiff, 2 vols)
Reid, Stuart (n.d.) *Officers and Regiments of the Royalist Army* (Partizan Press, revised edition, 5 vols)
Richards, Thomas (1920) *A History of the Puritan Movement in Wales*
    (1923) *Religious Developments in Wales 1654–1662*
    (1925) *Wales under the Penal Code, 1662–1687*
Roberts, M.K. (1981) 'Local Government reform in England and Wales during the Interregnum' in Ivan Roots (ed.) *Into*
    Another Mould (Exeter)
Roberts, S.K. (2000) 'Office holding and alleigance in Glamorgan in the Civil War and after : The case of John Byrd'
    Morgannwg 44, 11-31
    (2003) 'How the West was won : Parliamentary politics, religion and the miltary in south Wales 1642-9' *W.H.R.* 21,
    4 (December 2003) 646-674
Robinson, W.R.B. (2002) *Early Tudor Gwent 1485–1547* (Welshpool)
Roy, Ian (1978) 'England Turned Germany?: The aftermath of the Civil War in its European context' *Trans. Roy. Hist.*
    Soc. 5th series, 28 (1978), 127-14
Smith, T.S. (1978) 'Herefordshire Catholics and the rites of passage' *Trans. Woolhope Naturalists Field Club* 42, 235-43
Spurgeon, C.J. and Thomas, H.J. (2001) 'Caerphilly Castle: The Civil War redoubt' *Arch. Camb.* 147, 1998, (2001), 181-
    93
Steegman, J. (1962) *A Survey of Portraits in Welsh Houses Vol 2 : South Wales* (Cardiff)
Stoyle, Mark (1994) *Loyalty and Locality : Popular Allegiance in Devon During the English Civil War* (Exeter)
    (2000) 'Caricaturing Cymru: Images of the Welsh in the London Press 1642–1646' Dunn (ed.) 162-179.
Thomas, D. Aneurin (1971) *The Welsh Elizabethan Catholic Martyrs* (Cardiff)
Thomas, Keith (1971) *Religion and the Decline of Magic* (new ed. 1997)
Tucker, N. (1966) 'Colonel Roger Whitley' *J. Flintshire Hist. Soc.* 22, 9-24
Tribe, Anna (2002) *Raglan Castle and the Civil War*
Underdown, D. (1960) *Royalist Conspiracy in England 1649–1660* (Yale)
    (1973) *Somerset in the Civil War and Interregnum* (Newton Abbot)
    (1979) 'The Chalk and the Cheese: contrasts among the English Clubmen' *Past and Present* 85, 25-48
    (1985) *Revel, Riot and Rebellion : Popular Politics and Culture in England 1603–1660* (Oxford)
    (1987) 'A reply to John Morrill' *J. Brit. Stud* .26 (1987), 468-79
Wakeman, T. (1863) *Sheriffs of Monmouthshire 1541–1864*
Walker, J. (1714) *An Attempt Towards Recovering the Account of the Numbers and Sufferings of the Clergy of the Church*
    of England ... who were Seqquester'd, Harass'd etc in the late ... Grand Rebellion
Wanklyn, M.D. and Young, P. (1981) 'A king in search of soldiers : A rejoinder' *Hist. J.* 24, 147- 154
Warlow, W.M. (1899) *The History of the Charities of William Jones* (Bristol)
Warmington, A.R. (1997) *Civil War, Interregnum and Restoration : Gloucestershire 1672* (Royal Hist. Soc.)
Washbourne, J. (1825) *Bibliotheca Gloucestrensis* (Gloucester)

Waters, Ivor (1955) *Chepstow Parish Records* (Chepstow)

    (1964) *The Unfortunate Valentine Morris* (Chepstow)

Whittle, E.H. (1989) 'The Renaissance Gardens of Raglan Castle' *Garden History* 17, part 1, 83-94

    (1990) 'The Sixteenth and Seventeenth Century gardens at Raglan Castle' *Mon. Ant.* 6, 69-75

Williams, Glanmor (1962) *The Welsh Church from Conquest to Reformation* (Cardiff)

    (1974) ed. *Glamorgan County History Vol IV. Early Modern Glamorgan* (Cardiff)

Williams, J.G. (1988) 'The Castles of Wales during the Civil War' *Arch. Camb.* 137, 1-26

Woolrych, A. (2002) *Britain in Revolution, 1625–1660* (Oxford)

Wright, Arthur (1942) *The Church Bells of Monmouthshire* (Cardiff), originally published in seven parts in *Arch. Camb.* 92 (1937) to 96 (1941)

Young, Peter (1967) *Edgehill 1642. The Campaign and the Battle* (Kineton)

Index

Abbott, George 133, 136
Abergavenny 10-11, *11*, 13-15, 29-31, *30*, 45, 48, 72,
      82, 84, 86-87, 90, 96, 97, 101, 102,
      103, 111, 123, 136, 145, 160-162,
      164-167, 169, 172, 173-5
    Hundred 31-32
    St Mary's Priory 136
Act for the Propagation of the Gospel in Wales
(1650) 134
Act of Supremacy (1518) 8
Act of Uniformity (1662) 155
Aberystruth 39
Agriculture 34-35, 40, 42
Allen, William 8
Andrews, Thomas, Catholic priest *139*, 166
Anglican clergy 17-22, 130-136, 153-155
Anne of Denmark, Queen 9
Arnold, John 10, 43, 52-53, *158*, 159, 160-169, 172,
    173-175
    of Llanthony 54
Astley, Sir Jacob 35, 89-90, 94, 96, 97, 108
Atkins, Sir Robert 167, 168, 169

Backhouse, Major 78
Bailey, Captain 78
Baker, Augustine (alias David) 11, 13
Baker, Henry 15, 145, 155
    William 15, 56, *57*, 59, 97, 145
    William, J.P. 9
Baptists 133, 136
Barnes, Thomas 153, 155
Barry, William 95-96
Baskerville, William 42
Bassaleg 17, 82
Bassett family (Beaupre) 120
    Sir Richard 94, 101, 120, 121, 141, 163
    Thomas 175
Beachley 76, 79, *80*, 81, 86
Bedloe, William 161, 162, 167, 175
Bedwas 133
Bedwellty 18, 21, 134
Berrowe, Colonel 67, 149
Berry, Major General James 144, 145
Birch, Colonel John 101, 113, 122
Blackbrook, Skenfrith 42
Blackiston, Sir William 78
Blaenau Gwent 45
Blethin, William (Dinham) 38
Blethyn, Francis 144
    William 129
Blindman, Richard 35, 155
Bodenham, Thomas 42
Bonner, Anthony (Llanwenarth) 136
Booth rising 85, 149
Bostill House 86
Boteler, Alan 106-107

Bowen, Captain 103
Brabone, Robert, Monmouth 131
Brag, Thomas, surgeon 78-79
Brereton, Sir William 78, 108
Brett, Sir Jerome 66, 68, 69
Bridgwater 93
Bristol 35, 44, 91, 93, 98
Broughton, Colonel 129
Brown, Major John 142
Bryngwyn 20, *21*, 132
Burgess, Captain 127
Bye Plot 9
Byrd, John 3, 10, 17, 84-85, 88, 97

Caerleon 7, 8. 12. 15-17, 28-29, 31, 35, 42, 45, 62,
    63, 103
Caerphilly 93, 145
Caerwent 34, *36*
Caldicot 34, 158
    Hundred 31-32
Callendar, Lt. Gen. the Earl of 96
Cantrill, Parliamentary officer 124-125
Capel, Lord 66
Carbery, Earl of 66
Cardiff 93, 104, 145
    Castle 31, 52, 97, 141
Carlton, Bishop George 18
Carne, Edward 104
Carvine, Captain 75
Cary, Nicholas 155
Catchmay, Christopher 41, 58, 129
Catchmay, George 41
    John 58
Catholic recusants in Monmouthshire 7, 9, 10, 42,
    44
Cave, Sir Richard 72
Cefn On 93
'Chalk and cheese' model 47-48
Charles I 105, 113, 119, 120
    in Monmouthshire 90-98
Charles II 161
Chartists 176
Chepstow 12, 24, 26, *26*, *27*, 30, 31, 45, 64, 71, 72,
    74, 75, 82, 85, 86, 90, 98
    Castle 124, 125-127, 147, 148, 151
    George Hotel *74*, 75
Church bells 135
Christchurch 15-16
Cilfeigan 89
Clarke, William (Dixton) 131
Clegge, John 131
Clubmen 76, 89, 98, 99, 104
Coldbrook *58*, 84
Clytha 157
Coleford, skirmish at 67, 149
Collington, Nathaniel 20

Commissions of Array 63-64
Committee for Compunding 136
Compton census 17, 155-157
Convention Parliament 150, 175
Cooke, Sir Robert 67-68
Coningsby, Fitzwilliam 64, 66, 72
Corbet, John 67, 71, 76
Council of Trent 8
County armoury 61-63
    Committees 129-133, 136-141
    militia 61, 142, 144
Cradock, Walter (Llanvaches) 131, 133-134
Cragge, John (Llantilio Pertholey) 136
Crane, Sir Richard 56
Creed, Major Richard 134
Crick 92, *92*
Croft, Bishop 161-162
Cromwell, Oliver 117, 124, 125, 127, 144, 147
Crowther, John 104
Crump, George 19, 41
Curre, John 174
Cwm, Jesuit college at 15, 43, 51, 161-162

Dabridgecourt, Captain 88
Davies, John (Llangattock Lingoed) 84
    Rees (Bedwas) 133
Davis, John 60
Dean, Forest of 36-37, 46, 66, 79, 84, 88, 99, 100
Decimation Tax 144
Declaration of Breda 150
Dennis Wise's Bluecoats 69
Digby 93
Dingestow 157
Dissent, beginnings of 22
Dobbins, John (Llangattock vibion Avel) 20, 131
Dormer, Jane, Duchess of Feria 16
Douai, English Seminary at 8
Dracot, Francis 43
Drew, Abraham 86, 155

Earl of Glamorgan's Horse 74, 91
Edwards, John 20-21, 34, 39, 49, 131
Ernley, Sir Michael 76
Eure, Lord 11
Evans, Judith 140
    St Philip 14, 162, 163, *163*
    Thomas 20, 41, 140
Ewer, Colonel 125-126

Fairfax, Sir Thomas 93, 100, 106, 114-16,
120, 123, 150
Field, Bishop Theophilus 18
Fitzgerald, Richard 140-141
Fitzmorris, Colonel 99
Fleming, Colonel 100, 124
Foley, Thomas 41
Foster, Captain 100
Frampton, Robert (Bryngwyn) *20*, 21, *21*, 131-132

Gainsford family 10
    John 64, 69, 100, 143, 149
Games, John 132
Gamme, Colonel Conrad 87
Gerard, Sir Charles 79, 84, 88, 90-91, 93
George ap Howell, Edward 137
Giles, John (Usk) 74
Glamorgan, Countess of 116
Glamorgan Rising (1647) 119-122
Gloucester 66, 68, 73, 76
Godwin, Bishop Francis 8-9, 18
Goldcliff 15, 16
Griffiths, William, recusant 43
Grigson, Major 125
Grosmont 42
Gunpowder Plot 9-10, 50
Gunter family 4, 14, 54
    James 10, 90
    Richard 145
    Thomas 14, 139-140, 146, 162, 171, *171*,
        172, 173, *173*
    Blessed William 9
Gwehelog 112
Gwent Is Coed 32-40
Gwent Levels 32-34
Gwent Uwch Coed 40-44
Gwiliym, William 62
Gwithain, Thomas 64, 66
Gwyn, Howell 66, 72
Gwyn, John 159
Gwynn, William (alias Powell), Jesuit 4, 138
Gwynlliog 44-45
Gyrlinge, John (Caerleon) 22

Hardwick, The *139*
Harley, Colonel Edward 79, 81, 138
Harris, Captain Evan 112
Harris, James 146
    Jane 166
    Walter (Wolvesnewton) 41, 130
    William (Llandenny) 138
Harry, John (Dinham) 37
Heath (Cardiff), battle of 104
Henllys 44, 82
Herbert family 43, 49
    Charles 172, 174
    Edward, Earl of Glamorgan 36, 59, 60,
        64-81, 88, 142, 149
        negotiation with Irish catholics
        104-106
    Sir Edward (Chirbury) 18
    Edward (Merthyr Geryn) 146-7, *146*
    Sir Henry (Coldbrook) 53, 57, 63, 111, 130,
        141, 144
    Henry (Trellech Grange) 41
    Henry (Raglan) see Worcester, Earl of
    Henry, third Marquis of Worcester, first
        Duke of Beaufort 149, 150-151,
        155-156, 157-161, 172, 174, 175

James (Coldbrook) 151, 169, 174, 175
Philip, Earl of Pembroke 52
Sir Richard (St Julians) 63, 107, 127
Thomas (Usk) 29, 173
Thomas (Parliamentary Colonel) 101, 102, 117
Sir William (St Julians) 11, 17
Sir William (Coldbrook) 42, 71, 97, 111
Sir William (Llangattock nigh Usk) 57, 59
William, 4th Earl of Pembroke 31
William (the Friars, Cardiff) 75
Hereford 64, 72, 75, 93, 97
Hertford, Marquis of 67-69
Highnam, battle of 67-69
Holtby, Colonel Marmaduke 78
Hooper, Captain 112, 115
Hopton, Colonel 101
Horton, Colonel 124
Howell, Roger 15
Hughes, Charles (Trostrey) 35, 57, 108
Hughes, Michael (Usk) 130
Hughes, Thomas (Moynes Court) 35, 42, 57, 63, 99, 124, 130, 144
Hundreds 31-32, 61
Hutchinson, Lucy 138

Impropriations of livings 18
Iron industry 41-42

Jackson, Eleazer 14-15
James, John 167
Lewis (Bedwellty) 21, 134, 153
Saunder William 7
Walter (Trivor) 42
James, William and Dorothy (Caerleon) 160, 163, 164-5
Jenkins, Francis 174
Thomas 43-44
Jessey, Henry 39
Jesuits 8, 9
John ap John 69
Eleanora 7
Morgan ap 7
Jones family (Treowen) 54
family (Trivor) 43
Edmund (Llansoy) 64, 141
George, parish constable 37, 38
John (Dingestow) 43
Sir Philip (Treowen) 54, 59, 64, 92, 116
Lady 54, 116
Philip (Llanarth) 4, 101
Robert, Jesuit 9, 43, 51
Walter, Catholic priest 167
William (Dingestow) 131
William (Hardwick) 14, 138-139, *139*
William (Usk) 129, 131, 141
William, Recorder of Abergavenny 164
Joyce, Cornet 120

Kemble, St John 167, 168
Kemeys family (Cefn Mably) 44, 120, 159
Sir Charles 54, 55, 64, 69, 104, 120, 126, 127, 142
David, Dominican Friar 4
David 56
Edward (Bertholey) 159
Sir Nicholas 10, 20, 37-38, 53-54, *54*, 55, *55*, 59, 62, 64, 124-126, *126*
Sir Nicholas (junior) 143
(of Michaelchurch y Fedw) 54
Kemeys Inferior 7
Kyrle, Robert 35, 41, 64, 78, 99, 100, 103, 104, 112, 122, 123

Lancaut, battle of 87-88
Langdale, Sir Marmaduke 84, 87
Langley, George 15-16, 34-35, 47
Philip 16-17
Langport, battle of 93
Laud, Archbishop William 18, 19, 38, 59
Laugharne, Rowland 103, 104, 112, 121, 122, 124, 127
Lawdly, Sir Richard 66-67
Lawes, William 83
Laythorne, Captain Christopher 83
Lee, John Edward 70
Leslie, Alexander, Earl of Leven 96
Lewis family (Llandewi Rydderch) 54
Andrew 109, 110
Charles (Llanllowell) 131
St David 10, 13, 14, 43, 160, 162, 163-171, *166*, *169*
Sir Edward (the Van) 10, 38, 93
Esquire (St Pierre) 125
Morgan 10, *11*, 13
Thomas (St Pierre) 117, 159, 164
Major Thomas 112
Thomas, magistrate 62
Thomas 109
Valentine Jones 109
Lingen, Sir Henry 69, 73, 91, 124, 127
Littleton, Humphrey 10
Llanarth 103
Llandenny 112, 133
Llandewi Rhydderch 135
Llanfoist 164
Llangattock vibion Avel 20, 42
Llangibby 127, 133, 154
Llangua 42
Llanhennock 12, 18, 42
Llantarnam 154
Llantilio Crossenny 2, 109, 134
Llantilio Pertholey 40
Llanvaches 35, 36, *39*
Llanvair Discoed *39*, 55
Llanfihangel Ystern Llwyn 44
Llanvihangel Court *158*
Lloyd, St John (Trivor) 42, 163, *170*

Sir Marmaduke 70
William, Catholic priest 168
Long Parliament 150
Lord Charles Somerset's Foot 74
Loup, William 110-111
Lunsford, Sir Thomas 82, 84, 95, 99, 100, 101
Lydney House 75, 88

Machen 82
Major-Generals, rule of 144-146
Mansell, Bussey 103
Sir Edward 159
Mansfield, Elizabeth 89
Marquis of Worcester's Foot 74, 77
Horse 74, 103
Marshfield 157
Marston Moor, battle of 76
Marten, Henry 151-152, *152*
Mason, Edward 62
Massey, Colonel Edward 64, 68-69, 73, 75-81, 88,
90, 120, 138, 149
Captain George 87
Matthews, Colonel 98, 99
Maurice, Prince 66, 68, 72, 98
Meredith, Mr 'of Abergavenny' 9
Richard (Trellech) 154
Merthyr Geryn *146*
Milborne family 10
Henry (Wonastow) 4, 43, 111, 161, 162
John 64
Militia—see under County militia
Ordinance 62
Monck, General 143, 156
Monmouth 12, 26-27, *28*, 30, 31, 41, 42-43, 45, 61,
64, 71, 72, 75, 78, 79, 81, 82, 84, 86,
87, 100, 103, 123, 125
Castle 152
Dixton Gate 81, *82*
Great Castle House 152, *153*
Montague, Sir Walter 33
Montgomery, battle of 76
Moore, Nicholas (Crick) 92
William 8, 9
Morgan family (the Garn) 12
family (Llantarnam) 12, 15, 54
family (Penhow) 54
family (Tredegar) 44, 53
Anthony, Cilfeigan 71, 88-89, 98, 101, 106
ap John 7
David, recusant 15
Jacobite 44
Edward (Llantarnam) 8, 18, 50-51, 62
Sir Edward 51, 52
Edward (Pencoed) 99, 101
Giles (Pencrug) 12
Henry, buccaneer 44
Captain John 88
John, preacher 134
Lt. Lewis 44, 77

Colonel Myles 44
Philip (Ruperra) 93
Sir Richard, MP 42
Thomas (Llansôr) 64, 71, 138
Major Thomas (Peterston Wentloog) 44
Thomas (Machen) 44, 56, 59, 61, 62, 64, 66,
100, 101, 103, 126, 144
Thomas (Penrhos) 174
Thomas (Tredegar) 4
Colonel (later Major General) Thomas 69,
90, 103, 104, 111-113, 143, 150
Sir Trevor (Llangibby) 4
William (Machen) 51, 126
William (Pentrebach and Llantarnam) 50
Sir William (Penrhos) 51
Sir William (Tredegar) 15, 44, 56, 59, 63, 91,
97, 145, 133
William (Tredegar) 150, 159
William (Treddunock), churchwarden 153
Morris family (Piercefield) 35
George 9
Moston, Ambrose 22
Moulton, Robert 97, 99
Murray, Bishop William 19
'Mushrump Army' 64-69
Mynne, Sir Nicholas 74-76
Mynyddislwyn 18

Naseby, battle of 90
Newport 12, 29, 30, 31, 45, 82, 103, 133
Hundred 31-32
Nicholas family (Llanfihangel-Tor-y-Mynydd) 143
Edward (Trellech) 147
Lt-Colonel John 127, 144, 146, 147, 148,
149
Nicholas, Philip, Skenfrith 138
Northern Horse 76-79, 84, 90
Nott, Sir Thomas 121

Oates, Roger (Cefn Tila) 159
Titus 56, 161, 167, 168
Oldisworth, Mrs 121
O'Neill, Colonel Daniel 75
O'Queeley, Archbishop Malachy 105
Ormonde, Earl of 73, 74, 105, 106, 144, 161
Owen, Bishop Morgan 19

Packer, Thomas 62
Panteg *19*, 21, 135
Papal bull *Regnans in Exelsis* (1570) 8
Parliamentary taxation 130
Parry, Lewis 43
'Peaceable Army' 89, 94, 97, 98, 104
Penallt 133
Pembroke Castle 127
Pembroke, Earls of, power 198, 41
Penrhos 3, 109, 110
Peters, Hugh 117
Phillips, Edward (Chepstow) 86